George T. Wolz
St. Charles College
February 15, 1952

The Meaning of Civilization

THE MEANING OF

CIVILIZATION

BY

BOHDAN CHUDOBA

New York

P. J. KENEDY & SONS

MATRI PVLCHRAE DILECTIONIS

SEDI SAPIENTIAE

ET

CAVSAE NOSTRAE LAETITIAE

QVA

LAETABITVR DESERTA ET INVIA

ET

EXSVLTABIT SOLITVDO

Foreword

MOST of the first part of this book, concerned with the
conceptions of history and progress, was first drafted
during the summer of 1938, a time full of forebodings.
Austria was already in the hands of the Nazis. The
Czechoslovak army, partially mobilized since the
month of May, was guarding the frontiers. In my
spare time I could ride along endless forest pathways
of the frontier districts of Southern Moravia and think
not only of the political situation but also of its philosophical implications. The Germans, so I thought,
were a highly civilized nation. They knew all the historical facts. And yet their approach to them was
basically wrong. The meaning of history had escaped
them. They were conscious of what they imagined
was their role in history. But they did not listen to
what history might tell them. No wonder. Did not all
Europe—and the Germans especially—study history
from books in which the life of Our Lord was treated
as a "politically unimportant" event of the reign of
Tiberius?

I had already been studying the various conceptions

of history for some years. I now tried to put my medi-
tations on paper. They were published as a booklet.
But by the time the copies reached the booksellers the
Nazi military units were parading along the streets
of Czechoslovak towns and singing:

> *Heute gehoert uns Deutschland und morgen die
> ganze Welt. . . .*

> Today, we are the masters of Germany, tomor-
> row we shall govern the world. . . .

The un-Christian conception of progress had won another battle. Not long afterwards the copies of my
booklet were seized by the Nazi police.

As to the second and the third parts, concerning the
ancient civilizations and the various aspects of Christian civilization, my ideas about them began to emerge
nearly seven years afterwards, out of a days-long, almost unintermittent discussion with a Soviet officer,
in whose unit I served for some time. He was younger
than I but higher in grade and an excellent soldier. He
was as conscious of his role in history as the Nazis had
been. But he lacked their erudition. Almost all his
facts were wrong. Not only his interpretation of history, but his very knowledge of history was faulty.
And such was the case with all his comrades. Soon
afterwards, their spirit, the spirit of nomadic ignorance, invaded the Czechoslovak schools. It was necessary to fight it. That was why I started writing the
remaining two parts of this book.

I could, however, finish the manuscript only in
exile. But even then, my work should not be in vain.
The defense against totalitarian philosophy and igno-

rance—of which the positivist enmity against Christian doctrine has been but an overture—is not an exclusively European affair. On the contrary, it is perhaps more necessary to fight it in countries where it has not yet taken root than in those which have already experienced its despair and misery.

My aim in writing the first part of this book, bearing the title "The Creative Activity of Man," was to restate, in a general way, the Christian concept of history, so much neglected in our times. As the Christian criticism of the idea of progress has recently been well sustained by scholars like Christopher Dawson, I was able to retain it in a few conclusive paragraphs only—in order to keep the whole argument comprehensive—and to concentrate on the criticism of historical evolution and, more positively, on the idea of history as drama, which seems to me the core of the theme.

The second part, "The Ancient Background", aims at a survey, not of the events which preceded the birth of Our Lord, but of the values which, directly or indirectly, have been inherited from the various ancient civilizations by our own civilization. Such a survey, undoubtedly, must be done, partially at least, in a narrative way. But it is not history in the true sense of the word.

The third and main part of this book, "Aspects of Christian Culture," is perhaps nearer to the ideal unity obtainable only in a purely narrative work through the temporal sequence of events. But even there our own needs and our own problems form the central pivot. It is not so much the individual facts of history as its significance and its value as a whole which is misunderstood. If this book is able to help to clarify these, its mission will be fulfilled. I am persuaded that, to a large extent, it is because we do not realize the meaning of history and of civilization—which, after all, is a living history—that there are so few great historical narrators among us.

I would like to add that I know of the inevitability of two kinds of criticism which this book will provoke: one which will point out a gap between my analysis of the ancient civilizations and my study of the Christian civilization; another which will doubt the objective value of my rather impassioned treatment of the present world situation.

As to the first objection I would like to stress that I am well aware of the fact that even many Christian historians of the present day, having been affected by positivist thinking, regard the tremendous event of Our Lord's Incarnation as a development which can be placed side by side with other so-called milestones of history. Consequently, it is possible for them to connect the events which preceded the beginning of our era with those which followed it in one uninterrupted story. To me, however, the exceptional character of the events narrated by the Evangelists seems much more real than the most fluent arrangement of a textbook whose author does not recognize any exception from the so-called normal course of history.

Regarding the second objection, perhaps I may be allowed to point out that there is all the difference in the world between two concepts of history one of which considers it a drama and the other a series of events which has no beginning, no middle, and no end. The ultimate victory of Christ can not be doubted by a Christian. But the temporal annihilation of values which we have witnessed during the recent years does not leave one untouched who loves a value because he knows that, in history, it is unique. Of course, people who believe that every value is replaceable by another one just as one link of a chain is replaceable by another, may act as cool, dispassionate observers. The question for them to answer, however, is why should one observe at all if one does not care.

Larchmont, N.Y.
on the Vigil of the
Feast of the Assumption, 1950

BOHDAN CHUDOBA

Contents

I

THE CREATIVE ACTIVITY
OF MAN

Clio at the Crossways

1:

THE INQUISITIVE PILGRIM in Comenius' book *Labyrinth of the World*, after he had visited the streets of several other learned professions, arrived at last into the street of historians. He found them bent behind their periscopes through which they were trying to look into the past. They assured him that it was rather of advantage to anyone to be able to use such a periscope because, from the past, one could always learn something about the present time and about the future. The pilgrim asked them to let him see for himself. Several historians eagerly offered him their instruments. Yet what a disillusion! The pilgrim could not conceal the fact that through each of them he saw things differently. The historians immediately started quarreling because each of them was sure that the perspective of his instrument was the right one.

If quarrels are usual among the servants of Clio, the muse of history, no wonder that she has found herself at the crossways, unable to catch up with the other muses or at least find a way for herself. History in itself will hardly bring peace among men. Memory is

so short, outlooks are so different, and the capability
to perceive is not always developed to the same degree.
But there is a lot of unnecessary quarreling among the
historians—just because some of them think, as Comenius puts it, that, from the past, one can always learn
something about the present time and about the future. The classical maxim *"historia magistra vitae"*
does not mean to them that knowledge of the past may
enrich our own experience. They mean by it rather
that history can predict our experience.

To be able to predict one has to find out some similarity or regularity and then to formulate laws according to which the regular changes take place. How dis-
appointing it is to try to do such a thing in history
may be seen in the frustration which met the ingenu-
ous theories of Hippolyte Taine or Oswald Spengler.
However learned their books on the "laws of history"
might have been, they are scarcely ever mentioned
nowadays. The laws which they have discovered are
found no more useful than the historiometrical calculations of a professor who spent many years in measuring coins, statues and many other monuments of the
past to be able to predict the future. The secret of the
easiness with which such theories are born lies in
the arbitrary way in which their authors choose their
examples. However fantastic the predicated law may
be, it is always easy to find several examples from the
past to support it. But the very moment we choose another set of examples the law turns into ashes.

Another aspect of this confusion concerning the difference between history and science is the refusal of
quite a number of historians to distinguish between
condition and cause. It so happened that in the last
century when science was accomplishing prodigious

triumphs some historians who had lost their way in the labyrinth of pagan philosophy began to envy the scientists. Having tried in vain to formulate laws and to predict as the scientists did they started to "play science" at least by establishing the so-called causal relations between various events in history.

Undoubtedly, *cause* is a word which symbolises something very important. Pascal even speaks of the *dignity of causality*. But do we, for instance, mean the same thing when we say that the river was the cause of the flood or that the defenestration of Prague was the cause of the Thirty Years War, and that the sculptor was the cause of a statue?

The scientist is, of course, perfectly entitled to take the greatest interest in the chains of material events. By establishing their regularity and expressing it— mostly in a mathematical way—one can not only predict what will happen after this or that event has taken place but also start similar chains and reconstruct events. There is a saying in science that we know more about the event R if we know at the same time that R is the last event in the chain of the events $M, N, O, P. \ldots$ It would be perhaps truer if the scientists would say that, by knowing the chain, they have more power about the event R so that they can reconstruct it or place it in different surroundings. But what is the use of choosing one historical event which has preceded another event and declare it the cause of this other event? Do we really know more about the First World War if we know about the Agadir crisis in 1911? Knowing about Agadir we certainly know more about the general atmosphere in which the First World War started. But everything could have happened in 1911 as it really happened without there being any necessity for the war to come.

What is the use of having one historian assure us that the First World War was exclusively caused by a bad distribution of property? In a few days another historian will appear on the scene with the theory that the only cause of that war was the irresponsible journalists. Then the first historian would either defend stubbornly his own opinion or he would declare that his colleague had not grasped sufficiently all the threads from which that important event had been woven. And no one, of course, can stand up to such a criticism. If all the conditions of the First World War, that is, all the preceding events which had some relation to it, had to be enumerated, hundreds of historians, working all their lives, would not be able to do it. They would have to include, for example, the private life of the parents of the pastor who taught Wilhelm II his catechism because one never knows what would have been the policy of that ruler, had there not been this or that complex in his teacher's mind.

There are historians who know very well that the conditions of any historical event, however unimportant the event may be, are innumerable. And yet they do not hesitate to call them "causes," to arrange them and—what is even worse—to choose between them according to their own imagination. The French historian Seignobos, for instance, is of the opinion that there is a difference between the *main cause* and the *secondary causes* and that this difference can be ascertained through a sort of sympathetic insight. There is a lot of such *déterminisme par sentiment* in modern historical books. It has not been made more critical by those who, following the example of John Stuart Mill, tried to select the real cause among the conditions by a series of complicated arguments. There is no such thing as a regularity in history. Therefore none of the conditions of any event can be declared more necessary than the others.

Approaching this subject from the philological point of view we can compare three words which are usually employed in the same sense as the English word "cause": the Germanic *ursache*, the Romanic *raison*, and the Slavonic *pričina*. *Ursache* is evidently something which stands at the beginning of a chain of events. The electric bulb glows because the electric current comes into it; the electric energy is released by the force of a river falling from the mountains; the river assembles its waters from places where it has rained; we can say that the rain is the original thing, the *ur-sache*. And, of course, we are free to proceed farther and look for other events in nature which have preceded the downfall of the rain. The word *raison* is of another affinity. It is connected with the verb *raisonner* which means to think, to invent. When speaking of something as the *raison* of something else we usually have in mind an act of thinking over, of pondering. And that can not be done by a rain. The word *pričina* includes the word *čin* which means an act resulting from a deliberation. It may be compared with the Greek word *aitia* which besides meaning a "cause" means also "responsibility" and presumes therefore that the effect of the act in question has been premeditated.

Thus it is evident that the word *cause* can be translated in different other languages by terms which do not mean precisely the same thing. Of course, philology can only give us some idea about the complexities of the language. It is the purpose of logic to help us to find correct and true words. If we employ the word *cause* as symbol of the relation between Napoleon and the collection of laws which he deliberately induced to be published, we can not employ it correctly as symbol for a relation in which there is no question of a knowing will. The river has not wanted to cause a flood because it could not know the meaning of a flood. Even the caterpillar which cuts leaves along a very precise curve can not be considered the cause of the cuts because it acts according to a given instinct and has no idea of the mathematical qualities of the curve. In a similar way, the crisis of Algeciras had no idea of the First World War. Therefore, the First World War can not be "explained" by the Algeciras crisis or by any other event which has preceded it. It can only be explained by the wilful actions of the Austrian government and of Wilhelm II.

There is only one causality, the real causality, and that is the relation between a knowing will and the effects of its actions. The medieval philosophers were quite right in discerning the *causa efficiens* "the real cause" from the *causa materialis* "the condition." A book of plays may have an indefinite number of conditions like paper, ink, pen, the author's experiences, but only one cause, the playwright's will. Among the events in nature and among the conditions of our own acts, each may be conditioned by a number of preceding events, but each has one cause only, the knowing and loving Being which has created all the events and all their regularities. A scientist may not be interested in this cause as scientist—but he should be interested in it as man. He may be satisfied with knowing the conditions and he may even speak of them as necessary conditions, forgetting the old maxim of David Hume

that we call the regular chains of events in space and
time necessary only because we are accustomed to
them. But in history, whenever we speak of a cause,
we can mean only man or God.

There have been yet other attempts to change history into a sort of science. The German philosopher
Wilhelm Dilthey has divided history into departments
each of which covers the field of a special branch of
science. Military history, for instance, can not be
studied without a good knowledge of physics; and
physics is a science. In that way the whole domain of
history was distributed among special sciences. There
remains, in Dilthey's opinion, a certain amount of
basic history which consists in chronological arrang-
ing of events. But is history just an enumeration of
days and years or is it just the sum of our knowledge?
In the same way we could divide art into chemistry,
for painters, psychology, for poets, and physics, for
sculptors, architects and musicians. But if we do so,
what will remain of art?

Equally fallacious thoughts on history have been
developed by the younger followers of Hegel. According to Hegel's teaching there is an "unpersonal spirit"
in the background of all human activity. This spirit
is a power in comparison with which any single human individuality is as good as powerless. The successful people are able to divine what the "unpersonal
spirit" is after. Others, the unsuccessful, know nothing
about it. The younger generation of Hegelians enjoyed
this peculiar teaching perhaps even more than Hegel
himself did. We have not as yet forgotten, for instance,
the assurances made repeatedly by Nicolai Hartmann
in the years of Hitler's ascendancy that the "leaders

of the people" were exceptionally endowed to reveal to others the will of the "unpersonal spirit."

Another school of historiography has based its opinions on the assumption that at least some events in history do repeat themselves because some ideas rise in human minds under the influence of external, physical environment. The followers of this school usually spoke of large epochs of history in the flow of which they believed to have found a certain regularity. Some of them also spoke of the histories of different geographical areas as being impregnated, each of them, by the characteristics of the area in question. An attempt in that way was made in France in the 16th century by Jean Bodin. An Italian thinker of the 18th century, Giovanbattista Vico, who was also the first to speak about the "dark Middle Ages," called the regular ebb and tide of history, which he is believed to have discovered, "corsi e ricorsi." But somehow, since those days, history has not gone on along these prescribed lines.

A younger generation of this school is represented by Arnold J. Toynbee whose book, *The Study of History*, has brought up copious examples from various epochs of the story of mankind to prove that history can be dealt with in a "scientific" way. His examples are of secondary interest only. The general lines along which he approaches history is what matters in his learned work. All his conclusions are based on the assumption that the only intelligible units of history are the "societies," that is to say those social structures which we usually call civilizations. Now, civilizations are undoubtedly what we usually see before all other things whenever we look into the past. But, in the same way, the colored patches of woods and fields are undoubtedly what we usually see before all other things whenever we look upon a country. And if we choose to behave like realtors we can declare that woods and fields are the only intelligible units of the country, because there is nothing else which we could buy or sell. But would that mean that we know the country and know its life? In history, to consider civilizations as the only intelligible units is an even more prejudiced simplification. Toynbee himself has come to the conclusion that the progress towards self-determination is the only criterion of a historian according to which he can estimate the value of different societies. But there is no such thing as a progress towards self-determination in any civilization or other abstract unit. Man as an individual person is the only one who can progress towards greater liberty from his own instincts and from the other regularities of nature.

It is true that Toynbee was able to find quite a number of events in history which have taken place in similar circumstances. The nomads who no longer found any food in the desiccated steppes descended usually into the valleys of the rivers and started to build new agricultural states. But to what extent does the knowledge of this regularity help us to know the experiences —mostly very individual and dramatic experiences— of this or that ruler or legislator of such a newly founded state? In the same way an atomic researcher of our own age gets all the material required for his study only when his state is in danger from some external enemy. But that does not help us in following the development of his scientific ideas. All the conditions of human creative activity form only the background of history. It is that activity alone which makes history. It matters little whether, in the life of a creative individual, we perceive a condition which seems to have stimulated all his activity. We may find the same "stimulus" in the life of Roger Bacon or of Thomas Edison as in the life of thousands of other persons who have never dreamt of a scientific investigation. Little it matters whether a creative individual lives in a growing or in a decadent society and whether he seems—to use Toynbee's terms—to be a builder or a saviour. We shall hardly understand Rodin's statues better if we confer upon him either of these two titles.

What is perhaps characteristic of all the more recent imitators of science among the historians is their pessimism as to the fate of every civilization. The ultimate fate of every unit in nature is death. If history is made similar to nature what can be the ultimate fate of its own factors? Even Toynbee assures us rather sadly that all the values of any civilization can not escape ultimate destruction. Of course, he tries to make Christianity an exception—but in this he is not quite logical. But we can assure him that, not only the Christian creed, but also many other values created by free human will many centuries ago, are still known to us—thanks to tradition and to historians who did not despair of them because they did not try to change history into science. There is an immense richness in the variability of human progress and of human culture. Why should Clio look for other ways than for her own?

The task of a historian is twofold. He has to relate the drama of history and the dramas of the men who made history. He has also to choose among the innumerable historical facts which are known to him and select his material.

It is with a definite purpose in mind that we place the noble task of historical narration before that of the selection of material. The historians of our own times have an excellent possibility to choose what they would like to relate. It was not always so. There were times when chroniclers were anxious to get a new story which they could add to their sparse knowledge of the past. It may well be that a time will come when the future historians will know as little as their ancient or medieval predecessors did. But even in such times man does not like to be deprived of history. Even in such times history has to fulfill its mission. It is of small importance whether or not a lot of details is at the disposal of the historian. His first duty is to tell his readers about the glorious drama of history. Only secondary is his mission to rediscover the values of the past ages. This truth is often forgotten in our own age. We have quite a number of editors of documents, of scientific researchers into the past, and of historical sociologists, but we have very few real narrators.

Is history nearer to art than to science? Yes, it is. In the hierarchy of the branches of culture, history and art occupy a position much more elevated than those of politics, science, or any of those technologies which depend on science. Both science and politics look on the reality from very far away. They deal with generalities only: with the laws of nature or with the laws which man imposes upon himself. Medicine, in the realm of science, and education, in the realm of politics, are smaller disciplines which reach to the highest points in their respective realms. Both history and art transcend the generalities and reach directly the individual persons and also the individual times and places. As such they are capable of expressing not only the scientific and political experience of individual men but also their philosophical and theological ideas.

An artist, of course, has much greater liberty than a historian. He can indulge in extending the ways of creation and of the human will in fantasy. The testimony which the historian has to bring is much more disciplined. The events of the past are finished for him, although it is his task to revive their memory. Nevertheless even his testimony should be one of faith and love, not of knowledge only.

It is evident that, however diligent a historian may be, he can not tell all that he knows. He must select the facts which he is going to include in his narrative. According to which rules, then, must he choose them? On the preceding pages, we have criticized the mechanistic conceptions of history, especially that which impels the historian to select those events which would fit into a prefabricated theory about this or that regularity in history. We have equally refused to accept the false theory of causality and the so-called "causal chains." On the other hand we have tried to make it clear that the task of the historian consists in narrating the drama of history and in reestablishing the values which have been forgotten. This twofold aim is at the same time the criterion which the historian needs for the selection of his material.

The drama of history consists chiefly in classical works. A classical work is an activity which has surpassed the level of culture of its own time or at least represents the cultural results of its time most completely. We use the expression *classical* because the

educators used to call *libri classici* the books selected
for use in schools. A classical work may mean an
activity in any branch of culture: scientific, political,
artistic, historical, philosophical or religious. It may
be an activity expressed by the way of books or any
other sort of communication but it may also be an
activity known only from the testimony of others.

The broader the basis of a historical treatise or book,
the greater the number of classical works which may
be mentioned in it. If there is space enough we may
even study the minor classics whose scope of ideas
and of renown was not a large one. Such is the case
especially in historical studies devoted to the histories
of different nations, countries, epochs, generations,
persons, or branches of culture. In such studies we
may extend our enquiry even into the details of the
daily lives of the persons who took part in the events.
But there is a certain danger in this kind of historical
work. Historians engaged in it often overestimate the
general importance of their subject. How many histories of different nations have already been conceived
on the basis of a false assumption that the nation in
question had a Messianic mission in the history of
mankind. How many biographies have been based on
an exaggerated love of the author for his subject. It
was perhaps at this point that the historians have most
often crossed the frontier of their own domain into the
sphere of art. One criterion can be applied here,
namely the question whether the work which we are
studying was really classical in its own epoch or
whether, at least, it can have a classical value for
ourselves.

But speaking of the value which a classical work can

have for ourselves we touch upon the second task of
the historian: that of the selection of material.

The selection of material is always a personal one.
History would be a dead branch of culture, not a living one, if one expected the historians always to say
the same things about the past. But history, as we have
already tried to demonstrate, should be a living element of our own progress. And because every progress
is personal even history must be personal. The objectivity of the historian is given by the facts with which
he deals. Which facts he selects depends on the quality
and stage of his own progress.

The story of mankind consists, of course, of lives and
works—even classical lives and works—which are
very often directed against each other. Undoubtedly,
not only Winston Churchill's but also Adolf Hitler's
political work was classical. A mechanical conception
of history would assign to them equal space in a book
on modern political history. The duty of depicting the
drama of history forbids the historian to leave Hitler
out. But the historian must also revive values. And
this task brings him right into the middle of the cultural currents of to-day. Not only is he obliged to
choose, he is also obliged to defend his choice. He has
to stress everything that seems positive to him and
bring out those characteristics of the positive classical
works which he thinks important for our own progress. Of course his choice will depend absolutely on
his own formation and philosophy. This dependence
is unavoidable. But it is always better to acknowledge
this fact than to try to put the historian upon a throne
of immovable objectivity which, in reality, has never
existed. The so-called objective positivist historians
were, in reality, the most fanatical partisans in their

fight for positivism and against the Christian conception of the world.

The historian is here not to judge people but ideas.
Even if he does not pronounce any other judgment,
his selection of material is already a critical sentence.
It is not history which brings about our creative activity. It is, on the contrary, our creative activity which
brings about our interest in history and our judgment
of history. It is also our creative activity which can be
called the history of the present time. Thus history
finds its right place among the branches of contemporary culture. History is born out of the questions
asked by science, politics, art, philosophy and religion.
But, without history, not a single one of these cultural
activities would be able to attain its present stage.
Lacking history, there would be no civilization to
build upon.

2:

The starting point of every study of history must
inevitably be the study of the creative power of man.
If anyone chooses an abstract unity to start with he
has to come back to the human individual whenever
he mentions any creative act. And that means always
to choose the longer way.

Some thinkers have tried to arrive at the top of human knowledge by proclaiming, first of all, their lack
of interest in man. Some of them have even lost interest in their own existence or, at least, had some doubts
about it. St. Augustine had to remind them that we
would not be able to doubt, unless we existed. The
men of the 17th century, like Descartes, liked to
assure themselves in a similar way. They had to tell

themselves that they thought and that they could not think without existing; only then were they satisfied. And in our own times again there are some that doubt whether man, as something distinct from the regular flow of natural events, really exists.

Undoubtedly, there are situations in life which incline us to accept the theory of man as merely a bigger particle of matter—or energy. That is why some historians have tried to demonstrate that even history is regulated by the laws of nature. They have, of course, put themselves in rather a privileged position by declaring that they were able to judge these things from an objective, scientific point of view. The question for them to answer is what reason can we have for studying a law of nature if we can not escape it. If, however, we can escape it, are we really subject to it?

Dealing with history we have to think and speak about the real man. No abstract picture of a man who has never existed can be of any help to us. Perhaps, by asserting this, we are going to make history more difficult. It would be much more simple to declare, for instance, that the activity of man consists of a certain number of habits and that we have only to know them in detail to be able to reconstruct the story of mankind. With the real man the whole affair is much more complicated.

Undoubtedly, man is rather interesting even when considered as just an animal. That is why the scientists have never lost sight of him. But there is a personality in every man and that is what escapes science. It matters little whether many or few scientists are ready to acknowledge with the Swiss psychologist C. G. Jung that the psyche originates from a certain spiritual principle which can not be analysed. In history we have to deal with the full nature of man, not just with this or that part of him which is adaptable to our theories.

The real man stands alone in the world. Everywhere else the regular processes of nature seek their own fulfilment. The disintegration of minerals, the ripening of fruit, the building of nests, everything is based upon a regular unchanging order. The spiders weave their webs as they have for thousands of years. The bees do not change their social organisation. But people who lived under the same conditions as that under which the spiders and the bees lived have added television to hieroglyphs, symphonies to simple songs and the complicated administration of the modern state to their basic social norms. Man certainly lives in nature. But he also lives in history. Human existence is something more than ordinary existence in time and space. For man, *to be* means to know and to love. Even his capability to express his ideas exceeds by far the range of those words which are connected with the memory of the senses. And by means of this capacity man has got hold even of that which he can not grasp by means of his senses.

This is the portrait of man which every historian has to draw. Every single event in the story of mankind tells us about man's dual character: his organic life in nature and his spiritual life in history. For the historian there is no sense in the materialist's explanation of man, but there is also no sense in the idealist's explanation.

As to the materialist theory, in rejecting it we do not deny the very important fact that we can only create new values by using the regular processes of nature which are known to us. But if every process in space and time serves a definite natural purpose, human creative activity dares to ignore these purposes. The oxydation of metals or the life of a swarm of bees, even the death of an organism, all that fills up a certain prescribed way and is directed to a definite and natural purpose. History, on the other hand, means laborious research work of scientists who offer their health for the sake of their discoveries, the suffering of thinkers who lose everything and yet cleave to their ideas, the poverty of artists who are not willing to sell their abilities for some cheap purpose. It is true that man changes his environment by using the regular processes of nature. But not always does he change it to suit his own health or to suit an imperative instinct. On the contrary, the alterations which result from his creative activity usually deny all regularity and all instincts.

It is rather a remarkable thing that philosophers who looked askance on human history or even denied its very existence usually did not escape its powerful spell. On the first pages of their books they readily announced that man was just an organism behaving according to the laws of nature. But in the later chapters of those same books they showed that nature was behaving like man. They found, for instance, that storks had developed long and strong beaks because they wished to feed on frogs in the marshes. Their readers could almost wonder whether the primitive animals had developed eyes because they wanted to see something or stomachs because they were hungry. And when we read in a book on Spencer's positivist philosophy that the wind tries to choose the yellowing leaves to carry them off, we are almost surprised when we find that it was not meant as a poetical image.

Whatever way these thinkers chose to obscure the frontier between organic life and human creative activity, they always ended in a forest of words, sometimes very scholarly words but always only words. Is it not a neat and learned expression to say, like Freud, that poetry is a "sublimation" of sexual instinct? But we can say as well that the invention of the electric bulb by Edison is a sublimation of the selling of newspapers, or that the epistles of St. Paul are a sublimation of traveling by boat. What is always evident is that writing a poem is different from having an instinct and that having religious ideas is different from traveling by boat. Has the word *sublimation* helped us in clearing away these differences or has it helped us in getting nearer to the substance of poetry or of religion? It has done neither.

It seems hardly understandable that even a great thinker like Henri Bergson has indulged in this wordiness. Trying to represent animal instinct and creative activity as two branches of the same tree he asserts that some kinds of animals are endowed with instinct whereas others were given reason to use, and that man has become a reasoning animal in the same way in which he can become a good swimmer—that is, by jumping or falling into new circumstances and accommodating himself to them. But where are these new circumstances to which man has found it necessary to accommodate himself during the same periods when other animals continued to follow their usual ways? And where are the circumstances which force the human reason to invent newer and newer values? Some artists were hungry, others lived in comfort; some scientists were ill throughout their lives, others spoiled their good health by their research work.

Which circumstances have forced them to do their creative work?

But perhaps the most surprising characteristic of all these greater and minor apostles of the materialist interpretation of man is the fact that they usually consider man the top achievement of nature. Has all that introduction into science of terminology appropriate only to human activity served only for this purpose? Is that their reason for trying to clear away the distinction between will and instinct? Did they begin to speak about the evolution of nature and, in that way, establish a sort of history of nature just to be able to declare that man is the most accomplished of all the organisms nature has created? Why? Every ant is more progressive than man in his social life. Every bee knows how to organise economic production much better than the presumable descendant of the primates. And perhaps quite a number of plants have developed their instinct of preservation of the species to a degree inaccessible to man. Why then put him on the top of the universe? Perhaps the most logical conclusion of this rather "homocentric" reasoning has been that of the German philosopher Nietzsche who has announced the coming of the "superman." This prediction has been at least fulfilled: the supermen are already streaming into our life in their colored uniforms.

Thus the materialist explanation of man does not have any meaning for the historian. Neither does the position of the idealist. It means nothing to declare that only the spiritual nature of man is the real one and that everything in space and time is only an "image." It means one empty word more if I assert that the table upon which I write or the hand with which I write are only imaginative objects of my spirit. Here they are with all their material regularities. And everything I know from history has been transferred to me by this or that material medium: word, paper, stone or melody.

Man's creative activity contrasts with the substance of the natural processes. The whole realm of time and space is a sorrowful experience for him. The more he knows the more he is conscious of how restricted is his capacity to know. But his spiritual nature craves to know and to love. It is possible, of course, to find short periods of time in the daily life of anyone in which he is quite satisfied with the fulfilment of his material needs. But it would be wrong to base our whole account of the qualities of man on these exceptional portions of human life. And it would be also wrong to base it upon some dreams about an indefinite epoch in the future history of mankind when, as we are sometimes inclined to imagine, there will no longer be any sorrow or any craving in our spiritual life.

Man's strife with time and space is always of a creative character. Even if we sometimes do not know or have forgotten the values which have already been discovered and even when we by our own work put in danger much higher values which have resulted from the work of others, our own striving has still its creative character. The only way to loose this quality is to make ourselves a passive tool of the instincts. The only way we can get rid of our own personality is to declare ourselves in complete accordance with the irretrievable passing of time, of that time which invites us to death, of that time which is, to use Plato's words, only a moving image of duration.

The striving against time is the very heart of man's life. Those who do not recognise that this is so must spend substantial parts of their lives in persuading themselves that they are right. The German philosopher who reached the conclusion that the best thing in life was to commit suicide—that is to accept unconditionally the passing of matter—did not commit suicide himself but spent his life in preaching his doctrine. And even those who, in despair with the changing world, do destroy their own life, do so because they take death for a sort of existence behind the boundaries of time, forgetting with Hamlet that there is not only question of sleep but perchance of dream also.

By fighting with the changing matter we create certain values. We create them by using the regularities of the material processes. And by doing so we can —but we are not obliged to—express our own progress, our successes on our way to the full knowledge and the full love.

There are five main ways in which knowledge and love for what we know may be pursued.

We can aim at the understanding of the regular processes of nature and of the laws by which they may be represented. By analysing the processes of matter we may ascertain their systematic arrangements and similarities—in reality numerical similarities—in construction. Such knowledge gives us the power to reconstruct certain events, or rather construct similar events, and to predict similar happenings in time and space. By doing so we do not escape from the realm of the matter but we can at least rearrange its proceedings.

Or we can aim at our relations with the human

society and at its organization. The wills of other people are manifest to us by their conflict or consent with our own will. And because our own creative activity requires the greatest freedom possible we try to restrict the conflicts between human individuals and to get the maximum of mutual support. As means to this end we use education and legislation.

We can also aim at the beauty of things. Of course, that which we usually call beautiful in the sensual sense of the word is just the most accessible of those properties of things which arouse our astonishment. Every new contact of our mind with every kind of being is a surprise to us. And to find the fullest meaning of every being in the order of things, to reproduce it or at least to express it by means of symbols is the substance of art. And the more passing and momentous the character of a thing is, the higher is the value of the work of art by which it is adequately expressed. The highest purpose of art is to snatch away from flowing time the dramatic beauty of events which are singular and will never be repeated.

Again we can aim at the recovery of events and experiences of man which have been forgotten and we can discover again the values which have been lost. Not to judge people who are dead—to do so we have no right whatsoever—but to recover the dramatic value of their lives and to make their knowledge our own, that is the purpose of historical research work. And, evidently, our interest in human creative activities of the past can not be restricted to just one branch of human progress; on the contrary, it has to cover them all.

These four approaches to perfection—science, politics, art and history—are eligible to any one of us.

Hardly would we find a human being who would not take at least a slight interest in all of them. Usually, of course, an intense interest in one of these four branches of progress requires most of our energies.

But there is a fifth way whose lure nobody can escape. Every man has either to pursue it or to fight with it and try to deny it. This fifth course is the progress of man in the knowledge of the meaning of his own life, its sources and its final aim. We can not avoid giving at least some sort of answer to the questions referring to the ultimate sense of our own existence. We can use our own experience in doing it and make progress in philosophy. We can rely on testimonies which have been revealed to us and make progress in religion.

A remarkable fact is that these five branches of progress differ from each other as to the degree of their evidence in history. Nearly every discovery in the realm of science and technology has left at least some traces and therefore may be easily detected by the historian. Most of the changes in the organisation of communal life and of the human society as a whole are also traceable in contemporary documents. A number of works of art have been left to us although as many of them have been probably destroyed. To a certain extent also the testimonies of man's interest in the past are at our disposal. But very little indeed do we know of the philosophical and religious progress made by human individuals in the past ages. Thus a whole scale in the historical demonstrability of the five different branches of the progress of man can be established. If a man ploughs his field it is always evident to his neighbors. But if he goes through a religious experience very rarely does he succeed in expressing it.

But if one branch of human creative activity in the past is more traceable than the other it does not mean that it is also higher on the scale of values. Perhaps quite the reverse is true and the least manifest activity is the most important one.

In writing history, however, we have no other choice than to collect the evidence we can find. And we have to bear in mind that it is always through an individual human personality that a new value comes into the world. It can also perish with it. Or sometimes it can remain buried under the dust of time for years and perhaps for centuries. Only when other people get hold of it can we speak of it as of a factor in the process of history. When it is accepted as it is and perused without substantial changes or additions we can say that it became a part of a civilization. When it is developed and cultivated we can speak of it as of an element of a culture.

To distinguish between civilization and culture is perhaps more important than we usually think. Only clear words can help us to clear thinking.

If, for instance, we open an encyclopaedia we may find this definition of culture: "The sum of the activities of the people as shown by their industries and other discoverable characteristics." But what, then, is the difference between a culture and a civilization? Do we not, when speaking of a culture, mean something distinguishable from a civilization? Is there not a substantial difference between a civilization which is dead—and therefore discoverable—and another, living civilization the standards of which are being changed every day by creative individuals? Has not Arnold J. Toynbee, for instance, been forced to introduce into his *The Study of History* a similar distinction between "non-civilized societies"—which, however, would be called "civilized" by an archeologist—and "civilized societies," in which a constant alteration of standards is conspicuous?

We really need an expression by which we could designate any ensemble of ideas, works, instruments, customs, and institutions known to us only from historical research work, or one still existent in a state in which no change at all or only slight changes are perceptible. There is no better word for this purpose than the word *civilization*. The Latin word *civilis* has been always used to indicate somebody or something pertinent to a given, permanent order.

At the same time we need another word by which we could denote the living, creative activity of a certain group of men or of a certain epoch, the changing creation of new values—ideas, laws, instruments, institutions, works of art and so on. If we remember the meaning of the Latin verb *cultivare*, "to cultivate," or "to improve by labor or study," we cannot choose a better expression for this purpose than the word *culture*.

But those are already secondary subjects of interest for a historian. His primary subject remains the creative activity of man as an individual personality.

The Idea of Progress

❦

1:

EVERY DAY and every minute new values are born into this world. But at the same time many other values are being forgotten or destroyed. Everyone knows how many ideas which he has conceived become lost. And among those which he was able to express or to realize, how many remained until to-day?

Nevertheless the historians are often inclined to forget this rather important fact. They like to speak, for instance, of primitive societies and try to find examples of them among the tribes in Africa or in Oceania. But who knows whether the civilization of this or that tribe was not much more developed centuries ago than it is to-day? There are ruins of big cities buried under the sands of the Gobi desert. The civilizations of the so-called primitives may just as well be ruins of some much more complicated civilizations of ages past.

Were it not for the fact that we forget and destroy as well as create perhaps we would not need any history. But there are moral principles, works of art and technical instruments which, for us, have a much dif-

ferent meaning than they had for their inventors.
There are words and symbols which we understand in
a way contrary to that in which their authors have
understood them. The values are changing constantly
and everywhere. There is a small, however insignifi-
cant, cultural life in every civilization which has not
yet met its death in a catastrophe. Toynbee's conception of societies in which there are no creative individuals is a very theoretical conception. But cultural
striving may be directed in a way which is quite opposed to that of the people who have created the various factors of the civilization. We ourselves may testify
that it is so. How many noble ideas degenerate in
common use under our own eyes!

Sometimes we are ready to make other people responsible for things for which we are guilty to the
same extent as they. We like to depict our own times
as an exceptional period. The assertion that we live in
a time of unusual culture may be found very often in
our historical books. The bitter lives of thinkers, politicians, artists, and scientists in the past periods of
history are usually represented in such a manner as
to arouse the feeling that nothing similar could be
possible in our own century. Many historians of our
own epoch, however much they may differ in other
things, are of the opinion that a decisive change for
the better has occurred at the beginning of our own
era—that is in the 16th century. They maintain that
the bad times finished with the end of the Middle
Ages. They eagerly follow in the footsteps of Goethe
who described the Reformation as something unique
in the history of the world and of Michelet in whose
opinion the 16th century meant the discovery of man.

Even when this deification of the Renaissance and Reformation period is now being gradually abandoned, a feeling of the superiority of the modern epoch remains.

Let us accept this assumption for a while at least. Let us suppose that the character of history has really changed in such a way. Where does such a change lead? Where will it bring us?

It is remarkable that one of the most conscious efforts to answer this question is to be found in the work not of any historian but of a scientist. The German biologist, Hans Driesch, who became famous through his studies of organic life, had more courage than many historians and philosophers when, trying to analyse the idea of common progress, he admitted that we did not know the true character of the cultural process and that we even did not know whether it might be explained as growth or only as an accumulation of knowledge. Driesch was also aware of the fact that historical events were just accumulations of physical circumstances which had not any creative power of their own. That was why he accredited history with a meaning of its own, inaccessible to the scientific method. In his opinion we can not inquire into the laws of history but we have to inquire into history as a law.

In comparison with Driesch, the philosophers and historians of the past two centuries cared little as to what was the exact meaning of the supposed improvement of history or progress of humanity, as they liked to call it. And the more often they used these expressions the more rarely they seemed to understand that it was facile to explain all human action as progress.

As to the word *progress* itself, the enlightened

Frenchmen of the latter half of the 18th century, Saint-Pierre and Condorcet, were probably the first to neglect the Christian conception of that idea. Instead of preserving it as symbol for the way to perfection of any individual human personality, they gave to the word a meaning which made it equivalent to that of the development of mankind as a whole. But it so happened that in the course of the following hundred and fifty years a great anxiety resulted from the belief in the golden future of this world and from all that despising of the past which the enlightened philosophers had introduced into modern thinking. We can read pages which are full of this fear of the fate of our own civilization in Oswald Spengler's famous book *The Decline of the West*, and we can meet it again in the volumes of Toynbee's *The Study of History*. There are many historians and philosophers today who have given up the idea of a constant progress in history. They have some doubts as to what can be the end of the ever quickening pace of the contemporary culture. They even have grown desperate of looking for its sense and direction in the years to come.

It seems as if history herself has had a laugh at her adepts who died only ten or fifteen decades ago. What the founders of the religion of progress really had in their minds was not a regular, uninterrupted progress but a sudden coming of a golden age. But their feverish visions were of help even to those who conceived of progress as equal to evolution in the Darwinian sense of the word. For a whole century they could have had the impression that history herself had accepted their theory. The immense development of science and technology supported their opinions. But then the military and economic catastrophes arrived and the number of the members of the Church of Progress began to diminish. On the contrary the number of its critics grew. Many a name famous in our times is among them: Sorel, Curtius, Inge, Dawson, Eliot, Zakrzewski, Huizinga—just to name a few of them.

But our duty should be not only to criticize the false interpretations of a concept but, first of all, to uphold the right one. The idea of progress is not new to mankind. It has a true meaning which has been lost but which can still be recovered. We should try to reestablish it.

The spirit of man used to manifest itself through his creative activity from the very beginning of history. There are innumerable traces of such activity—not only of individuals, but also of families, tribes and different other communities. Were it not for this creative activity there would not have been any story of mankind. Or, what we call the story of mankind, would be only an incomprehensible tragedy.

It is true that man often overestimated his capabilities. Many a liberty, for which people had been fighting for years, was changed into moral chaos and lawlessness. Many a human life was annihilated by the engines made to save other lives. Perhaps we shall not be any better. Our own imagination may be seduced by many a dream. But even so we can try to look on things from a realistic point of view—which has always been that of Christian doctrine. People around us like to exchange one extremist point of view for another. "Where the infatuation with the general progress has ceased and where the misery of this world becomes manifest we no longer find the old Christian conceptions of sin and its effects but an utter scepticism or metaphysical despair." These words of the German historian Ernst Troeltsch are perhaps the truest definition of the world we live in. But is it necessary to run from one extreme to another?

The interest in the meaning of creating and forgetting values is as old as history itself. We can already find it in the two civilizations upon which our own civilization and culture are based: in Palestine and in Greece.

The Jews were persuaded of the exceptional character of their national history. They were impatiently awaiting the day which they believed would be decisive not only for their own fate but for that of the whole world as well. Their belief in such a sudden change was, of course, not a homogeneous one. Some of them, like Isaias the Prophet, were aware not only of the necessarily spiritual character of such a change but also of its probable sorrowful realization. Others looked eagerly forward to a change which would give them power and which would make the earth a paradise. In the end and to the detriment of the nation, this second opinion prevailed.

As to the Greeks, their outlook was different. Herodotus called his books of narrations *historiai*. But Aristotle has also called one of his books dealing with the knowledge of nature *peri ta zoa historia*. The original meaning of the word *historia* is research. Even history in our sense of the word meant a kind of research to the Greeks, a research in the cosmic order of the universe to which the stories of men and nations were subordinated. The cosmos of the Greek philosophy was an eternal order which was being constantly renewed in regular phases. In this regular scheme the dramas of individual human lives were included. In Aristotle's conception identical civilizations kept on returning to the world. Herodotus, when dealing with a human tragedy, used to speak of the "jealousy of the gods," trying to avoid, by using this symbolical expression, the philosophical question which he could not answer. Later on, the wisdom of the stoics recognised only immutable fate moving in circles similar to those of the spheres of heaven. Even Thucydides, the man who started writing history as drama, has not escaped this atmosphere of resignation and despair.

So on one of the shores of the Mediterranean people waited impatiently to see the result of history. The conclusion they were awaiting was the only sense of history for them. On another shore of the same sea people thought it better not to await anything from the future. They did not see any difference between history and nature as far as both could be expressed in abstract symbols. Only some of them barely guessed that there was a mystery hidden in the story of human culture.

Such were the opinions of the world into which Christianity entered with its distinct views of the world and of the role of man in it. These views were based upon the tradition of the Jews and also—especially in the works of John the Evangelist and St. Paul —upon the rich terminology of Greek philosophy. But it was evident that they were quite new views.

The Christian view of man is also the Christian view of progress. Little it matters whether a man lives in poverty or in abundance. It also matters little whether he knows a lot or just a few things. What is important is the will with which he accepts his being and his knowledge, whether his heart is full of love or of fear, of joy or of hatred, of assent or of defiance. Life itself is not so valuable for a Christian as a manifestation of love. Life and knowledge pass, but love does not pass; such is the principle of martyrs. Loving assent is the core of man's relation to God. And reason can only follow that assent. Although, as St. Thomas Aquinas affirms, we can wish only that which we know, that is, what is grasped at least in some way by our reason, we have to give our assent first to be able to understand. This maxim has been repeatedly affirmed by Christian thinkers of different times. Hence Augustine's "You would not seek me, had you not found me already," Anselm's "Faith seeking reason," and Pascal's "Heart which knows better its reasons than reason itself."

This doctrine of the necessity of good will towards God and towards one's neighbors has created a new spiritual atmosphere in the world. Although affirming that the kingdom of peace which the Christians had to seek was not of this world it led people out of the passive indifference of the Greek stoics and taught them how to express their love in deeds. It gave them hope. But not the Jewish kind of hope in some distant future event. The Christian hope is centered around the ultimate result of everybody's own life, around the ultimate reward given to workers laboring in the vineyard of the Lord. And although not everybody was ready to grasp the full meaning of this teaching, such force was infused through it into the hearts of the people who accepted it that the resulting Christian culture began striding ahead of all the other cultures of the world.

To illustrate the difference between man living in the ancient civilizations and man of the more modern times who has inherited at least something from the Christian way of thinking, the Polish historian of Greek civilization, Thadeusz Zielinski, chooses two examples. In the first he compares the dialogues of Euripides' *Faidra* with the monologues of Shakespeare's *Hamlet*. In Faidra's case a healthy reason is seduced by an ill will. In Hamlet's case a healthy will is embarrassed by an unhealthy reason. In the second example he compares the two different conceptions of courage, one expressed by Thucydides and also by Plato in his dialogue *Lakhes*, the other expressed by Tolstoy in *War and Peace*. For the Greeks, courage is a result of reasoning. For Tolstoy's soldiers it is something which is not to be disturbed by unnecessary arguing. Perhaps these examples are not exhaustive. But they are true. The angels above the stable in Bethlehem did not sing for wise, sceptical people. They sang for the people of good will.

In that way a new capability was released in human minds which had been latent in them for ages. Whatever old language we study we always find in it some sort of distinction between the state of immobility—which may be cherished not only by primitives but also by stoics—and the state of creative activity. Even the Chinese make a difference between *gi-shi* or *yang* and *ven-hua* or *yin*. That means that everywhere and in every time the process was known by which values are created or changed. But personalities like the Egyptian pharaoh Akhenaten who revolted against the fossilized religious civilization of his time or the brothers Gracchi who tried to reform the Roman organization of land property at the cost of their lives— these examples are rather rare in the pre-Christian times. Christian culture, on the other hand, has proved incomparable in creativeness and has conserved a vivid memory of its original source. Even the most sceptical businessmen and the most selfish Communist or Fascist dictators of our own times call their dealings a service to humanity.

By teaching the importance of good deeds in the life of everyone Christianity has formed a conception of progress. Creative love has taken the place of the sceptical stoicism of the Greek philosophers, of the "will not to will anything" of the Buddhists, and of the considerate resignation of the Chinese wise men.

Thus the original and the only real meaning of progress in the Christian sense of the word is every change in the life of man which exceeds the realm of the laws of matter and of instincts, and, by doing so, creates new values. First of all there has to be a progress of a certain individual or of many such individuals and only later the progress of a family, a community or a nation. The origin of any new value in this world is a personal one.

Therefore whenever we speak of progress we mean something which, in the first place, concerns ourselves. To anybody who is not a historian by profession, the past events which do not concern him personally are more or less indifferent. The demand for the knowledge of things which have happened in the past has its source in the problems of our everyday life. We need our shadow to be able to control the direction in which we walk. If we lose it, we are embarrassed not because it has been our shadow but because we have lost a good compass by means of which we have been able to check the course we have taken. If anything is of value in history it can only be so because it has at least some value now. Our own conscience of history is a factor in our own progress.

And to progress means, of course, to undergo a certain amount of suffering. This is perhaps the point of the Christian doctrine of progress which is the most important for our own times because it is the most neglected one. The principle that whoever wishes to make some progress has to bear his cross became the stumbling block for many people who would otherwise have readily accepted the Christian message of hope.

Man would like to get rid of suffering. If he does not forsake the fulfilling of his duties he would like at least to rearrange the world in such a way that there would not be any duties in it. And that, of course, is an illusion. To-morrow, forever to-morrow. The waves of the sea come running to the shore and break against the rocks. And again and again they keep on coming and breaking themselves. In how many dreams this illusion has already crept into man's mind! Some spoke about the restriction of infectious diseases and forgot the accidents brought about by the machines. Others preached the prohibition of private employment and forgot that man might fall into servitude of the state. It is true that man, in Plato's words, craves good and immortality at the same time because his love wants to possess the Good forever. But there is no duration in the world. The substance of time and space is change and death. Which morrow may be expected to bring them in accordance with human will?

We have to accept the inevitable reality. The fight with time is the core of our creative activity in this world. We can not get rid of this fight and remain active. We can not get rid of something which was in the prescience of the Cause of the world. This has been explained already by the author of the book of Job and elsewhere in the Old Testament, and it has been fully manifested by that central event in history which took place in Palestine two thousand years ago.

Some people may find it difficult to seek wisdom in Judea or among the fishermen of Galilee. They prefer to accept the Greek conception of life as unexplainable tragedy or to obey Buddha's commandment to look for the way to Nirvana. Some others may try to transfer progress from the life of individual men into the distant and misty future in the rather vain hope that a time may come which will not pass. But neither of these ways can bring us any real understanding. The fishermen of Galilee knew better. They took into consideration the real life of man with all its sufferings. They learned to know God who had become man because of the same love for the sake of which our sufferings are necessary. They healed themselves through his pallor.

Love is the only reason for any real progress. And it is also its only purpose. "I may give away all that I have to feed the poor," says St. Paul, "but if I lack love, it goes for nothing." All other motives can find their fulfilment in time and space. Love exceeds their frontiers. Love begs for eternity and for contemplation which, according to Dante, will replace every longing. And because the progress which originates from love makes man more free from matter, it is also the source of true liberty. When acting according to his instincts, man acts as a prisoner. When he acts from love, he is free. And only because he is free, he lives in history. An act of love is a decision of will in favor of liberty.

It is also a victory against the power of the instincts. The enlightened philosophers who conceived the distorted idea of progress as a general improvement of mankind used to ask with some irony: "If God has spoken why is man not persuaded?" Had they really studied the Christian doctrine they would have known that man is not persuaded precisely because God has chosen to speak and not to impose His will. Had He wished it, He could have created a splendid robot who would have been certainly persuaded. But God wished love and His word was made flesh and we had sight of His glory.

For those who did not yet know the gospel of Christ progressive activity was a strange thing. They could not understand anything which exceeded plain justice. Plato tells us how one day Socrates who was about to leave Peiraieon was invited into the house of Cephalos where he started to discuss justice with Polemarchos. When Polemarchos tried to represent the just man as an ally in war who helps his friends and damages the enemy, Socrates interrupted him by asking him whether he thought that in time of peace a just man could not help his friends. By that question he revealed the shallowness of the pre-Christian wisdom which considered even justice as a static virtue. The Christian answer to this question was that about the greater joy over one sinner who repents than over ninety-nine justified who have no need of repentance.

It happens also rather often that the justified ridicule the progressive. Many new and good ideas have scandalized the world. "Whoever has got some character is apt to be sullied; only mediocre people are safe in that respect," we may say with the Czech critic

F. X. Šalda. But everyone has to make his decision. One can not create and live in peace at the same time.

It is always possible to choose tranquillity. It suffices to use the instruments which are already known, to serve the state and not the man in politics, to repeat what has been already said in art, to deny history and to forget that our ways have to bring us nearer and nearer to God. But a truly progressive life knows no boundaries, no order, no necessity. It emerges from the loving and free acts of man in a similar way to that in which the universe emerged from the act of God.

2:

The Christian idea of progress has impressed itself upon the minds of the Europeans. It has been accepted as a part of European civilization. And it conserved its power even in the times when Christendom went into the profound moral crisis of the so-called Renaissance. But every moral decay usually distorts ideas. That was also the fate of the idea of progress in the 16th century.

The humble and anonymous chroniclers of the Middle Ages used to describe one event after another because they were of the opinion that every one of them could be of service to the reader and enhance his personal progress. The general atmosphere of the Middle Ages was a realistic one and there was little historical pride in them. The medieval people never spoke of their own time as of something superior to other epochs. The coming of the Renaissance marked the beginning of a period of a very different character. The superiority of the present time used to be mentioned everywhere and people began to speak of an even greater superiority of the times to come. They began to write and read utopias.

Among the authors of the different utopias not everyone was able to treat the subject as we are wont to treat a pleasant dream. There were poets among them like St. Thomas More, but there were also ambitious organizers like Campanella. And among the scientists of the 16th and 17th centuries there were not only men who, like Blaise Pascal, were able to distinguish between the law of things and the law of man, but also people desirous of power like Francis Bacon. In his treatise *De Dignitate et Augmentis Scientiarum* Bacon expressed the opinion that nature itself was interested in the knowledge and power of man and, what was even more characteristic of his line of thinking, that human history was a part of the realm of nature. The pride which was inherent in these thoughts then grew and the distorted idea of history gradually gained ground. We can trace its influence in the works of several authors of the 17th and 18th centuries, particularly in Voltaire. At last it became predominant in Iselin's treatise *Sur l'histoire de l'humanité*, published in 1764, and in Condorcet's *Tableau du progrès de l'esprit humain*. In these works there is no more a question of the moral progress of individual people but of the permanent progress of humanity as a whole.

In the 19th century this false doctrine of progress made another step. It became the foster-child of science, something which Francis Bacon would probably heartily approve. Already in the works of the German philosopher Herder the idea was expressed of an eternal movement in nature which revolves gradually around the most perfect type of each species. This idea was seized upon and developed not only by the scientists but also by the philosophers of the 19th century. We know it to-day as the theory of evolution. Karl Marx and Henri Bergson are the thinkers who are most often connected with it although some other philosophers were, in their time, more popular as its apostles.

If, in future, we shall call the 19th century and perhaps also our own times the age of science, it will be not only because of the great number of inventions which were made in these years but also because this age believed in science. It believed in science to such an extent that it considered it unnecessary and even useless to believe in anything else. There was no place for religion, philosophy, and history. Science was considered able to replace them all.

But such a scheme never could be in accordance with the character of man. Human culture is by its own nature multilateral. Shorn of any of its branches it grows them quickly again. And that is why the scientists of our age have developed their own religion and philosophy and even their own history. Only they did not call them by their proper names. They called them *evolution*.

In the beginning it was rather an artless theory. Many people who took a fancy to Pierre Simon Laplace's mechanical cosmogony or, a little later, to Charles Darwin's thesis on the origin of species, were naive enough to think that they could get rid of the Cause of the universe by simply pushing it as far back as possible. What would we think of a man who, seeing that house B has the same sort of roof as house A and a staircase very similar to that of house C, declared that he had found proof for his scientific assumption that house C developed from house B and house B from house A? Such an idea would not even enter the head of a man who had never seen an architect. It could only occur to a very simple man who either dislikes the architect or who is so proud that he does not like to give credit to anybody besides himself.

There was, of course, the famous argument of Immanuel Kant. Kant assured his pupils that, proceeding from an effect to its cause, then to the cause of this cause, and so on, we would never be able to reach an absolute cause which would not be itself an effect of still another cause. There was no such cause, he said, which would not have been a priori bound to its effects by a certain law. There would have to be still another cause which would precede our absolute cause in time and form also its relations with its effects. And so farther and farther back without end.

What was the critical value of such a reasoning? The very judgment that every event is the effect of another event preceding it in time is an incomplete judgment. But even in accepting it, we must not forget that the succession of events itself is an effect of a cause. Necessarily there must be a cause of the time and of every change. And such a cause is itself the law of logic to which every existence is subject.

But the 19th century was evidently too fond of Immanuel Kant to be able to resist his argument. Thus it happened that our grandfathers and fathers came to consider the theory of evolution a new and more critical sort of history. It was rather a curious sort of history. It consisted chiefly of statistics and did not interest itself in individuals. In its views human history and the past existence of nature were one. Accord-

ing to it, new values came into the life of man in the
same way as new species came into the life of nature.
For a long period of time an animal would take baths
in water until finally it became a fish. In like manner,
a man would transport his possessions on the fallen
trunks of trees until the trunks developed into a
wagon. Sometimes it is really amusing to read popular
treatises on evolution written during the past hundred
years, such as that by Friedrich Engels, published under the title *Einteil der Arbeit an der Menschwerdung
des Affen*—a touching story of a group of apes, sitting
in a tree and cracking nuts, who suddenly felt inclined to have a chat and from that whim started the
whole history of human language.

At least subconsciously, the scientists themselves
could not have been satisfied with the simplicity of
such assumptions. The theory of evolution was
changed and reconstructed several times. After Lamarck's theory of assimilation and Darwin's natural
selection by survival of the fittest came de Vries'
hypothesis of sudden mutations. And even that was
not yet the end of ever changing explanations.

It was quite easy to believe that the time will come
when we shall know all the laws by which the regular
processes of nature are governed. It was much more
difficult to explain the substantial differences not only
between the various results of human activity but also
between the various species of organisms and between
the various epochs of evolution. Gradually it became
clear that having refused to consider history as an independent branch of knowledge and having changed
the science of nature into a sort of history the scientists
have embarked on a task which may prove insoluble.

To the student of the development of science in the

19th century it seems almost a pathetic story how the apostles of evolution stuck to their creed and tried to defend it by constantly putting off the most serious problems which kept heaping on their path. In the last decade of the century, for instance, Hans Driesch discovered the tendency of organisms to form wholes that are more than the sum of their parts, by demonstrating how certain embryos whose structure had been damaged were able to complete themselves. One could expect that it would have been a serious blow to the theory of mechanistic evolution. It was not. Most scientists declared that it only proved that the causes of evolutionary effects resided in the environment of the organisms as well as in the organisms themselves. Thus the problem has been put off and, of course, the theory remains a theory.

Today, very little remains of the original conception of the scale of evolution—from the smallest particles circulating in the primeval mists to the complicated organisms of man, as the 19th century textbooks used to say.

Today, the very beginning of the scale is a point of interrogation because we know almost nothing about the smallest particles which we call electrons and whose presence we can ascertain only when they change their positions. The second difficulty is the indisputable principle of entropy which points towards a universe nearing to its end, not towards an evolutionary one. The third problem is that of the origin of life. We have no definition of life which the majority of scientists would approve. If we accept the definition of life as the capability of an individual unit to adapt itself we may almost accept the opinion that electrons are alive and that so-called dead matter is only a great number of living units. But if life is something else then it is at least evident that it has not come into the world as the result of a chance, because that would be mathematically improbable. The fourth problem the solution of which is yet to be found is the evolution of species. No paleontological proof has been discovered as yet of the development of one species from another. Some intermediate specimens have been found among the mammals. But even there all the main species are fully represented already at the beginning of their epoch. As to the others, the reptiles, the fish and the birds or others, every species among them has descended upon this world instantaneously and fully represented. No initial or intermediate specimens are to be found among them. And then there remains the fifth and perhaps most conspicuous difficulty: that of the human history and of its place in the general plan of evolution.

Facing these problems the scientists of to-day have to envisage the theory of evolution in ways which differ substantially from those of the scientists of the 19th century. They remain, nevertheless, true to it.

The biologists, above all, attempting to do for the entire field of science what has been done by researchers in thermodynamics for physics, namely to unify it into a single, ordered whole, have remained faithful to the theory of evolution as the most apt basis for such a unification. If science needs a common methodology surely there are several ways in which it could be obtained. Here again we find ourselves in the presence of the subconscious striving of man to complete his culture and to have at his disposal not only science— no matter how developed from the methodological point of view—but also a philosophy and a history at the same time.

That is probably the reason why the doctrine of evolution survives even in face of difficulties of which its founders never dreamt. In mechanistic evolution, so cherished by the scientists of the 19th century, a rather beautiful picture was presented to the general public—beautiful because of its homogeneity. Nowadays the evolutionists have to deal with several different realms of nature, the common basis of which is yet to be found. There is the realm of microphysics with its protons, electrons and quanta, the realm of macrophysics, the realm of organic life with its mysterious teleology and, last but not least, the realm of the human creative activity. The great theatre of nature is much more rich in human eyes than it was fifty years ago, but it has lost its uniformity.

And more than that. Modern science, however reluctantly, has had to drop some of the devices which she had been using for years. Thus the possibility of the development of the first organic molecules from dead matter under the influence of thermic changes had to be put aside. Also it had to be admitted that there was no proof by which any other factor than pure chance could be excluded from the changing scene of nature. Besides that, the scientists found it difficult to defend the doctrine of chance as a decisive factor in nature against the objection of the logician that if everything is a result of pure chance even the conclusions of a scientist are a result of pure chance and in that case they may be as wrong as right.

But one idea which the founders of the doctrine of evolution appreciated remained firm in its place, namely the idea of causal connections between various events in nature. Notwithstanding its logical falsity it is still the cherished instrument of scientific reasoning. The evolutionists of to-day try to avoid the old fallacy of representing the effect as being included in the material aggregates of the cause. On the contrary, most of them are ready to accept the existence of an unknown law which forces evolution to produce more and more independent beings. They also are aware of the fact that even with the best instruments in hand they can reconstruct events which are only similar to those which they have observed. Events which have already taken place in a certain time can not be reconstructed because their particular time can not be reconstructed. Therefore it is necessary to drop the old axiom of the positivist that only those problems can be dealt with by science which can be repeatedly dealt with by our experience. But the illusion of causal relations between subsequent events remains in force in the minds of the scientists. They even refuse to take the real causality into consideration. The very idea that the result of a chemical experiment is caused not only by the material ingredients of the experiment but also by the will of the chemist who has started the experiment is quite unacceptable to them. By introducing such a psychological element into our calculations, they say, we would make them impracticable.

Yet the centre of the kingdom of material "causality" has been transferred from the sphere of physics into the sphere of biology. The 19th century scientists used to explain evolution by the laws of physics, based on statistics. Now some laws of biology or "evolutionary concepts," as Lecomte de Nouy calls them, have to be discovered. One of the most important physical laws, the second law of thermodynamics, is usually considered the best starting point for this ideal task. According to this law, a constant diminution of free energy, the energy which is capable of doing some work, is evident in this world. It is accompanied by an equally constant increase of the bound energy or *entropy*. To the physicist this principle means that the world is in every moment nearer to a state of immutability in which the warmth will be equally distributed in all its parts. Most biologists do not raise any objections to the inevitable rule of this law in the realms of statistical physics. On the contrary, Lecomte de Nouy is of the opinion that precisely the occurrences expressed by this principle give us the experience of flowing time and entitle us to speak of the evolution of nature. But if the world is approaching a point when it will be unchangeable what can be the sense of evolution?

That is the crucial question for every evolutionist. Many are of the opinion that the second law of thermodynamics, as well as any other purely statistical principle, can not be valid for all that takes place in nature. That, undoubtedly, is the only way out of the blind alley. If there has to be an evolution and if the second law of thermodynamics is valid in the sphere of physics, there has to be another sphere in nature where that law is not valid. If there has to be a theory and if the reality which we know does not respond to this theory, another sphere of reality is to be found which would respond to it. We can only wonder what the 19th century positivists would have said to such a dilemma.

Two scientists of our own generation, Lecomte de Nouy and Joseph Needham, have decided to save the doctrine of evolution at any cost. Their reasonings follow the same line. We can summarize them in three points: 1. There is, without any doubt, an evolution of nature, which is explicable by itself. 2. The laws of physics are incapable of expressing this evolution in its completeness. 3. It is necessary to express the entire order of the evolution in a new and as yet unknown way. But as to what this new way should be, Needham and Lecomte de Nouy differ. Let us examine their answers.

Joseph Needham is a fervent follower of the teaching of Karl Marx. His terminology is based mainly on that of N. I. Bukharin and only partially on that of A. N. Whitehead. His conception of the world is an *organic* one. According to this conception nature is a whole, the parts of which are organically connected, dependent on each other and organized in so-called "societies." The living cells of a body as well as the citizens of a state are such societies. In all these societies a certain "mentality" is inherent which, of course, is "latent" and "non-operative" in inorganic nature. Although one in substance, nature manifests itself in qualitatively different forms and especially in different forms of movement. Every one of these movements is governed by a special set of laws.

A law which has been formulated to express one kind of movement in nature is not capable, according to Needham, of expressing another kind of movement of the same nature. A number of stones may be arranged, according to their sizes, in a certain order. We can disperse them and we can also build a house from them. No matter which one of these two possibilities we chose, both of them, judged by a physicist, mean disorder in the sense that it differs from the original order. But to a biologist who is interested in functions it is clear that in the second case a house has been built and that by building it we have achieved a certain organisation. Every organisation is, in Needham's opinion, accessible to scientific analysis and measurement. In asserting this, Needham goes as far as to contradict J. S. Haldane, the author of *The Philosophy of a Biologist* whose opinions he otherwise accepts almost without reserve. He admits that he can not give us any example of how he is going to analyse and to measure the holistic organisation of societies. But he is sure that a way will be found to do it and, consequently, to measure the evolution of nature including the evolution of human society. His final conclusion is that an "upward trend" is evident in the evolution of nature in which lower stages of organisation are gradually replaced by the more developed stages. The purpose of scientific work is therefore to explain nature by defining the sense of its evolution and to give hope to mankind in its fight for a perfect organisation.

What are we to think of it? Let us push aside the question of how even the most perfect organisation will face the constant decrease of free energy—having the power to accumulate energy but not to create it. There are other questions which Needham does not answer. How is it possible, for instance, to distinguish between "order" and "organisation" and yet to speak of the measurement of the organisations? We can *measure* something only when it can be divided into numerical units, that is to say, a thing belonging to the physical order of things or, at least, belonging to it partially as a book does belong to it by the number of its pages. If "organisation" is substantially different from "order" how can we measure it? We can listen to a symphony but we can not listen to a picture. Whatever can Needham mean by "measurement"? If he is going to establish any kind of laws by it, it has necessarily to have a *tertium comparationis*, something similar to a numerical unit in physical measurement. What will be the *tertium comparationis* between two organisations, say between a maple leaf and an agricultural cooperative?

Then there is the question which is of utmost interest for a historian. If we accept Needham's definition of the human mind as "a phenomenon of high organisational level," we have to ask him what particular human mind or at least what particular kind of human mind does he mean by this definition. Certainly he could not have meant the human mind in general because there are greater differences between individual human minds as to their activities than between different species in the organic world. Now, was Plato's mind a phenomenon of lower level than the mind of Joe Smith? If not, where is the upward trend of evolution? It is true that sons of simple people are sometimes men of genius. It is also true that the sons of men of genius are sometimes worse than simple. Where is the upward trend? Perhaps Needham's answer would be that we are to judge the progress of the human mind only after its organisational manifestations. He likes to compare the transition from economic individualism to Communist economy with that of the transition from "dead" proteins to the living cell. Well, the living cell certainly has qualities which the dead matter has not. Perhaps we can even accept the assumption that dead matter is older than living cells. But as to the relation between the Communist and the capitalist economies two things are evident. First that the Communist organisation of society is much older than the capitalist organization; quite a number of tribes in Central Africa may testify to that. Second that we are at a loss in trying to find any indication of the direction in which the "upward trend" moves from one of these two sorts of societies into another. Does Needham, for instance, expect us to count and compare the starving unemployed in Switzerland and the tortured inhabitants of the concentration camps in Siberia—and if he does, what conclusion are we to make out of it? Needham's chief aim is to show us the way in which the perfect organisation of human society could be achieved. He does not tell us what that perfect organisation will be like. We have some suspicion that it will be something like the perfect organisation of bees. But, in any case, if such an organisation is the aim of nature, nature would undoubtedly achieve it without our help. And, if nature was able to accomplish such a thing among the bees many thousand years ago, why does she need such a long time in dealing with man? Why indeed?

Lecomte de Nouy's theory of evolution is in some aspects more critical. He distinguishes among four main realms of nature: 1. the sphere of the smallest particles governed by the laws of the mechanics of quanta; 2. the sphere of atoms governed by the laws of thermodynamics; 3. the sphere of living organisms governed, as he believes, by biological laws as yet unknown to us; 4. the sphere of human mind, governed by moral and spiritual laws. Thus he acknowledges the fact of the substantial difference between the creative activity of man and the realms of nature. But immediately afterwards he makes rather an interesting step. Although not giving up the false conception of the casual relations, he declares that evolution can be explained and fully understood only as a movement directed to a certain end. And because that end can not be that immovable state in which all energy would be equally distributed, Lecomte de Nouy has conceived the idea of what could be appropriately called prolonged evolution. The final aim of evolution is, in his opinion, the knowing and creating spirit of man. This brings him also to the conclusion that adaptation, natural selection, and mutations could possibly help the evolution but were not perhaps always real progressive factors. Especially adaptation could hardly ever be a progressive factor because, as Lecomte de Nouy puts it, adaptation seeks equilibrium and every instinct can achieve a state of balance with its environment whereas an intelligence usually finds out its own situation just to be able to cross its frontiers in the very next moment.

All that is rather interesting. Lecomte de Nouy went along his somewhat Bergsonian lines much farther than perhaps any other scientist in recognising the true nature of man. He went even so far as to formulate the question whether, by accumulating knowledge, man becomes more perfect or perhaps only more rich. His answer was that the mind of man becomes more and more complicated and also more and more free from matter. But does it? Where are the proofs? To have some power over nature and to be free from it are very different things.

Even if we accept this fantastic wish—that man might be made free from matter—as something which can be fulfilled, would not then the whole theory of evolution, as conceived by Lecomte de Nouy, be a sheer farce? If, from the very beginning, nature aimed at the creative spirit of man, there must have been somewhere in nature an intelligence capable of conceiving such a creative spirit and therefore more intelligent than any individual man. But man, even if he is free from any material laws, will only be intelligent enough to play with all the regularities and instincts of nature as he plays now with the acquired characteristics of the *drosophila melanogaster*. He will never be able, as Lecomte de Nouy himself says, to start another evolution. Thus, in the end, nature will itself change into something much inferior to what it was at the beginning of evolution.

Such is the survey of contemporary evolutionist thinking. One of its representatives assures us that evolution is governed by laws which we first have to discover to be sure that there is an evolution at all. The other says that we can understand evolution only from a teleological point of view which will show us that nature aimed from the start at changing itself into man who, however spiritual, would not be able to do what nature itself has done. And if we look back on the original mechanistic conception of evolution we may say, with some regret, that although it was as uncritical as these modern conceptions, it was perhaps easier to believe.

3:

There are problems and there are also mysteries in human life. A doctor may concentrate all his knowledge and all his memory in forming the diagnosis of a patient. But he is usually surprised to find how easy a task it has been when, all of a sudden, the atmosphere of hope and despair of a hospital ward appears before his eyes confronting him with the question of all questions: what is the sense and the meaning of a human life. There are problems of all kinds, technical, political, artistic, scientific. All of them can be answered, sooner or later, by this or that act or explanation. But there are also mysteries or, better to say, one mystery with many variations, the mystery of our existence.

Many of our contemporaries do not like the word *mystery*. They prefer the expression *problem*. They are of the opinion that every mystery is really a problem or, at least, that it can be solved as one. The word mystery is not a scientific word and therefore people living in the age of science do not employ it.

But even the scientists themselves can not escape it. In answering the scientific problem of the origin of the drops of water hanging on the surface of a window we can mention the steam in the atmosphere, the temperature of the glass, and perhaps many other circumstances and we can even prove the validity of our answer through an experiment. But if we ask what makes the various factors act in such a regular way that it can be expressed by a law, it is not a problem. It is a mystery. Of course, our answer can be that "chance" makes them act in that way. But to use the word chance is worse than to use the word mystery. By calling something *mysterious* we recognise that we hardly know the thing about which we speak. It is a veracious word. On the other hand, by using the word *chance* with its definite, assured accent, we pretend that we know everything about the subject to which we refer. The use of such cheap but pretentious words is what we reproach the so-called "scientific philosophies" for.

Let us consider, for instance, what the philosophers of the 19th century have done with the expression *progress*. To a Christian, the capacity of every man to know more and to love more always seemed a part of the profound mystery of his existence. The evolutionists, on the other hand, began to treat progress as a simple problem. Taking as a reality the assumption that history is a part of the evolution of nature, they arrived at the conclusion that progress is only another word for evolution. Instead of symbolizing the mysterious capability of human individuals, the word progress was employed by them as a symbol of the continuous advance of humanity as a whole. The existence of such an advance they took as evident. The problematic side of the thing consisted for them only in the task of finding out the laws by which that advance was governed.

In what way has this doctrine helped us? In what respect have the followers of Karl Marx or Henri Bergson made our knowledge more profound? It certainly makes some sense to say that the fruit has ripened to make the growth of new trees possible; although it would be better to say clearly that the Creator makes the fruit ripen to enable the growth of new trees. But what sense is there in saying that Smetana achieved his musical compositions that Dvořák might be able to achieve his? What sense is there in assuring people that each of us has to go through the sorrows of his life so that another one might be able to go through his?

And again, what sense is there in speaking about

Nature, Necessity, *Élan Vital*, Harmony, Humanity and all the other words which remain meaningless even when we write them with capital first letters? Karl Marx, for instance, assures us that the development of the forces of production cause the conditions of production and these conditions of production, in their turn, cause the development of the human knowledge through which new forces of production are being discovered. And to the question, why is that so, he answers: "Because of necessity." Which, of course, is not an answer at all. To say that man has to live in history because he necessarily has to live in history has no meaning at all—except that it means degrading a mystery into a problem of words only. And just how ridiculous such a degradation is becomes clear to us when we read in a Marxist text-book a phrase like this one: "To remain faithful to ourselves we have to bear in mind that we are only small links in the chain of Nature." Well, what will happen if we do not remain faithful to ourselves? Shall we cease to be links in the chain of Nature? And if not, why be afraid that we shall not remain faithful to ourselves and why write Marxist text-books?

From the Christian point of view, no such thing as evolution in human history has ever existed. We do not believe that people are better or more happy than they were a thousand years ago. And, of course, we also do not believe that they are worse or more unhappy. We do not even believe in what we can perhaps call the most curious conclusion of a desperate evolutionist, namely that people are more happy and, at the same time, more unhappy than they were a thousand years ago. We believe only that which is reasonable: that the story of the life of each human personality is a drama—which may be full of progress as well as of retrocession—and that the story of mankind is also a drama of its kind.

First of all we refuse to see the meaning of a man's life somewhere in the life or lives of other men. The drama of every human personality is enclosed in the frontiers of the individual human conscience. Inside these frontiers the dramatic experience of human life is started, developed and achieved. There are joys and there are also sorrows included in it as well as knowledge and creative activity. All that has certainly a meaning. It would be foolish to look for that meaning somewhere else in space and time. But, at the same time, it would be also inadequate to look for it exclusively in this or that part of the drama of life. We have to consider the human life as a whole to be able to grasp its meaning.

In a similar way while refusing to look for the meaning of history in the regular proceedings of nature or somewhere else outside history itself we insist on trying to understand history as a whole, as a drama which has its beginning, development and even its end. We would never grasp the whole meaning of history by dividing it into single civilizations or by just enumerating or depicting the changes which have taken place in its course. In doing so we would act like Zeno who was not able to grasp the meaning of movement because he had divided it into a series of imaginary points none of which had any space.

In the short period of our own lives we know from experience that the world has been repeatedly afflicted by catastrophes hitherto unknown to mankind. Millions of men died in wars and millions were put to death in concentration camps. People of good will, no matter how frank were their decisions or how strong were their efforts, were left far behind the striding giant of fate. And those who had all the experience of the terrors of war did not hesitate to plunge into another sea of blood and misery. That is the tragic reality of history. It is as real as future events are unknown to us and unpredictable. And whatever the future history may be, its past and present can not be changed. To understand what can be understood about history we have to deal with it as with a drama which, often enough, is a tragic drama.

This is not a problem. It is a mystery. By claiming our right to understand history we, at the same time, express the wish to understand the meaning of human life. It is in history where the creative activity of man is anchored. The answer, therefore, can not be given in cheap words which are easy to invent but whose content is so poor that they even do not resume the content of the question.

The first step towards a real answer to the mystery of history—although even then, an answer as insufficient as human answers always are—is the acknowledgement of the Cause.

Whenever an idea was realized—in the spheres of science, politics or art—it was realized because somebody wished to realize it. But man is not the only cause of his own deeds. He always has to use this or that part of the order of nature, this or that regularity which was evidently meant for his use. And not only that. To be able to create, or to change something, man must first grasp the meaning—or at least a partial meaning of his act. That is to say he must know his act. But neither the meaning of the things around us, nor the meaning of our own images, nor that of our abstract ideas has been created by ourselves. There must necessarily be a Cause of every meaning, including the meaning of time and of history.

Without the Cause there would be no meaning whatsoever. The world without the Cause is a logical nonsense. Not knowing the Cause I would not know myself, because the meaning of "I" is conditioned by the meaning of the Cause in the same way as the meaning of "my letter" is conditioned by the meaning of "I." This truth is not only a kind of analogy; it is much more. Not only because every human deed has its partial cause in man must the world as a whole have its Cause, but because every meaning includes a priori the Cause. No thing which has a certain meaning can exist without being caused to have that definite meaning, because otherwise it would not exist.

But do we not, in introducing the expression "Cause," just introduce another of the same group of words which we have refused as meaningless? Is not the Cause something similar to Nature, Harmony or Necessity? Not quite. There is included in it the meaning of a conscious will which is not the case with any one of the other symbols. But our argument is not yet finished. We are not satisfied with the expression "Cause." We are going to speak of God.

Why of God? Could we not choose Lao-tse's *tao*, Pythagoras' *to perainon*, or Bradley's *Absolute*?

The words which we use have to be correct and true. A correct word symbolizes exclusively the concept we have in mind and nothing else. A true word symbolizes all the relations, or characteristics, of our subject which are known to us. Our knowledge is a true knowledge. What is questionable are the ways we express it. The adequacy of the words to the subject is the central problem of logic. If we dream about a castle of silver there are two tasks to be undertaken by our reason. The first is to think—and to speak— about a dream of a castle and not, for instance, about some castle which we have seen in reality; this entails choosing a correct expression. The second is to think and speak about a dream of a castle of silver and not about a dream of any sort of castle; in doing so we choose a true expression.

We often choose a word which is correct. Lao-tse's or Bradley's expressions which we have quoted above are perhaps quite correct. The more difficult task is to choose a word which is true enough. Our knowledge is never complete, no matter how simple its object may be. There are always some qualities of our objects which we have only recently ascertained; and in ascertaining them we have to express them.

If, then, we have to find a true name for the Cause of history we have to remember all the dramatic characteristics of history. We have to remember the constant fighting of men against men and of ideas against ideas. We have to remember the eternal uncertainty of man who does not even know what knowledge will be granted to him the next day. We have to remember the sufferings of every child who has been born into this world and of every old man who has seen broken the things which he had strived to build up throughout his life. Only then can we give a name to the Cause of history.

How often have we chosen a wrong name! How often have we been influenced by poets who tried to reform God or, magnanimously enough, to forgive Him that He had introduced suffering into this world.

How often have we been seen among the multitude on Golgotha crying: "Come down from that cross, if thou art the Son of God."

The sufferings of man, the drama of his life, the drama of history, all that has a certain meaning. But what can it mean to the *élan vital*, to Nature, to the Absolute, or to Necessity? It certainly must mean something to the Cause. It does mean something to God. And that is why we have to return to the God of the Christians. We are not able to find a name for Him that would be not only correct but also absolutely true. His is the wisdom (*sofia*), ours is only the craving for wisdom (*filosofia*). But we know that calling him God we recognize in him the author of the freedom of human will which is, of course, the source of our sufferings, but which is also indispensable for love. And that is why we prefer the simple name of God to all the names chosen by the scientists. "If anybody claims to have superior knowledge, it means that he has not yet attained the knowledge which is true knowledge; it is only when a man loves God that God acknowledges him." (I Cor. 8, 2)

To understand the drama of history means more than to understand the situation of man in his natural environment. It means to understand his relation to his Creator. It means to understand his position between nature and God. The sense of drama was known to the Old Testament authors of the stories of Jacob's fight with the angel and of Judith's sacrifice. It was known to the Greek dramatists—although it was not much known to the Greek philosophers. But it was known above all to the Son of Man who, when teaching, never used syllogisms, and rarely aphorisms, but whose similitudes possessed a singular dramatic beauty.

To understand the drama of history means to understand that love can be born only in a heart free enough to deny it. It is rather a characteristic thing to read in Lecomte de Nouy's book *La Dignité humaine* [1] that love can not be included among the factors of evolution because, although often a motive, love never was the aim of evolution. This opinion expresses all the abyss which yawns between the evolutionists and the Christians. From the Christian point of view love is the only aim and the only reality. A lot of other values are being accumulated in history and again lost. Even in our own age, so proud of its knowledge, we can not be sure of what lies ahead of us—not to mention, for instance, the moral values which we have lost already. These other values have their own sense but it is only a secondary one. What matters is love. And love is individual. It differs with every human person. It may be born in any century and in any set of conditions.

That is the core of the Christian conception of history as a drama in which the love of each individual person may be manifested independently. A drama the culminating point of which is God's own manifestation of his love for man.

The ancient people who saw how the gospel spread through the world had some difficulty in grasping this idea which changes the natural existence of man into a participation in history. Take for instance Celsus against whose attacks Origen had to defend his creed. It was not so much hatred which led Celsus' pen as his astonishment at what seemed to him to be the simplemindedness of the Christians. He could not

[1] New ed. Paris, 1948 p. 164.

quite grasp how the Christians could be so foolish as
to honor a God who gave up his immovability and
even took part in human history. Such a thing seemed
to Celsus the precise contrary of the fixed, regular and
eternal order which was the highest ideal of antiquity.
Also the gnostic heresy which for some time looked as
if it would rapidly spread among the Christians themselves, did not recognise history; it taught a regular
recurrence of events and tried even to explain Christ
himself as just a symbol of the cosmic process. But
the Church remained faithful to the truth with which
it had been entrusted and stuck to the words of the
apostle: "In this has the love of God been shown in
our case, that God has sent his only-begotten Son into
the world that we may live through him." (I Jn. iv, 9)

Any drama has its end as well as its beginning.
Perhaps the chief difference between a drama and an
order consists in the opposition of this characteristic
of the drama to the unending validity of an order. The
"scientific" conception of history as eternal evolution
was originally based on the Christian idea of progress
but it has missed the chief point of this idea. According to Christian doctrine time, and every portion of
it, is directed towards a definite end. The flow of time
has a meaning which is given by what is fulfilled in
that time. The time of the life of each of us has its
fulfilment and so has the time of history. There is
no fulfilment in evolution. Seen from an evolutionist's point of view an organism lives to enable another
organism to live. Such a view, of course, was rather
unpalatable, and more acceptable explanations had
to be found; thus the Nazi and Communist versions
appeared. What then are we to expect? The victory of

the superrace whose chieftains will later engage in murdering one another? The Bolshevist organization of the world in which even the directors of the secret police will be afraid of each other? Or are we expected to have recourse to a third possibility invented by the American specialists in advertising, namely the idea of a future time which will be so progressive that anybody will be able to be born, insured and buried in a fragment of a second?

The Christian view of history is different. According to it there is an *alpha* but also an *omega* of history. "One thing, beloved, you must keep in mind, that with the Lord a day counts as a thousand years, and a thousand years count as a day. The Lord is not being dilatory over his promise, as some think; he is only giving you more time, because his will is that all of you should attain repentance, not that some should be lost. But the day of the Lord is coming, and when it comes, it will be upon you like a thief. The heavens will vanish in a whirlwind, the elements will be scorched up and dissolve, earth, and all earth's achievements, will burn away." (II Peter 3, 8-10)

"In the beginning was the Word." And through him God created man who can love but who can also refuse to love. Love is the only purpose of creation. It is the value of values. It can not be born without liberty. And liberty means the possibility of hell as well as the possibility of heaven. There was also the centre of history. "The Word was made flesh, and dwelt among us, and we saw his glory." And there will also come an end of all the times. "I am Alpha and Omega, the beginning and the end, says the Lord God; who is, and who was, and who is to come, the Almighty." (Apoc. 1, 8)

Therefore, a Christian can not deal with history as with a prelude to some other epoch of time. He can consider history a prelude to eternity, to the new heavens and new earth which will be the dwelling-place of holiness. (II Peter 3, 13.) History is not a portion of time, it is the whole of time, the whole of its meaning. In history time has found its fulfilment.

II

THE ANCIENT BACKGROUND

The Origins of Culutre

❧

How FAR BACK in the past can we reach for the beginning of history and for the sources of our own civilization? The written sources which are at our disposal
cover a little more than five thousand years. The further in the past we look for them the less frequent
they are. Only few of them concern the period before
3,000 B.C. and they are written in alphabets and languages with which even the best experts are not perfectly acquainted. What about that part of the story
of mankind from which there are no written documents? Even the oldest traditions known to us—the
Old Testament, for instance—which are concerned
with it, can not inform us about its real length; the
way in which they use the expression "year," for example, is more symbolical than historical. And have
the historians themselves not restricted their own field
by distinguishing the so called prehistory from
history?

It is true that the oldest epoch of history has to be
searched by other methods than the newer ones. The
specialists who are interested in it have to know more
about geology than about languages. The profession
of an archeologist is usually distinguished from that

of a historian. But, nevertheless, both deal with the
story of the same mankind. It would be, perhaps, more
logical to speak of protohistory than of prehistory. In
any case, it is not correct to say that history begins for
any nation or tribe from the time from which we can
trace its experience from its own records. History begins for mankind from the time from which we can
trace its experience by any way. Little it matters how
remote that time may be. Even today, only a part of
the creative activity of man is expressed by written
word. We can not restrict our interest to written documents without depriving ourselves of not a few
branches of human experience. We have to study
history in its entirety.

Besides that, we have now another method by which
we can add a great deal of knowledge to the results of
excavations and geological comparisons. We can study
the civilizations of the so-called primitives who still
live in our own world. Especially among the colored
tribes which have not as yet received the Christian
civilization we may find instances of civilizations very
similar to those about which we know from the excavations of the protohistorians. We have, of course, to
be careful in availing ourselves of the results of such
ethnological studies. The present civilization of this
or that tribe in Central Africa or in Oceania is not
always necessarily its original civilization. It may be,
on the contrary, a result of a long process of decadence
or of an equally long and complicated process of super-
imposition of civilizations which had originated in
other areas or with other peoples. That is also why,
perhaps, the name "primitive" is not well employed
in this connection. But if we distinguish the elements
of civilization which appear to be the earliest every-

where from all the other elements we may be sure that we have got hold of the really primitive results of human creative activity.

We can, therefore, deal with the advent of man and with his first achievements as with the first and not the least part of history.

If, however, we consider this period as the first chapter in the drama of mankind of which we have said that it has its beginning as well as its end, what can we say about its dates? Could we not, at least approximately, fix the date of the beginning of history?

In this respect, the answer of every critical historian has to be negative. History itself has no method by means of which it could obtain any result in this field. There are only the opinions of the geologist. And the geologist is, of course, ready to serve us with quite a number of theories and hypotheses about the date of the advent of man on this earth and about his early history. Only there is a major difficulty with all these geological theories—which some historians, however, do not hesitate to accept. Geology has a predilection for ciphers. Speaking about the beginnings of life on this earth or about the time when the earth began to cool, the geologist is ready to throw millions of years over his shoulder. In the same way, speaking about the advent of man, he is ready to calculate with tens or perhaps with hundreds of thousands of years. But if he is so sure that the basic biological or perhaps even physical conditions on this earth were substantially different some time ago from what they are like today, how does he know that the time which he uses in his calculations was the same as today? We know that the biological time differs from the physical one. We know that there is no such thing as an absolute time. Now, what, for instance, was a stellar year like ten thousand years ago? And is there any point in employing a criterion whose nature could have been changed much more than the nature of the things which we would like to measure with it?

In any case, we know that tangible remains of the existence of man appear for the first time in the strata dating from the time between the first and the second ice age, a period which may be dated at the very least 25,000 years before Christ. We also know that even the physical appearance of this *homo primigenius* differs by a number of characteristics from the anthropoid monkeys with whom he used to be put in relation by the evolutionists. For the last hundred years, it was rather interesting to observe the endeavours of the evolutionists to find some "missing link" between the apes and the man. Had they found a missing link between the mouse and the elephant they would not have been so full of joy as when some remains of human skeletons were found in Neanderthal in Germany with heavily protruding eyebrow arches, similar to the eyebrow arches of some monkeys. Unhappily for the evolutionists, such eyebrow arches are nearly or altogether absent in the skulls of women and children of the Neanderthal type. Besides, there is further evidence of the substantial bodily difference between man and the animals who are nearest to him from the anatomical point of view. The remains found in 1911 in Piltdown, England, in 1933 in Swanscombe, England, and in Steinheim, Germany, and in 1951 in Behshahr, Iran, are, without any doubt, from a period much earlier than that of the Neanderthal man. But their high foreheads and only in some cases slightly heavier eyebrows do not differ in any substantial characteristic from the form of skulls of modern man. It has to be noted also that these remains are older than the fragments of bones which can not be attributed with certainty to any type of animal or man, but which some anthropologists have named *sinanthropus* and *pithecanthropus*.

It is quite possible, on the other hand, that, in his early stage, man was endowed with the capability to differentiate rather quickly into races which differed from each other to a much greater degree than the human races of today. The influence of different physical conditions of the various regions into which the different tribes had migrated is also not excluded. There are all sorts of evidence—common mythological traditions, relatedness of languages, traces of former geographical conditions—to the effect that not only have there been contacts between peoples now separated in space but also that all the different human races came from a common single source. But if the migration of peoples between the 4th and 8th centuries after Christ had a much greater extent than any move of population today how much more extensive could have been the movements of different tribes and races in the dawn of history? Why then could not the relatively small differences between the *homo primigenius* and the *homo sapiens*, the anthropological name of the man of today, be explained as differences between two races which existed—perhaps together with other human races, now extinct—at the same time? Some of those races might have met the fate of the Australian primitives or the North American Indians of our own times. In the recent excavations on Mount Carmel in Western Palestine there is some

evidence that members of two very different protohistoric races lived not only at the same time but also
in the same places. In Europe the sudden appearance
of the homo sapiens in the course of the Fourth Ice
Age coincides with the gradual disappearance of the
men of the Neanderthal type. Also the civilization of
man in the protohistoric epoch changes in a way
which is far from simple; a certain level of material
civilization is associated, in Europe, with man of the
Neanderthal type, whereas in Eastern Central Africa
the same type of implements is usually found with
the remains of a race much nearer to the modern type.

As yet, we know very little indeed about the first
epoch of human history to be able to establish the
order in which the various races of men occupied
different territories. The fact that in Europe the race
of homo sapiens in its oldest remains is already found
subdivided into three rather different types—those of
Brno, Cro-Magnon, and Grimaldi—is in itself sufficient to demonstrate the immense variety of races
with which we have to deal. And perhaps the custom
of the archeologists to name the different races and
their civilizations after the places in Europe where
they were found for the first time does not help us to
get a clear view of things. We have to wait until we
shall know more about the protohistory of other
continents.

What is, of course, of much greater interest to us
than the complicated migrations of men during the
first stage of history, is their creative activity. If the
number of human races of those times was great, the
number of their civilizations was even greater. And
perhaps—although we do not exclude the influence of
physical conditions in various regions on the forma-

tion of different races—the different types of cultural activity of protohistoric man may have been also important factors in the origin of races. Especially if we take into consideration the long centuries during which those races probably developed, we may find it quite reasonable to suppose that it was the kind of life which a tribe used to lead and the values which it used to produce which changed its physical appearance, and not the other way around. Today, some people even affirm that they can discern the development of a Nazi and a Bolshevik type of man, each of which has not only its distinct moral but also, it would seem, conspicuous physical qualities.

What then were the general aspects of the creative activity of man in the first stage of history? And what are the values which he has created and which are still worth something for us?

A number of historians—and especially those among them who had taken a fancy to the theory of evolution—used to treat primitive man as a kind of brute who mastered his savage instincts and began to think only at the end of a very slow process. Besides being satisfied with such a characterization because it matched perfectly with the evolutionist theory, they had only one argument in support of it, namely that the protohistoric man was not capable of any abstract thinking. And that, of course, is an absurdity. The greatest invention of primitive man was language. And no language is possible without abstract thinking.

The primitive man was, undoubtedly, ignorant of many things. But does that mean that he was less human than the self-satisfied engineer of to-day? The child which regards a clock does not know anything about its mechanism or about its purpose. But, sooner or later, it will express the joy it feels at the discovery of a new interesting thing, the same joy which the sophisticate man of the 20th century has lost. Is it less human for doing so—even if it is ignorant as perhaps the primitive man was?

The astonishment, the joy of learning to know things was the obvious source of human language. Had the primitive man behaved like the animals, we would today possess a number, and perhaps quite a great number, of cries which would express all sorts of feelings and emotions connected with the various instincts. But the substance of human language is quite different. It can also express feelings and emotions but at the same time and first of all it expresses things. A human expression—it can be a word and it can also be a phrase—means that the attention of man has been concentrated on one thing or on one event and that he has conceived the wish to fix the sense of that thing or event and even to communicate it to others. And all that is a manifestation of astonishment and of joy.

The students of language who have tried to reconstruct its origin and development in accordance with the theory of evolution as a development from the quite simple, monosyllabic words to the modern languages with their fixed grammars, found it always very difficult to explain why it is that the farther back into the past we go the more complicated are the languages we meet. And to put down the innumerable rules of the languages of the primitive tribes which still live in the remote parts of the earth is a task in comparison with which the study of the grammar of any modern language is the easiest thing. But we need not employ any such artificial theory because we do not have to prove at any cost that primitive man was a brute. On the contrary, we find the most natural explanation of the complicatedness of old languages in the fact that their inventors were real personalities, men capable of untiring observation and—if we may be allowed to say so—poets in the best sense of the word. If we compare the present tendency of every modern language to express the greatest amount of things in the simplest way possible with the efforts of the poets who are dissatisfied with the basic language of daily life and try to find words and expressions which would say more than the usual idioms, we can guess in what sense the linguistic efforts of the primitive man differed from the linguistic indifference of the common man of today.

It is true that the primitive expressions were probably quite concrete and specialized in meaning. But they were, all the same, the very foundations of abstract thinking. To express the sense of a thing means already to be able to abstract that sense. On the other side, the primitive expressions, symbolising a concrete experience, were much more personal than any of our own expressions. The results of ethnological studies confirm the fact that the older a language is, the more important is the role which the intonation plays in its grammar. It is not improbable that the primitive languages were more sung than spoken. And to sing is a much more personal way of expression than to speak. It is also, in a way, a much more communicative way of expression. We have just to remember the important role which singing played in the communal and family life of our forefathers. Have we not, in forgetting it, lost a value the lack of which is perhaps one of the roots of the growing spread of mental diseases in our age? Such a loss is perhaps irreparable. But we can still preserve another value inherent in human language from its beginnings, namely its personal character. If we allow our modern languages to degenerate into a sort of newspaperman's slang consisting only of prefabricated phrases, would it not mean a degeneration of the whole creative life of man? We must not forget that language is not only a means of communication but also the indispensable couch of human thoughts.

The early history of language will probably always remain hidden to us. Although all the languages might have had a common origin, their differentiation followed without much delay. In greater communities one of the dialects was usually accepted as means of common understanding; but such selected dialect did not necessarily oust the other dialects; sometimes, on the contrary, it even lost its distinguishing qualities in contact with them, forming thus a new, national language. Such at least is the process, of which the ethnologists tell us rather often.

One other invention of the genius of the primitive man is connected with the development of language: the pictographic script. We can only propose various conjectures as to the occasion when a series of pictures was for the first time used to convey a message. But it certainly took a long time before the pictographic writing developed into linear syllabic or alphabetical writing in which each sign represented a syllable or a letter. The first European alphabet was formed on the basis of the older linear alphabet which had been brought to Crete and the neigboring islands from Egypt, and of the Phoenician script whose signs sym-

bolized consonants only. To reach the century in which
this occurred—probably in Palestine or on Rhodes or
some other island in the Eastern Mediterranean—we
would have to go well into the historical epoch, to the
end of the second millennium before Christ.

The connection between language which sprang up
from astonishment and joy and the development of
script leads us to another branch of cultural life: art.
If anybody had any doubt about the human character
of the primitive man and even if he supposes that some
human races in the first stage of history were *homines
alali*, men unable to speak, he can not feel uncertain
about the primitive man's love for art. In excavations
uncovering the remains of any human race of the past,
implements are found which bear more or less developed ornaments—something which no animal instinct
can achieve. And we have to remember that objects
made from stone and bone and later from copper and
bronze superseded those from wood, the material
which is most apt for artistic purposes but which is
also of the least durability so that nothing of the
wooden objects has been preserved until our own
times. If we speak of the stone age and bronze age, we
can certainly guess at the existence of a wooden age
and, calculating from the number of objects of art
made from stone or metal, we can imagine how vast
the field of the creative activity of primitive man was.
But even those of his artistic creations which we know
are sufficient testimonies of the depth of his feeling.

There were at least two lines along which the artistic attempts of the primitive man were directed. The
first of them is his interest in geometrical ornaments
of which he profited in making weapons as well as in
making vessels. The predilection for different sorts of

ornaments varied from tribe to tribe but changed very rarely inside the tribal community. The second line was much more free and personal. It was the interest the primitive man took in the beauty of things which astonished him, in the swiftness of a stag or in the force of a bison. Anybody who regards the wall-paintings of the primitive man in the caves of Altamira or at Fond de Gaume has the impression that something profoundly human led the hand of the artist who worked there several thousand years ago: the longing for the beauty of the quickly passing moment.

As to what concerns the other arts, architecture, poetry, and music, we have, of course, very little to say. Of the architectural achievements, if there were any, we do not know any remnants. Of the poetical and musical works of the primitive man we know probably something. At least the similarity between some mythological poems of the Near East and the myths of the Indians of Central America or the similarity between the Basque and the Ukrainian songs can be explained only through the contact of these distant tribes somewhere in the dim past of the protohistoric era and can be regarded, therefore, as proof of their antiquity. But, naturally, we can not distinguish the poetical and musical achievements of those remote times from the additions and changes of the later ages.

But let us now ask a question concerning a subject of utmost importance. If the primitive man was capable of such profound joy from which sprang his language and his art, what were his religious ideas? What opinions has our civilization inherited from him concerning the belief in God and the meaning of human life? In this respect, the results of excavations give us only one assurance, namely that the primitive man believed in some sort of life after death. The flat stones which used to be placed into the graves to protect the heads of the dead, the vessels placed beside the bodies, such are the only testimonies of his religious or philosophical thoughts. The answer of the ethnologist is a much more complete one. According to the results of his research, everything in the world is, in the thoughts of the primitive man, a manifestation of a spiritual power. Perhaps we can not go so far as to say that man has already at the dawn of history grasped the idea of cause and effect. We have no testimony of complicated reasoning before the first millenium before Christ. But the primitive man was as near to the basic realities as we are or perhaps even nearer. Just as the primitive tribes of today are conscious of the sensible meaning of everything around them, so was he conscious. And therefore he looked upon things as upon evidence of spiritual, creative activity. And, what is even more important, he knew that there is only one, indivisible creative activity in the background of all things. In some cases or in some times, his world was inhabited by many spirits of lower grade and many a regular event in nature was looked upon as the result of the activity of a special god. But even in those cases the initial and all pervading activity of the Creator remained present in his mind. The Creator was the giver of the moral law and with that law were connected the ideas of sin, sacrifice and prayer.

Religion was the unifying spiritual aim of all the cultural activity of primitive man. It was the given and universally accepted basis of communal life. Through it the fundamental social order was sanctioned, namely the order of the family. The duty of obedience towards the parents and the obligation of mutual help among the members of the family were always, as we know from the ethnological studies of the primitives, represented as insoluble bonds imposed by God himself. The family was led by the oldest father; and so was the tribe, a group of a certain number of families. The substitution of the father by the mother was exceptional and, according to the myths preserved in many countries to more recent times, it was regarded as abnormal. Enterprising individuals were usually respected, and their memory—like that of Prometheus the firebearer—remained living in the mythical poems, but human life had more communal character than it has today. In the natural order of the family a safe common ground was given to the life of every one of its members.

What remains rather a forgotten part of the story of mankind is the great revolutionary change in the social organization which occurred in China, India, Mesopotamia, and Egypt and perhaps also in other places from the sixth to the second millennium before Christ. In this period the hunter and nomad tribes established themselves in the valleys of great rivers and, by starting an intensive agricultural life, created little town states on which all the subsequent political history of the ancient times was based. It is quite possible that some changed natural conditions made it necessary for men to look after a new way of life. But it could be as well only a result of the free enterprising spirit of man. The primitive man was by no means restricted in his activity to the area inhabited by his own tribe. The presence of stone axes made from a certain kind of stone in the settlements in regions where that kind of stone can not be found in nature, and, later on, also the presence of amber, gold, tin, copper, and jadeite in regions distant from their places of origin, bear witness to commercial undertakings of not a small extent. And commercial enterprises could possibly stir up also new cultures based on irrigation and cattle breeding.

Numerous inventions which today serve us as a basis of our own material civilization were undoubtedly made already in the time when the primitive men tried to find their living on the steppes and in the forests as hunters of deer, bison, and mammoth, and perhaps also of the giant-like elasmotherium, the unicorn of the myths. Not only the use of fire but also different types of tools and weapons like the axe, the bow and the fork are among them. Later on, when many tribes were already engaged in various sorts of agriculture—according to the climatic types of the regions in which they had settled down—the technological abilities of man developed even more quickly. The potter's wheel, the manufacture of sun-dried bricks, the implements necessary for cattle-breeding, and, finally, the draining of marshes and the construction of canals leading to the control of the flood waters of the great river-valleys marked the final achievements of the primitive man.

Tribes and Empires

THE EPOCH covering the last three thousand years before Christ and the first three centuries of the Christian
era was full of decisive changes in the political organisation of mankind. The details of these changes escape
even the most minute inquirer. But the political history of those times can be summed up in three classes
of events. The first of them was the rise of the cities as
centres of tribes who had chosen intensive agriculture
as their chief way of obtaining food. The second was
the growth of imperialism and the successive creation
of various empires of which the city states became
parts. The third was the origin and growth of the
Roman Empire in the Mediterranean area and of several other centres of different civilizations in Asia and
in America.

As was already pointed out, the cities as centres of
agricultural regions began to spring up mostly in the
valleys of great rivers like the Nile, Euphrates, Tigris,
Indus, Ganges, Hoangho or Yangtse or in rich regions
in proximity to the warmer seas like Italy, Yucatan or
Peru. We know, of course, much more about the events
which took place around the Mediterranean or in the
Near East than about the early history of India, China,

Central America or Peru. Perhaps we are not wrong in concentrating our attention on the Mediterranean and the Near East, and that for two reasons. The first is that the civilizations which developed around the great centres in Asia and in America have since those times produced very little cultural activity. The second is that our own civilization has accepted very little from them and that, on the contrary, they have been already superseded or are in the process of being superseded by our own civilization.

Of the regions which later became parts of the Roman Empire, Egypt (the valley of the Nile) and Mesopotamia (the valley of the Euphrates and Tigris) were those where the cultural development was the fastest one. The history of Egypt, where the two originally small agricultural city states of Memphis and Thebes formed the basis of a united kingdom, was perhaps not so complicated as that of Mesopotamia, where great states were successively formed around the cities of Lagash, Ur, Babylon, and Niniveh. Both tried repeatedly to get under their influence Palestine, where the Hebrews and the Phoenicians had their towns. And both, Mesopotamia to a greater extent than Egypt, were from time to time attacked by tribes coming from the north, from the dark mainland of Eurasia, like the nomadic Hyksos in the 18th century before Christ or, several centuries later, the Hittites, who had already organised their own empire in Asia Minor. In the 6th century before Christ, both these territories, the Semitic Mesopotamia and the Hamitic Egypt, became parts of a new vast empire, organised by the Indo-European Persians who had settled down in Iran.

Contemporary with the ascendancy of the Persian

power is the advent of the Greek tribes to the western shores of Asia Minor and to the southern part of the Balkan peninsula. The Greeks, after they had destroyed the, to us, rather unknown Minoan civilization on Crete and other islands of the Eastern Mediterranean, organised their city-states on the shores of the Aegean sea and defended them with success against the Persians. Then, in their turn, under the leadership of one of their kings, Alexander of Macedonia, they made an attempt to unite all the countries around the Eastern Mediterranean in one empire. After this attempt had failed, Greece and the Near East remained, for a short time, divided into smaller states and were then included into the Roman Empire.

This empire, the final political achievement of the pre-Christian era in the Mediterranean area, developed gradually in the last few hundred years before Christ from the Italic city-state of Rome. Having reduced under their rule the Italian peninsula and defeated powerful Carthage, a Phoenician colony on the North African shore, the Romans secured for their empire not only Greece and the Near East but also Central and Western Europe. The northern boundaries of the Roman empire followed the frontier between England and Scotland of today and the rivers Rhine and Danube.

From a group comprising the descendants of one family wandering through the forests and plains to the complicated administrative system of the Roman Empire is a long step. No wonder that such a change took four to six thousand years. It was, however, not a destroying change. The institution of the family might have seemed submerged in various critical moments of those times. But at last, in the social structure of the Roman Empire and in its legal system, we find it again as the basic unit of political organisation. The moral adjustment of the mutual relations of its members is again considered the essential factor in the life of any society. The value of the family is permanent.

It was different with the tribe. The historians can submit only hypotheses as to how the tribes came into existence. It is quite possible that they were the product of the migrations. A group of families speaking one language naturally sticks together when it finds itself surrounded by people speaking strange languages. But whatever the origin of the tribes might have been, it was not an institution which would have made itself a permanent element of civilization. In the times with which we deal, the tribal organisation was left to the outer world, to the inner regions of the continents, which nobody had as yet explored. Anything might have been expected to come from those regions. And the difference between the culture of the attacking tribes from behind the frontiers of the empires and the culture of the empires themselves was immense. The tribal organisation could be considered the chief characteristic of a stagnant civilization in which there is only a very small amount of culture. That was why the ancient people were so afraid of the barbarians who, of course, remained in majority. They were to remain in majority and to attack the frontiers of the empires throughout the ancient epoch of which we speak and even for a large part of the Middle Ages. Then, by changing themselves gradually into nations, they became nearly all of them heirs of the civilization upon which they once acted so destructively.

The tribes which founded the agricultural centers did not change directly into nations. They changed into city-states. A clearly perceptible consciousness of nationality, that is, consciousness of a tradition common to everybody who speaks a certain language, was an unknown thing as yet—with the exception of the Jews, whose exclusive religious tradition made them a real nation. There was a certain national feeling among the Greeks, but it never attained a force which would be able to shape their political organisation. A Chaldean from Ur, an Egyptian from Memphis, or a Greek from Corinth might have been conscious of his native language, but above all he was conscious of his citizenship or of being a subject of this or that king.

A town was the origin of every ancient state. A town or a city is synonymous with the process of social differentiation. In a tribe leading a nomadic life all kinds of work were common to all the members of the tribe. In a tribe which had settled down a permanent division of work was soon introduced. Besides the farmers and cattle-breeders there were the workmen, the merchants and also the king and the priests. The difference between the farmers, the cattle-breeders, the workmen and the merchants sprang up from the growing quantity of knowledge. A sequel to this differentiation was also the actual building of the town as a central place for all the villages and farms. With the growth of religious and scientific knowledge a difference was established also between the patriarch of the tribe and the priest. And at last, as the final accomplishment of the whole change, comes the consecration of political power in a formal institution, the change of the patriarch into the king.

The gerontocracy of the nomad tribes has always

had a religious authority about it. The eldest of the fathers it was who used to "walk with God." This authority was transferred to the men who were the descendants of the patriarch in direct line. They were the "sons of God who took wives of the daughters of men." As the whole society was based on kinship— if, for instance, a man was banished, his family was banished with him—there was a particular reverence for the "eldest family." But not everywhere to the same extent. In Egypt or in Mesopotamia the power of the kings soon became absolute and the kings used to be represented as descendants of the Divinity. That was also the case wherever an empire was built by the personal endeavours of this or that king. With the Greeks the institution of kingship was in many places superseded by the oligarchy of a few noble families who secured for themselves a monopoly of office, or even by the democracy of all the citizens, that is of all the members of the original families which had founded the town. But even in these towns strong citizens used to seize power by force and hold it as tyrants. And at the end of the most glorious period of its history even Greece changed into an imperialist state governed by a royal family. The fate of the Roman republic was a similar one. It is evident that however deep the differentiation of the ancient society was, the custom to look upon society as upon a development of the family remained prevalent throughout the ancient times.

Gradually, however, the town as center of production outgrew the town as center of a tribe. The manifold production of textiles, leather wares, tools, jewels, and other commodities, conducted in work-shops owned by private proprietors, led to interurban exchange and to further development of commerce, an activity known already in the protohistoric era. In many places the merchants, coming from other towns, enjoyed certain privileges—this, beside the right of hospitality, was the beginning of international law—and a special peace protected the places where the markets were held. The use of metals as media of exchange became common although not exclusive. In some countries, as in Mesopotamia, for instance, even the priests became directly interested in business and it is quite probable that the primitive banking functions like exchange of foreign moneys, accepting of deposits, and making of loans, were their inventions. In Greece, special banking houses developed with nets of agents in other towns so that merchants going abroad could get letters of credit on the security of deposits at home. Also some of the Greek towns used to entrust prominent citizens in other towns with the protection of their citizens.

If, already in the earlier times, fishing became one of the important food producing activities, with the rise of commerce between distant countries the art of sailing developed rapidly. The ships of the Phoenicians and the Greeks, first hugging the coast or sailing from one island to another, soon traversed the Mediterranean from one end to another. But although ships from the Mediterranean went sometimes as far as to the shores of the Baltic and although sea routes were established between Egypt and East Africa, the Mediterranean area was really a self-sufficient economical unit.

In the Near East and in Greece production remained in private hands and the number of people employed in the workshops rarely exceeded fifty men for one factory. That was perhaps also the reason why the Greek law never recognized a corporation as a legal person. The farms, too, remained mostly in private hands. There was the danger that the farmers, trying to avoid the risks of bad harvests, would seek help with the town businessmen and forfeit their land, but legislation prohibited this process mostly with success. In Roman society, however, the distribution of property became one of the major social problems. Considerable accumulation of agricultural and industrial property was not stopped by reforming attempts like that of the brothers Gracchi in the latter years of the second century before Christ. It only diminished with the general decline of prosperity in the civil wars preceding the foundation of the Roman empire in the last years of the pre-Christian era. But later on, under the emperors, the system of vast agricultural estates, owned not only by rich individuals but also by a sort of joint-stock company, the *societates publicanorum*, gained ground once more. Many a region, not only in Italy, but also in more distant provinces, was cultivated by small tenants (*coloni*). Also the agricultural and mining enterprises owned by the emperors themselves, if they were not exploited directly by slaves under the supervision of an imperial procurator, were usually leased to private capitalists or to capitalist societies.

It is also interesting to note that the rise of capitalist production brought with it the formation of special associations not only of proprietors but also of employees. The professional guilds in which the proprietors of enterprises of the same craft were grouped were originally organised for charitable purposes and mutual aid. But gradually they began to exert a definite influence on local markets and also to influence municipal politics in their towns. Although much suspected by the Roman imperial government they became, at last, veritable state institutions which were entrusted with various public services. All citizens engaged in trade and industry were then obliged to enter these guilds. As to the confraternities of the workers, the organizing of which was supported by the Roman emperors, they never served any more important purpose than paying funeral expenses for deceased members and similar social activities.

It is nearly impossible to analyse the circumstances under which conflicts arose between the tribal towns, the consequence of which usually was the loss of independence of the defeated town. There used to be conflicts between the nomad tribes, some of which resulted in complete annihilation of the defeated tribe or in enslavement of the vanquished. Some remaining traces of this tribal warfare may be found in the clashes between societies which had already settled down to agricultural and industrial occupations. Such was, for instance, the Babylonian captivity of the Jews in the 6th century before Christ, when the Jews were transferred by force from Palestine to Mesopotamia. In some cases, the previous experiences of a tribe had made its culture preponderantly martial and aggressive. No wonder that flourishing towns were an enviable prey for such tribes and that their riches used to attract the leaders of these tribes. Some of them, even when already settled down, preserved the warrior character of their culture; we have just to quote the case of the Greek town of Sparta and, to some extent, even that of Rome. In other cases, personal political ambitions of the rulers were of decisive importance.

The most interesting among the great political units of the ancient epoch are undoubtedly those whose governments were based on a more or less unrestricted discussion of public affairs by their citizens.

Such an attempt took place, for instance, in the Greek city of Athens. There, at the peak of the city's ascent, the great critical debates were conducted in the *ecclesia*, the assembly of all the citizens. There most of the public officials were elected, their term of office being but one year. But out of the probable 250,000 inhabitants of the city at that period, only about 100,000 were its legal citizens. About 50,000 were people who had moved into Athens from other Greek cities or even from overseas and were therefore classified as *metics*, that is, people who were not members of the original tribe and who were not entitled to the rights of citizens. And about 100,000 were slaves, that is people who, in consequence of their defeat in this or that war, were forced to come to Athens and to live and work there as property of the citizens. The foreign policy of Athens, however, after having tried to assemble a certain number of other Greek city-states under Athenian "leadership," ended in the disaster of a bloody and enervating war between the most influential Greek city-states which destroyed more than it accomplished.

But another such story culminated in the creation of the Roman Empire, a political institution which not only lasted several hundred years, but remained a durable idea in the political thinking of Christian culture. This singular accomplishment is connected not only with the military tradition of the Romans but, to an even greater degree, with the Roman ability of juridical organisation. The gradual extending of partial and then of full Roman citizenship, with all the advantages of its legal perfection to the allies and also to the defeated enemies of Rome, was undoubtedly a policy of mature statesmanship. It ended, in the reign of the emperor Claudius in the first century after Christ with liberal granting of Roman citizenship even to the inhabitants of the most distant provinces.

When the clash between the Roman senate and its ambitious generals ended in the establishment of permanent dictatorship, and when, as Tacitus stated, no other remedy for a distracted state was found but the rule of a single man, it did not mean that the political tradition of the city-state was forgotten. It had been impressed in the minds of men too strongly, and it was also preserved by the Roman piety, which meant not only obedience to parents and other authorities but also reverence for the established order. Rome itself became *urbs urbium*, mother of the towns. The Roman empire had a single military command. It had a single official language, the Latin language, and a single intellectual language, the Greek language, in which also the business transactions in its eastern part were conducted. The emperor, through the governors of the provinces, whose functions for a long time were hereditary, had a supreme authority over the life of each single inhabitant of the empire. Yet, at the same time, each inhabitant was conscious of the difference between the empire and the town of his own native region. The land-tax and the tax on personal property were collected by the local communities, which were responsible for their fixed quotas. And the communal governments, although deprived of any possibility to indulge in international and military politics, had still other duties for which there was no central authority. The region of his native town was still the *patria* of every Roman citizen. If there was any bond besides the omnipotent emperor, which was really common to inhabitants of the Roman Empire no matter of what region they were, it was their citizenship. And the citizenship was a matter of law.

No such thing was known in primitive society as the exercise of an authority by the power of the stronger. Wilful acts might have been committed in a nomadic tribe as well as later in a city-state. But, as we know from historical as well as from ethnological studies, the men responsible for them almost always tried to make them look legal. There was always a customary law, even if it was perhaps restricted to the power of the father over his children. The family was considered an institution imposed by God and so was the law. When Demosthenes, the Greek statesman, spoke of it as of invention and gift of the gods or when the Roman philosopher Cicero called it the highest reason implanted in nature, they expressed a primeval tradition. Even the lawgivers who had really existed were later surrounded by myths which deified them.

The original equality before the law arose from the unity and solidarity of the family and of the tribe. And, of course, it depended on the discipline in the social unit in question, whether this or that judicial action had the mediatory character of arbitration or the compulsory character of adjudication. If we are to believe the oldest traditions—the historical narratives of the Old Testament for instance—certain crimes were always regarded as offences against the community and were punished in a more exemplary way than was asked for by the accuser. We can find traces of this primitive discrimination between the civil law and the criminal law in such customary punishments as that which, according to the Roman law of Twelve Tables, was inflicted upon any destroyer of standing grain. But the main characteristics of the early law were that of a civil law in the modern sense of the word. Even physical violence was usually regarded as a private wrong and punished according to the principle of an eye for an eye.

Later on, in the city-states and in the oldest empires, when much of the primitive consciousness of tribal solidarity had already vanished, the archaic law had to protect the family. It had to deal in detail with questions of marriage and care of children and also to introduce the institutions of pledge and suretyship. But in its basic conception it remained for a very long time the law of the tribe, of a small community all of whose members might have been present at the court of justice. It conceived every process as a judicial duel, in which both sides, the accuser and the defendant, directly participate; no judgment could be given by default. And although some of its technical aspects developed rather quickly—the procedure and terms of the commercial law in the archaic codes of the Mesopotamian empires, for instance—many others persisted on the traditional level. The claimant, for example, had to secure, perhaps even by violence, the presence of his opponent in the court of justice. And, what was even more important, the ancient law remained always a tribal law in this respect that it was considered valid for people who were by birth members of a certain society and not for people who lived in a certain territory. A merchant from Athens was under the protection of the Athenian law not because he lived in Athens but because he was a member of an Athenean family and therefore a citizen of Athens. When he came to Ephesus he was at the mercy of the magistrates of that city but he was not entitled to the benefit of the law of the Ephesians. It was one of the achievements of the Romans that they put an end to this state of things by a twofold way: by the formation of the so-called *ius gentium* and by the gradual granting of Roman citizenship to the great majority of the inhabitants of the empire.

Roman law was in its beginnings a customary tribal law like all the other laws in the ancient times. But its principles were developed in a way unusual in other town-states. They were developed not so much by legislative activity of the senate as by the constant adaptation to current needs, which was regularly done by the *praetors*. The Roman magistrate who bore this title used to issue every year an *edict* in which he set forth—often with important modifications—the principles that would guide him in his judicial activity. In this way, the modifications and experiences of the praetors being nearly always accepted by their successors, a system of law gradually arose, which gave ancient society a firm basis. It included regulations concerning the authority of the father in a family, property, succession and inheritance, the forms of transfer of property, marriage and guardianship, obligations, contract, public and private offences. It also included precise prescriptions of judicial procedure, the so-called *legis actiones* which, under the emperors, were supplemented by written decisions of the praetors whether the action of this or that plaintiff should be granted and according to which style it should be treated. The development of the Roman law was also much enhanced by the custom of the citizens to ask for legal advice and assistance in the conduct of litigation. These used to be given, in the early days of the Roman city-state, by state officials. Later, the assistance in legal questions passed into the hands of experienced laymen (*iurisconsulti*) whose professional advance was chiefly based on the activity of standing judicial commissions (*quaestiones perpetuae*).

Besides forming their own civil law the Romans made the first step towards the creation of the international law. As early as the 3rd century before Christ they appointed a special magistrate (*praetor peregrinus*) to deal with cases in which foreigners were involved. And soon these special praetors in their edicts began to mix the basic principles of the Roman law with principles taken from the laws of various Greek, Mesopotamian and Phoenician city-states. That was the origin of a system of law called the law of the nations, or *ius gentium*, which became so popular that even the Roman citizens began to use it in their lawsuits before the ordinary praetors.

In their origin, all the customary laws were oral laws. Only after they became too complicated it was found necessary to arrange them into collections. Such codes of law have been probably published in many ancient city-states; the famous code of the Mesopotamian king Hammurabi, the detailed code of Moses in the first books of the Old Testament, and the Roman law of Twelve Tables were among them. The inventive activity of the Roman magistrates and the annual publication of the edicts made, for a long time, a new codification of Roman law superfluous. But in the 2nd century after Christ the making of law was seized by the emperors who also reduced the edict to its final form (*edictum perpetuum*) which, from those times onwards, was only supplemented by juristic activity or imperial enactment. Later on, even the expert enquiries of patented jurists ceased and only the emperor himself or his deputies could interpret the old law or promulgate a new one.

The perpetuation of every civilization may depend on external events. Natural disasters or wars have put an end to many a flourishing centre of civilized life. But an equally important factor may be found in the cultural creativeness inherent in every civilization. And such creativeness, evidently, depends on the amount of consideration given, in each particular civilization, to the freedom of human personality from which all new values originate. In this respect the ancient civilizations were—with one single exception —engaged in an accelerating process of decay. Even the wisdom of a Confucius which, since the 5th century before Christ, has permeated large circles of the Chinese society, was full of scepticism as to the capability of man to attain truth and to propagate it in society. He and many other ancient thinkers were imparting their thoughts to a few select pupils, restricting thus by their own will their cultural influence.

The only exception were the Jews. Their laws, although not transcending the character of an essentially tribal legal system, and although far below the technical level of the Roman law, were singular in their social implications, tending to the protection—

even economic protection—of human personality. Laws such as those of the 25th chapter of Leviticus or the 15th chapter of Deuteronomy, prescribed that all landed possession which had been bought should return to its ancient owner in every fiftieth year—the year of jubilee—and that every person who had come into a state of slavery should be made free on that occasion and should be endowed by his employer.

The Jewish education was of a similarly exceptional character. As education is one of the creative joys of man, there is no doubt that parents educated their children from times immemorial. After the formation of the city-states, schools used to be founded by municipal authorities and by kings or by individual famous teachers. They were, however, not open to everybody but only to those young people who, according to the social situation of their fathers, were expected to play important roles in society. Only the public instruction of the Jewish youth was open to all classes of the Hebrew population and was striving for a high moral ideal, which was also exceptional in the ancient history. In some other tribal states, where instruction of youth outside family was prescribed and conducted by the state, as in the Greek city of Sparta or in Persia, it was a military and civic training, not education in the proper sense of the word. The Jews concentrated on the moral perfection of man and on his knowledge of God, things which can comprise his other capabilities, whereas even the best Greek teachers of the 5th and 4th centuries before Christ held only man's physical abilities and his wit and critical expression as the proper goal of instruction. If, therefore, speaking of education, we mean an activity perfecting the human character, the ancient Jewish teachers, especially the

Prophets, are more entitled to be called educators than the Greek philosophers. A special characteristic of the Greek education, however, was the love for competition in athletics and also in art, not only between the youth of one city, but also between competitors from various Greek cities assembled at Olympia in western Greece or in other places. The high level of the Greek competition was lost again with the Romans. The cheap and sometimes even bloody amusements, the "bread and circuses" with which the Roman imperial and municipal authorities supplied their citizens, had not even any instructive value.

The Secrets of Nature

THE ANCIENT BIOGRAPHER Plutarch, speaking of the Greek mathematician, Archimedes, said: "Repudiating as sordid and ignoble the whole trade of engineering, and every sort of art that lends itself to mere use and profit, he placed his whole affection and ambition in those purer speculations where there can be no reference to the vulgar needs of life." If these words were not exact in reference to Archimedes, they were true when applied to Greek science as a whole. And Greek science was one of the glories of the ancient times. What the Romans achieved in legislation, the Greeks accomplished in science and in art. They brought ancient culture in these two disciplines to perfection. And they established the frontier between technology and science in the proper sense of the word. As a matter of fact, they nearly brought these two branches of one knowledge into opposition. That was, at least, what Plutarch meant by speaking of the ignoble trade of engineering and of the speculations of pure science.

Such an opposition between science and technology could be, of course, only an artificial one. It seemed to be more evident to the Greeks than it is to us, but it

was no more real than it is today. Idealistically speaking technology may be considered the lowest branch
of science and medicine the highest one. But they
spring from the same interest of man in the regular
processes of nature. And they have also one historical
source: the astonishment felt by primitive man at the
wonders of nature which surrounded him.

As we have already pointed out, primitive man
looked at nature as a manifestation of an amazing
spiritual activity. Not only the various branches of
science but also science and religion were narrowly
related to each other in the thought of the ancient
people. Long before the sceptical Greek scientists tried
to trace down the immutable laws of the material universe, the priests of the Egyptian and Mesopotamian
city temples had already discovered many of the practical applications of those laws. And perhaps some of
the most practical discoveries, especially in the technology of agriculture, were objects more of religion
than of science. Was it the domestication of the bull
which led to its being worshipped in Egypt or did its
worship, springing from the astonishment at its force,
lead to its domestication? We do not know, but neither
of these possibilities can be excluded.

A great amount of technological knowledge had
been assembled by the ancient peoples before the beginning of the Christian era: weaving of wool, use of
flax and hemp for the manufacture of textile products,
weaving of cotton cloth—preceded by the introduction
of cotton-bearing shrub, brought probably from India
—irrigation machinery, operated by hand or by ox
power, production of coloured glass-ware, different
kinds of glass-blowing, use of alabaster slabs for the
decoration of walls, provisions for water-supply and

drainage system in towns, heating of big houses by hypocausts, various methods of wall painting, selection of sites of theatres according to acoustic principles, and many other technical inventions of greater or lesser importance.

Some of these inventions have been, since then, forgotten. Others, like the net of Roman military roads covering half of Europe, can still arouse our curiosity. But there are some among them which serve us as they have served their inventors. The paper upon which we write is similar to the papyrus of the Egyptians, which superseded the tablets from earth and wax. The canonic laws of architecture, assembled by Vitruvius Pollio in his treatise *De Architectura*, as well as the various irrigation and drainage systems, are still used by the builders and farmers of our own times.

But the main heritage of the scientific research of ancient times does not consist in its results. It consists in its method. The most important scientific achievement of the ancient times is the discovery of mathematical reasoning which sprang from the Greek predilection for abstract, unchanging concepts and for clear, precise thinking. It was this predilection which made the Greek mathematicians and astronomers look askance on technology. In the long course of time, after being neglected for centuries, it aroused the interest of the European scholars again at the height of the Middle Ages and, developed by them, it proved to be more fruitful precisely in the field of technology than the Greeks had ever supposed. But, after another series of centuries had elapsed, it proved also an insufficient method for research in what is perhaps the most substantial domain of nature, namely organic life.

If there ever was a distinct national characteristic or tradition in any branch of creative activity, it was the Greek love for abstract thinking. Although citizens of different city-states and often divided politically, the Greeks found in abstract thought a common bond. We can study its development from the very beginning of their scientific research, in the teaching of the Ionian philosophers of the 6th and 5th century before Christ, such as Thales, Anaximander, and Anaximenes and, later on, Heraclitus. They were interested not so much in the origin of the world as in what it had been made of. They did not like the heterogeneity of things. They wanted to get hold of something basic, immutable. And when Heraclitus proclaimed that everything was flowing, he was preparing ground for the atomic theory of Anaxagoras and Democritus as well as for the abstract principles of geometry taught by his contemporary Pythagoras. If any one of the so-called elements like fire or water—which to the most ancient scientists seemed homogeneous—could not be considered the source of all matter, then at least the atoms could be imagined as homogeneous. Or, if it had been found difficult to analyse matter, then at least its shapes and forms could be analysed and reduced to abstract principles.

That is why the Greek achievements in physics and chemistry were comparatively small. A greater interest in these two branches of science appeared later on, in the time of the Roman ascendancy. The scientists living in the Greek merchant-settlements in Southern Italy and in Sicily and especially in the hellenized Egyptian town of Alexandria, were more willing to indulge in experiments than their predecessors in Miletus and Athens. But even the most celebrated among them, Archimedes and Hero, accomplished little in comparison to the results of contemporary mathematicians and astronomers. Most of their knowledge concerned the abstract formulas of the simple mechanical laws. Already Aristotle, in the 4th century before Christ, was able to define the law of the parallelogram of forces and the law of the lever. Archimedes, who discovered such abstract notions as the centre of gravity, was chiefly interested in hydrostatics and optics. Hero's experiments on the elasticity of air and of steam led him to the construction of wind-driven compression pumps and other simple machines, but his chief interest was also in the field of elementary mechanics.

As to chemistry, the imagination of the Greek atomists was incomparably greater than the experimental evidence they had at their disposal. It was easy to say that the atoms were homogeneous, indivisible bodies of infinite variety of shape, which moved through a vacuum. But there were no experiments which could have proved the validity of such an assumption. Aristotle refused to accept it. He contented himself in constructing the theory of form and matter which, however abstract, can serve a modern physicist perhaps even better than it has served older generations of research workers in the same field. But that was, of course, just a theory, more philosophical than scientific.

Biology, the hidden science, remained inaccessible to the ancient world. Some of the regularities of the organic world were certainly known to the ancient inhabitants of Egypt and Mesopotamia. Aristotle tried to make a methodical observation of animal life; his pupil Theophrastus did the same for plants. Dioscorides, a surgeon in the Roman army in the 1st century after Christ, laid the foundations of systematic botany for medicinal purposes. But the interest in organic life as a basic domain of nature remained restricted to the research work of the surgeons.

For those who had been schooled in the dialectics of logicians—men like Heraclitus and, later in the 5th century, Socrates and his pupil Plato in Athens and Parmenides and Zeno of Elea in Southern Italy—it was not the substance but the forms of nature which attracted their attention. Systematic thought, a flair for founding the underlying principles of thinking and, above all, the critical study of the human ways of expression was characteristic in the development of Greek intellectual life. In the 4th century before Christ, when Aristotle, Plato's younger contemporary, summed up the dialectical attempts of his predecessors in his *Logic*, there were already several schools of Greek logicians who had devoted their studies to the natural forms which could be expressed by numbers. Aristotle, himself not a mathematician, did not pay much attention to their endeavours. But the results of their work spoke for themselves; and that notwithstanding the fact that the study of mathematics was considered, in the Greek cities, an occupation accessible only to a few. The pupils of Pythagoras, for instance, formed a secret society. Also the distinction between abstract and applied mathematics was more and more emphasized.

There were ways of counting and even definite number systems in every one of the countries through which ancient civilization had spread. Multiples of five were used in many tribes because, probably, counting was done on fingers and toes. In Mesopotamia, a sexagesimal system was employed, based on the division of the circle into 6x60 parts. Mathematical solutions of practical problems and even such formulae as that the area of a circle equals πR^2, with π equal to 3.16, or that a triangle with sides of three, four, and five units was right-angled, were known in Egypt and perhaps also in other countries. But the knowledge of the ways by which these truths had been reached, was probably shared only by a few temple-priests, who have never put it down or revealed it.

The Greek endeavours in mathematics surpassed these first steps very quickly. As there was no adequate symbolism for arithmetic, the Greek mathematicians, for several centuries, concentrated their attention on geometry. The geometrical induction was easier and it also appealed more to the Greek appreciation of the beauty of form. After definitions had been formulated of the fundamental elements of geometry, such as line, angle, or surface, the various methods of determining area and also the properties of parallel lines were studied. That led to the formulation of more complicated theorems resulting from the application of one surface to another. The relations of the sides of the right-angled triangle, the properties of the regular polygons, the proportionality of the areas of circles to the squares of their diameters, the quadrature of the circle and the trisection of the angle, the quadrature of the parabola, the conic sections—such were the problems which interested the Greeks. They are connected with the names of Pythagoras, Parmenides, and Hippias of Elis, who lived in the 5th century, and with that of

Apollonius of Perga, who flourished in the 3rd century.

Many of these geometrical discoveries, but not all, were included in the book which was to be, for many generations to come, the most learned and exhaustive treatise on geometry, the *Elements* of Euclid. Its author, although a man of great systematizing ability, who taught in Alexandria at the beginning of the 2nd century before Christ, did not intend to make a condensed account of everything that had been achieved in geometry by his predecessors and contemporaries. He rather remained faithful to the endeavours of the Greek logicians and used geometry as a preparatory course for general philosophical studies. That was no doubt also the reason why he avoided such concepts as that of infinity or of fixed infinitesimals, which did not seem to him clear and logical enough.

Had the attitude of the Greeks towards geometry been a more practical one, they would have been more interested in the existence of incommensurable magnitudes. It was undoubtedly clear to Pythagoras or to his pupils that if, for instance, the length of the equal sides of an isosceles right triangle was taken as 1, the length of the hypotenuse is irrational, because it can not be adequately expressed by any whole number or fraction. Zeno's paradoxical story of Achilles who was not able to overcome the tortoise because the tortoise was always able to cover at least a part of the distance which he ran, led also into the sphere of irrational mathematics. And so did the attempts of other Greek thinkers to square the circle by inscribing in it a series of regular polygons of an increasingly greater number of sides. But the Greeks did not like mathematical quantities which were not wholly explicable.

That was why their mathematics did not reach the employment of algebraic symbols. Diophantus, the author of the celebrated *Arithmetic*, who worked in Alexandria at the very end of the ancient epoch, in the second half of the 3rd century after Christ, knew the value of such symbols but did not employ them systematically. And that was also why Euclid, restricting his *Elements* to the study of the properties of those geometrical figures which can be constructed with ruler and compass, did not pass from the variable to its limit. But notwithstanding that, his work, practically unchanged, remained for more than two thousand years one of the basic text-books of mathematics. And although the mathematicians of today do not accept all its axioms and treat it as only a limiting case of a more general system, they know that the geometry of small spaces remains always at least approximately as the Greeks had conceived it.

Compared with mathematics, ancient astronomy was a much more practical science. It was also, undoubtedly, an older science and therefore more related to religion. In Egypt, the stars were worshipped no sooner than they were observed, because they were considered the symbols of the intelligence which determines the planting of various crops and the regular behaviour of the river Nile. In Mesopotamia, the priests of the city-temples who studied the stars were interested not only in their relations to the regular courses of nature but also in their influence on the characteristics and fates of the people who had been born under their various constellations. Thus the primitive science of the stars could be named astrology as well as astronomy.

And everywhere, even in the ancient Asiatic and American civilizations, solar and lunar eclipses were predicted and the times of new moon were computed, together with the calculated intervals as to the first visibility of the crescent, from which the beginning of each month used to be reckoned. The lunar months were in all likelihood the basis of the oldest calendars. It was found, however, rather difficult to combine lunar cycles with the solar sequences. The best solution of this problem was probably that of the ancient Mayas in Central America. But their calendar was not known in the Mediterranean area. The Egyptians had a calendar year of twelve months of thirty days, to which five additional days were added at the end of the twelfth month. In Mesopotamia, they were also able to determine, at least approximately, the length of the year and, in addition, they divided the day into twelve double hours which were subdivided each into thirty minutes. The Greeks were more conservative; they preferred the old lunar calendars to the solar year and they never accepted the system of hours. A very old practice, the origin of which remains mysterious to us, was the division of time into weeks of seven days. It is probable—and the theory is supported by the names of the seven days in Latin—that this division had something to do with the number of the seven planets: Sun, Moon, Mars, Mercury, Jupiter, Venus, Saturn.

But their knowledge of geometry and their experience in seafaring led the Greeks to other discoveries. By the sixth century they had recognised the properties of the circle which the sun describes in virtue of its apparent motion and they came to regard the earth as a sphere suspended in space without any support.

Two centuries afterwards, the hypothesis was reached of the earth rotating around its own axis. All such theories, of course, were regarded as assumptions only. Other assumptions, as that of the crystal spheres which act as the vehicles of the heavenly bodies, were equally accepted by the Greek men of genius. The Pythagorean theory that earth was revolving once each day around the same center, was developed in the 3rd century before Christ into the heliocentric system by Aristarchus of Samos, who tried in addition to measure the distances of celestial bodies on geometric principles. But this theory was set aside by most of the Greek scientists with disapproval. When, in the 2nd century after Christ, Claudius Ptolemy, an Alexandrian Greek, wrote his *Syntaxis*, a treatise which summed up the results of the Greek astronomers, he based it still on the geocentric system which, of course, from the point of view of geometry, was quite acceptable. But, by then, Greek astronomy could pride itself on other discoveries of permanent value, especially on those made by Eratosthenes and Hipparchus, who lived in the 3rd and 2nd centuries before Christ respectively. Eratosthenes succeeded, by a method which is still frequently applied by the geodesists, in forming a close estimate of the circumference of the globe. Hipparchus, who was interested in spherical trigonometry as well as in the construction of astronomical instruments and who also made a classified catalogue of the stars, discovered the motion of the axis of the earth in space, an achievement which, perhaps, can be called the most difficult of ancient science.

Eratosthenes can also be considered the originator of mathematical geography. The earlier geography was based almost exclusively on the reports of explorers like the merchant-sailor named Pytheas who, in the 4th century, set out from the Greek colony of Marseilles (Massilia) along the coasts of north-western Europe. The following epoch of Alexander of Macedonia, the founder of the short lived Greek empire, had stimulated geographical curiosity and men like Eratosthenes and his colleagues in Alexandria tried to use their knowledge of geometry in the drawing of maps. We know their work from the writings of two systematizers: Strabo, who lived at the beginning of the Christian era, and Ptolemy, whose astronomical *Syntaxis* we have already quoted. And it is interesting to see, even in such a practical science as geography, that mathematical speculation had the upper hand on real research and observation. Nevertheless we owe to these men our basic knowledge of geographical projection.

Compared with the scientific endeavours which were based on logical abstraction, the story of medicine in ancient times seems to be the story of a distant and different branch of research. In the modern era of human history, many great investigators in the field of medicine have been well versed in physics and chemistry in spite of the tendency of the modern physical sciences to become more and more mathematized. In the ancient epoch, the mathematical approach to nature was somewhat of a danger for the physicians. It tempted them to establish various theories on subjects which were not known to them from practical observation. When Aristotle, for instance, taught that the object of the brain was to secrete humors to cool the overheated heart, he was indulging in such a theory, plausible enough to the philosophers but worthless for medicine's own purposes.

That, however, was not the first obstacle which the ancient physicians had to overcome. Their first and main difficulty was connected with the origin of their own branch of science. Medical practice in protohistoric times undoubtedly involved more sympathy for the patient than theoretical interest. And, what was even more important, all the medical experience which had been gained in the first stage of history remained, after the division of work had taken place, with the priests. There is no doubt that there was a lot of knowledge and practical skill in this experience. The number of trepanned skulls which have been found in the excavations—trepanation used to be applied in cranial injuries but perhaps also in the case of some diseases—and the extensive use of animal remedies in ancient Egypt and Mesopotamia, testify to the high level of protohistoric surgery and to a great practical knowledge of physiology. But as the religious thinking of the ancient peoples gradually descended from the consciousness of the all-pervading presence of the Creator to a jungle of superstitions, medical practice shared in this decadence.

That was why, for instance, in Egypt, a substantial knowledge of anatomy—resulting from the practice of embalming the corpses—and an advanced bone surgery were closely connected with the use of incantations which had already lost their quality of prayer and had been changed into superstitious recitals of meaningless words. Such was the state of medical practice in the area of the Eastern Mediterranean even after a new progress in the division of work had put medicine into the hands of laymen. Various branches of the medical profession were separated from one another, but that did not improve the general state of things. On the contrary, such specialization decreased the knowledge of the basic facts about the human body and its various functions. And the primitive use of natural medicaments deteriorated into charlatanism.

It was again to the credit of the Greeks that the critical basis of the science of medicine was reestablished. Hippocrates, a native of the island of Cos, who flourished as healer and teacher in the beginning of the 4th century before Christ, can be called the father of the Greek physicians. Faithful to his principle that where there is love of man, there is also love of the medical art, he was more interested in the real conditions of his patients than in his own fame as a learned disciple of some old and perhaps corrupted tradition. It is true that when he described the general origin of diseases as due to disturbed conditions of the four "basic humors" of the body (blood, phlegm, black bile, and yellow bile) he was conceding too much to the love of his countrymen for geometric symmetry. Nothing remains from this artificial theory except the terms sanguine, phlegmatic, melancholic and choleric, which are still employed, although in a quite different way, by modern psychologists. But the importance of Hippocrates' work lies in his capability for objective observation. The case-histories which he relates in his *Epidemics* make him the founder of clinical medicine. His aphoristic principles concerning the ethics of medicine, his interest in general therapeutics and in climatology and balneology in particular only added to his stature as a scientific observer. His teaching was embodied by his pupils in the *Hippocratic Corpus*, the foundation stone of medical literature.

There were several other famous scientists among the Greek physicians. Two of them worked in Alexandria: Erasistratus, who was interested in experimental physiology, and Herophilus the anatomist, who discovered the nature of the pulmonary artery, classified the nerves, and named a number of organs hitherto unspecified, as for instance the prostate or the duodenum. Others, by the beginning of the Christian epoch, lived in Asia Minor and in Rome itself, like the famous Galen, whose books used to be studied in the medieval universities, although he also was too fond of theoretical completeness to admit the limits of his experience.

It must not be forgotten that during ancient times and even at the height of the Roman administrative system science was not asked to answer any social problems. The overwhelming majority of people led a natural life which enabled them to endure the difficulties which modern man tries to avoid. The inhabitants of the towns preserved at least some of the physical exercises which had been natural to their forefathers in their sports. The bullbaiting, popular in the Minoan civilization, and the Greek competitions in discus and javelin throwing, running, jumping, wrestling, boxing and horse and chariot racing required a careful training and helped to establish high standards of physical ability. These aptitudes were not completely lost even in the luxurious life of the centres of the empires.

The Harmonious Arts

MOST OF the artistic achievements of the protohistoric epoch were probably the spontaneous result of an inspiration which could have come to anybody. As there was no division of work, there were no artists in the professional sense of the word. But there were undoubtedly people whose special endowment for art was evident to their contemporaries. And, if we take into consideration the primitive man's consciousness of the all-pervading presence of God, no wonder the artistic vision used to be explained as an inspiration of supernatural character. The Greek origin of our own word *poetry* contains the idea of considering the capacity of man to create (*poiein*) as a sort of participation in the mysterious activity of God. The Latin word *carmen* also means much more than a song or a poem in the modern sense of the word; it means a prophetical, God-inspired song.

The story of art in the ancient epoch is not only the story of a gradual separation into various branches, but is also the tale of its estrangement from this primeval idea of God-inspired activity. Wherever this idea was completely lost, the artistic initiative gradually disappeared and a progressive decline of creative

power took place. Whenever the striving after the
transcendent character of the art was renewed, it resulted in a revolutionary artistic activity as in the case
of the Greek drama of the 5th century before Christ,
or, to choose an even earlier example, in the renaissance of the Egyptian art in the times of Akhenaten,
the pharao-reformer of the 2nd millenium before
Christ.

To some extent, the varying achievements of the
ancient artists depended upon the equally varying developments of the religious institutions. The stylistic
conventions which we find in full power in Mesopotamian and Egyptian painting at the very beginning
of the ancient era, were probably not all of the artist's
own choosing. Many of them were imposed upon him
by the stiffening prescriptions of the temple-priests.
On the other hand, the defence against the empty religious formalism of their neighbours led the Jews to
the prohibition of figural sculpture and painting in
their country.

With the Greeks whose achievements in art were
equal to those in science, it was again their preference
for clear reasoning and their distrust of intuition
which made them search for the prototypes of absolute
beauty. In their belief that "God ever geometrises"
and that every art is primary mimetic they kept on
insisting firmly on the so-called laws of art. Thus even
their greatest men of genius were bound not to exceed
certain prescribed forms and, what was perhaps more
important, not to abandon for fancy's sake observation
of the world surrounding them. The art of the brood-
ing, inward-turned man, which had flourished among
the Greek lyrical poets of the 6th century before
Christ, ceded to the predilection for outward propor-

tions. This did not mean, of course, a final victory of formalism. Although the ability to formalize beautifully was brought to perfection, the sense of the dramatic, unproportional beauty of life remained present in the mind of the Greek artist. Even if it was not always strong enough to break its own creative ways as it did in the works of Aeschylus or Euripides, it succeeded, at least, in achieving many a work of unconditional realism. And it has always been difficult to exclude the sorrowful, unharmonious experiences of human life from any truly realistic art.

The basic achievement of ancient art remained, however, the discovery of the various ways in which man's astonishment at the life and things around him may be expressed. The diverse applications of painting and sculpture, their relations to each other, and also their use in architecture were explored. Architecture itself was enriched through the development of all the basic forms, of which the modern architect can still avail himself. The simple forms of music were put on the firm basis of a classification of tones and series of tones. From the unwritten treasure of songs and narratives a multiform literature was developed in which lyrical and epical poetry, drama and novel were included; historical compositions came to be regarded as a special form of epical recital and they were developed along their own lines so that they almost reached the stage of complete independence.

There was one quality in sculpture which the ancient people used to value very highly and which has its admirers even in our own times. It was grandiosity. But it is sometimes difficult to distinguish it from a real grandeur. Perhaps the stately figure of Zeus in

Olympia, made by Phidias and looked upon with awe by generations, really expressed the majestic calm of the chief of gods in a way which was full of inspiration. But there was a lot of boastfulness and unspiritual propagandism in the various sculptural monuments of the ancient times which makes us a little suspicious of their real value.

Certainly there was not much art in the repetitive statues of the Egyptian gods and pharaos or in the Mesopotamian steles commemorating the military successes of long-forgotten kings. Only exceptionally, as under the reign of Akhenaten, did the vivid expressions of the faces overcome the superficial, decorative effect of the rigid attitudes of the bodies.

Are not the so-called minor applications of sculptural art in many cases much more full of genuine love for the beauty of life? From the faience reliefs and figured gold cups of the ancient Minoan art to the examples of the typical Roman skill of cameocutting we can find many a work of genius, distinguished by the way in which its author knew how to appreciate the charm of bodily movements or of the disposition of figures in space.

It was undoubtedly in the age of Phidias and Myron, the Greek sculptors of the second half of the 4th century before Christ, that ancient sculpture reached its apogee. Although restricted by a code faithful to the proportions of the ideal human body and striving to glorify exclusively the physical appearance of man, the creators of the Parthenon in Athens and of the "Discus Thrower" set up a hitherto unsurpassed standard of harmonious art. They did not indulge in an ostentatious display of muscles which could be found in the much earlier Mesopotamian sculpture. In a sober and realistic way, aiming above all at movement, they expressed the likeness of man as physically so perfect that he could be presented as god. Their exquisite sense of movement was shared also by several artists of subsequent centuries whose names we do not know but who could create works like the striking "Victory of Samothrace." On the other hand, some of the Greek sculptors of the later generations, whose names have entered history, such as Praxiteles, the author of "Hermes with the Infant Dionysus," pushed the striving for harmony so far that their statues became too pretty to be beautiful even if judged according to the standards of corporeal harmony.

The same artificial prettiness, although executed in a much more rude way, can be found in the bas relief panels with which the Romans used to cover their triumphal arches and tombs. But the sculptors who lived under the Roman Empire were great realists in lifelike portraiture, a remorseless, uncompromising art. Their device was still perfect imitation, but not perfect harmony. They did not hesitate to transcribe in their busts the vices and even the sorrows of man.

The bas reliefs of the Romans had their predecessor in a much older technique, nearer to painting than to sculpture, namely the Mesopotamian glazed terra cotta reliefs. The animal figures on these mural decorations, with which the towers and halls of the Mesopotamian palaces were lined, are rather remarkable for their accomplished realism which did not shun even the depicting of pain of the wounded beasts. Some of the high coloring of these bas reliefs passed later into the mosaic decorations of the Roman period which were used not only to cover walls but also floors and bottoms of basins in public baths and central halls of private houses.

Of actual painting in the ancient times we know very little indeed. Most of it has been preserved in Egypt. There we can trace its development in the adornment of walls and wooden objects. Throughout the history of the independent Egyptian state the painters of that country represented men and animals in stereotyped attitudes and nearly always in profile —perhaps for the sake of the ornamental value of their pictures, which were beautifully spaced and colored. Their interest comprehended almost every side of human life, from harvest scenes and workshop incidents to battles and religious ceremonies. Later, under Greek cultural predomination in the Near East, the art of realistic portraiture was developed in Egypt and the portraits on the wooden coffins, in which the inhabitants of Egypt of that epoch were buried, are almost the only examples of Greek painting which we now possess.

There was, however, another branch of the art of painting which flourished in Greece, and of which there are many instances preserved today, namely vase painting. Pottery and its decoration was a popular heritage from the protohistoric times. In Egypt and especially in the Minoan civilization it developed into a luxurious art. The Greeks, although they brought the architecture of the vase to perfection, preferred earthen vessels to those of more expensive materials precisely because they could illustrate them. If monotonous in coloring, their decorations testify to a high development of drawing, at first stylized, but later spirited and full of emotion, illustrating all the possible sides of their life, real as well as poetical.

Speaking of the ancient pictorial art, let us also remember the Chinese landscape painting which, although not a part of the ancient Mediterranean civilization, has later influenced the modern painting in Europe and elsewhere. Based on an ancient tendency of Chinese art, it developed fully only in the 11th and 12th centuries of the Christian era. Its extraordinary sense of movement and decorative qualities are subject to an absolute spirituality. The Chinese painters, far removed from Greek realism and rationalism, attained a mastership in expressing not just realistic visions of mountains and waters but impressions full of feeling and reticences, an art for which Europe had to wait a long time.

Three kinds of material were used for building from the beginning of the ancient era: wood, stone, and brick. The plans of the ground-floor buildings did not vary much. The square and rectangular shapes were the most frequent ones in the Mediterranean area. If they had any access of light, it was usually through an opening in the roof, which served also as an escape for smoke from the hearth. Pillars were frequently used to support the roofs. The use of the arch and the vault was restricted to some countries only; the Etruscans, a large tribe which had settled down in central Italy, were perhaps the first to introduce these two advanced elements of architecture.

The private house did not change much during the three or four thousand years of the ancient era. At its end, houses of several stories were built in great commercial centres. But the ordinary private house was developed rather on the ground-floor level, its rectangular rooms assembled on the three sides of a central courtyard and a garden added on the fourth one. The same elements, walls and pillars or columns, from which the private houses were built, were used by the architects of the public buildings, palaces, and temples. The simple repetition of court and colonnade, arranged, when the terrain required it, on terraces, was the usual base of the architectural planes. In some periods and places an exuberance in ornaments could be witnessed, especially on the heads of the polygonal pillars.

A branch of some importance in ancient architecture was the building of tombs. From the very ancient "beehive tombs," many of which had been built underground, to the sepulchral monuments of the rich families along the Via Appia in the proximity of Rome, many occasions were offered to the architect, in which he was not restricted by any utilitarian considerations. Perhaps the most famous examples of the ancient tomb-architecture are the pyramids of the Egyptian pharaos. We can only guess how many slave-workers were necessary to erect these simple, but immense and carefully calculated structures.

Greek architecture strove also for monumentality. But the horizontal accent and the more modest proportions of the temples in Athens and elsewhere made it necessary for the Greek architects to seek grandeur through the perfection of harmony. The temples they built—the Parthenon in Athens is the most famous of them—were based on a simple pillar and beam construction, their proportioning was carefully determined by mathematical symmetry, and the ornamental elements employed in them were derived from an earlier functional treatment of the wooden members and were never too numerous. Everywhere in the Greek world or wherever the Greek influence was

dominant, the main characteristic of the temple buildings was their oblong shape with the short sides, and
later on with all four sides, adorned by columns forming porticoes. There were three distinct orders of
columns: the heavy and stable Doric, the slender
Ionic, reposing on a ringed base, and the even more
delicate Corinthian, the capital of which was richly
adorned by carved decorations. What we have to point
out, however, is that the Greek temples did not have
the appearance they have to-day, namely that of grey
structures on a green background of olive woods; their
marbles were painted in polychrome and, of course,
we are now not quite sure what their colors looked
like.

In the Roman Empire, architecture developed along
two quite different lines. On the one hand, the introduction of the circular plan made possible the building
of small and graceful ornamental structures like the
temple of Sibyl at Tivoli near Rome. On the other
hand, the use of the arch and the vault, learned from
the Etruscans, helped the Romans to develop monumental architecture, in which engineering played an
even much greater role than in the Egypt of the
pharaos. That was perhaps also why in Rome the
erecting of public buildings was no more an anonymous business, let out by the city in small sections to
individual masons and sculptors, as had been done in
Greece. The Roman period was an era of great architects, whose audacity of structural design was sometimes surprising. Roofing an immense circular building like the Pantheon in Rome by a simple vault,
spanning a deep valley by a bridge or an aqueduct,
covering a hall in the Baths of Caracalla which could
accommodate several thousand visitors, or erecting,

story above story, big amphitheatres like the Colosseum, such were the works of the Roman architects. One of the last, but not the least important among them, was the creation of the basilica type of public building. It consisted of a rectangular central nave divided by rows of columns from two side-aisles and covered by a flat roof; sometimes a semicircular bay was added at the shorter end opposite the entrance. Its original purpose was that of an assembly place, where administration of justice, public meetings or even trading took place.

The two main kinds of poetry, the lyrical and the epical, existed probably side by side from times immemorial. They were never fully separated from each other. Neither were they for a long time severed from religion. The spiritual nature of the order of things was always present in the mind of the primitive man. His reminiscent narratives, which were often changed into poetical myths, spoke again and again of the creation of the universe. His feelings and momentous impressions led him frequently to the contemplation of Him who, in the words of an old Egyptian song, "is good in will and in word and whose affection encompasses all hearts."

Thus, if we take lyric poetry first, we see the oldest songs and hymns full of profound poetical comparisons, so fresh and far-reaching that it is hardly imaginable that they are several thousand years old. But, at the same time, their thoughts are almost always interwoven by ideas flowing either from religious inspiration, as in the Psalms of the Old Testament, or from religious instruction, as in the hymns preserved upon the Egyptian steles, or from the conscience of a cultural mission closely connected with religious persuasion, like in the Old Testament Song of Deborah. Even lyrical compositions which could be perfectly well explained as worldly songs of love, like the famous biblical Song of Songs, were from the very beginning considered as symbols of a much profounder, religious contemplation.

It is in Greece of the 8th and 7th centuries before Christ that we first meet the songs whose poetical parables deal with the beauty and sadness of things without reaching directly the sphere of religious thought. In China lyrical poetry of this kind was born in even earlier times; but only the Greek and, later on, the Latin lyric became a part of the civilized life in the Mediterranean area. Curiously enough, its best representatives among the Greeks were the poets living at the very dawn of Greek history; namely, Sappho and Alcaeus. Later, towards the end of the 6th century, the religious vein emerged again in the hymns sung by the choirs at various solemn occasions such as the festival of a god or a celebration of a victory in some athletic competition. Pindar of Thebes brought their elaborate rhythm to perfection and remained the master of the ancient lyrical poets, unsurpassed even six centuries later by the Latin poets Horace and Catullus.

Lyric poems were sung with the musical accompaniment of the flute or, as one can perceive from the term *lyric*, of a lyre. It is, however, a debatable question whether and to what extent all the ancient lyric poetry originated in some form of song. It is probable that the two main elements of musical expression, rhythm and melody, were not everywhere put on equal level. Even today, some of the primitive tribes are more interested in rhythm than in melody. Perhaps the melodious song and the rhythmical recital developed side by side. It is also probable that an intermediate way was in many places found in the rhythmical, but monotonous, recitals of long lines with only a cadence as a melodious ornament at the end.

The Greeks studied conscientiously the scientific basis of music in general and of the different tonalities in particular. They did not, however, invent any special musical signs, being apparently content with indicating the notes merely by letters of the alphabet. That is why we do not know much about their music. Maybe they liked the theoretical study of music more than its practical application. They held it certainly in great esteem as may be seen from the fact that the term *mousiké techné* was used comprehensively for all the arts taught in the Greek schools, as contrasted with the *gymnastiké techné* which meant physical training.

All the ancient narratives tended to rhythmical expressions because, originally, they were not written and therefore not read but learned by heart. It was easier to memorize rhythmical phrases than plain prose. Handed down orally, from one generation to another, such epic poems contained everything that was worth knowing. The story of creation, the memories of tribal migrations, the deeds of heroes, various events which happened in the course of military expeditions, the experiences of hunters and farmers, the teaching of priests and philosophers, all was embodied in epical verse or in rhythmic prose. All of it was the poet's material to be transposed into parables and comparisons. And what had been considered a mere comparison by one generation, changed into a myth in the course of another generation.

Epic narratives of all kinds could be found everywhere. Some were fabulous and romantic like the tales of the Egyptian papyri or the legends of ancient India and China. Others were crude like the Mesopotamian sagas glorifying the heroes Marduk and Gilgamesh or sober and didactic like the first books of the Old Testament. No one among those which are known to us tells its tale with such a poetic insight and such a richness of images as the two romances of warfare and adventures on the sea, *The Iliad* and *The Odyssey*, composed by Homer, a Greek rhapsodist, some time before the 7th century before Christ. But Homer's interest, as well as that of the older epic poets, whoever they were, was directed toward the past. At the very end of the ancient epoch another master of poetical narrative arose, whose vision was inspired by a sense of destiny. It was Virgil, whose *Aeneid* is a poetical embodiment of many achievements of the ancient times and whose famous Fourth Eclogue testifies to a prophetic presentiment of a coming decisive change in history.

Besides long epic poems or rhythmical narrations, there were also shorter tales or novels, some composed in verse, others in plain prose. Most of them dealt with mythological subjects, reflecting the romantic atmosphere of the very old stories, each of which contained a seed of historical truth covered by the imagination of many generations. The Roman poet Ovid assembled them in his *Metamorphoses*, the Greek novelists Longus and Heliodorus developed them into plots of nearly dramatical power. Many others can be found in the remnants of the Egyptian civilization or in the poetic traditions of India and China.

In the long inscriptions on the walls of the Mesopotamian palaces and Egyptian tombs, celebrating the
deeds of long dead kings, as well as in the most ancient
inscriptions on the ruins which have been discovered
in India and perhaps also in the undecipherable texts
of the Maya temples in Yucatan we find still another
kind of epic narrative, namely historical prose. But
the all-pervading inclination towards poetical adornment and dramatic interpretation makes it difficult to
distinguish between epics and history in the ancient
epoch.

Various longer or shorter chronicles, recording the
important events of the past, were composed in Egypt
and Mesopotamia as well as in the Greek towns on the
western coast of Asia Minor and in Sicily. The professional narrators—the Greeks used to call them the
logopoioi—used to relate the more recent events as
well as the old myths to their audiences. But very little
of all that has been preserved to our times. Herodotus'
book of *Histories*, written in the 5th century before
Christ, is the oldest of the Greek attempts to discern
history from the mythology. The books of the Old
Testament dealing with the origin and the early history of the Jews constitute even an older attempt.

In the last centuries of the ancient epoch, the link
which kept history in close connection with epic
poetry was not so much the esteem for poetical comparison as the tendency to dramatise the related
events. Such was the obvious aim of Thucydides, the
historian of the wars between Athens and the other
city-states in Greece at the end of the 5th century before Christ. Such also were the aims of Polybius who,
two centuries later, recorded the final loss of Greek
independence, and of Tacitus, whose *Annals*, written

in the period of the Roman Empire, put into sharp contrast the traditions of the Roman city-republic and the policy of the emperors. Even the speeches of the famous orators like Demosthenes the Athenian, who put up a noble fight for the independence of his city at the close of the 4th century before Christ, stressed the dramatic qualities of the most recent events. And, naturally, the various *Lives* of famous men, that branch of historical literature brought to great perfection by Plutarch and Suetonius at the very end of the ancient times, exploited every human conflict which could add dramatic coloring to their material.

From dramatized narrations and reports to a real drama is a big step. The Indian and Far Eastern cultures did, later on, develop their own theatrical art as a kind of entertainment. They never reached the idea of catharsis—which means the spiritual purification of the listener—because they did not have any dramatists; they had merely playwrights.

The ancient culture in the Mediterranean area made the step which is necessary to reach a real drama. It could make it because it developed its art in an age of intensive religious thought. That was why it reached the most unusual depth already in its first dramatic work, the Jewish *Book of Job*. Undoubtedly, we may find similar dramatical dialogues also in Mesopotamia or in Egypt. But nowhere else was the problem of human suffering stated with such insight into the human nature; and nowhere is to be found a dramatic answer of such a beauty and power as in this dialogue of the Old Testament.

The Greeks put drama on the stage. Some of the Greek gods used to be honored by choral songs narrat-

ing various scenes from their mythical lives. The
chorus, consisting of trained dancers who accompanied their songs by melodramatic dancing, was usually divided into two parts, as may be seen from the
division of their songs into strophes and antistrophes.
Nothing could be more natural to the poet than to
change his epical declamation into a dialogue. The
leading part was recited or even played by the poet,
the other two parts by the leaders of the divided
chorus. When these leaders developed into actors, the
poet himself was replaced by a third actor. Later on,
the role played by the chorus substantially diminished. Such were the origins of the serious drama,
which the Greeks named tragedy. In a parallel way,
the comic drama developed from scenic dancing at
the vintage and harvest feasts.

The 5th century before Christ and the beginning of
the 4th, the age in which Greek tragedy and comedy
flourished, was a period in which the elevated moral
consciousness of the poets, dissatisfied with the cheap
answers of the myths, looked deeper into the nature of
the human life in search for truth. The ultimate truth
was for them ultimate beauty. The mysterious reality
of sin and punishment and the even more manifest reality of suffering from the conflicts of human wills con-
stituted for them the substance of tragedy. In the *Prometheus Bound* and the *Oresteia* of Aeschylus, which
were probably the highest achievements of Greek
drama, the vision of the poet surpassed the usual expli-
cation of suffering as punishment for pride and found
the positive meaning of pain. Aeschylus did not need
surprising plots to seize the very heart of his listeners;
it was sufficient for his poetical art to create a simple

situation and to light it up with his lyrical similes to make all its dramatic implications manifest.

The moral conflicts in Sophocles' *Antigone*, the diabolical self-assertion portrayed by Euripides in *Media*, but also the gentle heroism of the same poet's *Iphigenia in Aulis*, such was the material from which the Greek drama was built. In its realism as well as in its imaginativeness it was followed by contemporary comedy, the masterpiece of which was Aristophanes' *Birds*. But once the interest in the ultimate problems of man had ceased, the exquisite poetic beauty of the ancient drama vanished. In the Roman comedy of Plautus and even in the pieces of the more refined Terence entertainment replaced art.

In Search of the Unknown God

~⁓~

WHEN DISCUSSING the development of the political life, the science and the art of the ancient epoch of history, we had frequently to mention their close relations to the religious thought and institutions of that time. From the very beginning the religious development has been of decisive importance for all the other branches of cultural life. But what kind of development was it?

Its story is by far not a simple one. Not only had the religious ideas a strong influence upon the political organisation, the art and the science, but also these three branches of culture exercised, in their turn, a compelling influence over religion. Thus the religious development of the ancient era was a twofold one: on one hand, there was, in every country, a growing religious tradition preserved by the priests, whose business was not always an exclusively religious one; on the other hand, the purely religious thought had its own way by which it frequently arrived at results diametrically opposed to the principles resulting from the accrued tradition.

The most conspicuous result of the growth of religious tradition was undoubtedly the gradual unfolding of polytheism. The original consciousness of a spiritual power permeating the universe and manifesting itself in the various activities of nature was slowly superseded in the mind of the ancient men by a belief in a multitude of divinities. There were probably several different reasons for this change. It is not possible to know them all in detail, nor are we able to reconstruct the series of smaller steps which were necessary to accomplish such an important substitution. It seems, however, quite probable, that the first step toward this disparaging goal was made by the oblivion of the personal character of the Creator. Not every country in the ancient world has preserved such a pure idea of a personal God, quite distinct from nature, as have the Jews. On the contrary, in many places such an idea has been superseded by a vague consciousness of an impersonal power, whose manifestations in the physical world have been slowly identified with the subjects or events in which they used to take place. Such manifold spirits—or *numina*, as the Romans used to call them—were then personified and changed into divinities, which had all the virtues and also the vices of men. Thus, in Greece, the spiritual power which makes the grain grow became Demeter, the goddess and giver of corn, and the power which sends the rain was changed into Zeus, the god of rain. Another factor in this development was probably the cultural intercourse between the various tribes or agricultural centres; it has not been found easy to identify the names or symbols of the divinities of various tribes or towns; it was much easier to accept them as different divinities. And still another, although probably quite exceptional, factor in this development may be seen in the natural theology which sprung up in various places from the primeval religious tradition. The pharaoh Amenhotep IV (Akhenaten), who tried to reestablish in Egypt a kind of monotheism in the exclusive cult of the Sun, succeeded merely in introducing into his country another deity, hated by the servants of the older gods and suppressed by them immediately after the pharaoh's death. The Persian priest Zoroaster (Zarathustra), who, in the first half of the last millennium before Christ, speculated upon the origin of evil, finished with recommending to his countrymen the belief in two almost co-eternal deities, the principles, respectively, of the Good and the Evil.

What was characteristic of the religious life in all the ancient countries, however, no matter how humanized and subject to the laws of nature were their deities, was the constant presence of the conception of a cosmic law, from which all things emerge. Sometimes this conception used to be personified. Such was the case of the Mesopotamian god Marduk whose functions as creator, conservator and judge used to be identified with the names of various contemporaneous divinities, or the case of the Egyptian Ptah, who had "fashioned the gods and set them on their holy places." Sometimes it was an abstract idea. The Greek conception of fate—*Moira* or *Dike*—the Persian *Asha*, the Indian *Rita* were such vague but ever present notions of eternal Providence. Even the Chinese, when their primeval religion had been corrupted and materialised, preserved the conception of the eternal Principle, the *Tao*.

There were periods of religious decadence in the ancient world as well as periods of progress. But there was always a tradition which none of the newer developments could efface: the tradition of man's personal

experience of God. The biblical Shem and his sons
introduced many idols into the religion transmitted
to them by Noah, the preceding patriarch, and Abra-
ham had to eliminate them again. He could do that
only because he knew God; he knew Him from tradition and he knew Him also personally.

If there is a branch of religious thought, which we
may be sure existed already in the protohistoric epoch
even though we can not infer it from any excavations
but only from ethnological studies, it is liturgy. The
primitive man's experience of God was an astonishing
experience. And liturgy, not abstract thinking, is the
first and most natural expression of astonishment. At
the beginning of the ancient epoch, the rites and
sacred techniques were already fairly established.

Every liturgy is based on two primeval conceptions:
on the idea of the holy and on the idea of the sacrifice.
It is probable that the original meaning of the word
holy was "that which is different, unusual." It was
meant, undoubtedly, to signify the experience with
the Spiritual Power and its manifestations, but very
soon, perhaps from the very beginning, it was also
used to indicate the sites in which such experiences
had taken place or were expected to take place. As
long as the tribe led a nomadic life, the characteristic
of a holy place used to be attached to a site only, a
mountain or a sacred grove, the trees of which must
not be cut down. In the towns, special buildings were
erected, the temples, to which the notion of holiness
was transferred. And in a similar way, as the holy
places were accessible to the patriarch of the tribe only
or to men selected by him, so the temple usually had
a sacred room that could only be entered by the priests,

to whom the religious duties of the patriarchs were usually transmitted.

By religious duties the ancient people understood above all the offering of the sacrifices, to which even religious instruction was considered secondary. We can only guess what the original idea of a sacrifice was: a symbolical acknowledgement of the Divine Power and of the gifts which the hunter and the harvester had received from it. In many places, however, the sacrifice itself took the place of the object of sacrifice and its offering developed into a sacred ritual of a mysterious character. And at this point, the ways of the religious development were divided. On one hand, religious civilizations of the Greek type were unfolded, in which the office of a priest was considered an elective office accessible to any citizen and in which nobody took care of the logical consistency of religious tradition. On the other hand, there was the exceptional religious civilization of the Jews, in which, for a long time, the religious thought got the upper hand of the liturgy and—maintained and developed by the prophets, the *nabi 'im*—overruled all the other branches of the Jewish culture. Between these two extremes and perhaps the most common type of ancient religion was the cult of gods established in local temples, to which professional priests and frequently also landed properties were attached. The priests of these temples had too many occupations to be able to devote their intellectual capabilities to all of them. Their activities were mostly influenced by all sorts of cultural trends. Their interest in the laws of nature, especially in the movements of the stars, resulted in the establishment of complicated rituals, tainted by magic and sorcery, based on superstitious belief in the hidden meaning of natural events or actions. Their religious opinions were soon changed into complicated mythologies.

Myths are undoubtedly younger than liturgical rites. At least, that can be said about the myths in the proper sense of the word, that is narratives which, by poetical license, connect historical persons or events with the Supernatural or add purely fictitious stories to the religious tradition. Such myths vary from country to country and from tribe to tribe, but are not to be found everywhere because some tribes had no taste for mythical transposition at all. From them we have to discern the primeval traditions adorned by the garb of poetical parallels and symbols but containing the reminiscences of events which might have really happened in the dawn of history. Such primeval traditions, about the original paradise on earth or the great flood, for instance, may be found in all the most ancient civilizations on the various continents. In such ancient narrations we can from time to time discover a scattered seed of a tradition which had usually little relation to the teaching by which it was surrounded but which can be later found again in the New Testament. Such are, for example, the doctrine of the incarnation of God, the prophecy of the birth of the Saviour from the Virgin, and the doctrine of the three persons in one God. The presence of such notions in various ancient civilizations can not be explained, of course, by the natural growth of knowledge. It could be, perhaps, explained by poetical inspiration; but poetical inspiration, as we have already seen, was considered by ancient people a kind of religious revelation.

The later and sometimes very crude mythical transposition, by which the primeval traditions were in many places gradually superseded, was centred around the historical figures of famous men and women. Their lives and works on this earth were, seen from a historical perspective, regarded as a blessing for mankind. The Greeks called them "epiphanies" or manifestations. What, however, sprung up from a disinterested reverence and poetical fantasy, was soon changed, with the advent of city-states and empires, into a sort of political publicity. Not only successful commanders of armies but also living heads of states whose political records were very poor, used to be recognized as gods; altars were set up and priests were appointed to their honour.

In the times when the patriarch used also to be the priest of the tribe, the moral principles of the tribe bound him even in his political and judicial actions. With the division of the functions in the city-states these things underwent a substantial change. Not only were the heads of the states much more free in their dealings, but also the moral principles of the religious traditions were exposed to corruption which was much more dangerous in a hereditary monarchy or in a city-republic than it ever had been in a patriarchal society.

How the ancient politicians treated religion is evident from the growing syncretism which, in the empires, became soon a common political custom. Each town and each empire admitted gradually all the foreign gods which they knew to their *pantheons*— usually to manifest their good will toward foreign towns or empires or to stress the political relationships which they had succeeded in establishing with them. Naturally, very little regard was given to the various,

more or less corrupted moral principles, inherent in
the accepted cults.

In this regard, also, the position of the religious tradition and its teachers among the Jews was an exceptional one. When Plato, the Greek thinker who was very
much interested in the problem of the moral government of the state, tried to practise his prescriptions in
a town-state in Sicily, his attempts ended in disaster.
The religious influence on politics in the Jewish state
could be, on the contrary, expressed by the words of
the Psalm: "He chose David his servant and took him
from the sheepfolds." Religious thinkers and preachers
used to set down the main lines of the Jewish political
life from the beginning of its history. And even in
times when religious syncretism and moral decadence
seemed to be victorious in Jerusalem, prophets like
Elijah and his successor Elisha, prevailed and preserved the uncompromising monotheism together with
its moral principles.

No ancient code of moral prescriptions went into
such detail as the principles of the Jewish book of
Deuteronomy. They enjoin justice towards the widows
and the orphans as well as towards the slaves and the
foreigners, take care of a fairly equal distribution of
property and often transcend the rational legality into
the sphere of charity. This dynamic spirit of the Jewish moral thought was lost only at the very end of the
ancient epoch when it was set aside by strict legalism,
the Pharisaism of the Gospels.

Certain moral standards, however, based on the
moral code of the family, were present in the customs
of every ancient civilization. Their imperativeness
used to be supported even by polytheistic religions as
may be seen, for instance, from the so called negative

confession of the Egyptian *Book of Dead*, in which the deceased affirms the moral integrity of his preceding life. Such standards were often insufficient; it was not considered such a big crime to kill a foreigner as to kill a kinsman. Sometimes they were corrupted by the decadent customs of the city, which also influenced the cults of the local divinities. But their validity was made doubtful only when the affirmations of the religious tradition began to be doubted. "Nobody returns from below; who can say what has happened? Therefore be joyful and follow thy desire as long as thou livest," says an inscription upon an Egyptian tomb.

It was only natural that such rational doubt easily took root among the Greeks, whose religion, as we have already pointed out, was based almost entirely on myths and was not connected closely with any moral instruction. The only moral rule the Greeks were able to abstract from their mythology was that only by self-restraint can man avoid pride which usually provokes Nemesis, the jealous goddess of retribution. But precisely where the pride begins and, consequently, where self-restraint is necessary, that was the question which several generations of Greek moral philosophers in the 5th, 4th, and 3rd centuries before Christ, the so-called Sophists, tried to solve. Some of them based moral duty upon unwritten traditional principles which can be forgotten but which may always be rediscovered through reasonable analysis of the nature of man. Such was the doctrine of Socrates, the teacher of Plato, who, however, has not escaped condemnation because of alleged want of reverence to the gods. Others denied the existence of any such natural principles and stressed the conventional character of every moral rule. It was natural that the teachers of moral

philosophy who, denying the natural law, taught
that the moral conceptions should be accepted and
observed, made any morality a strictly personal affair.
Two schools of practical ethics were founded by the
most prominent among them, Zeno the Stoic and
Epicurus, both flourishing in the 3rd century before
Christ. Their main precept was that of restraint from
any interference with the affairs of others. The Stoics
imposed a disciplined calm upon their followers; the
Epicureans admonished them to make profit of anything which could be of advantage for their own happiness. The Stoics became especially popular among
the Romans, where the philosopher Seneca and the
emperor, Marcus Aurelius, were its chief propagators.

The discussions of moral philosophy established, undoubtedly, one of the main ways of the philosophical
approach to religion. This approach, however, contrasted sharply with the decadence of religious institutions in many countries. Gradually, philosophy was
going to develop all its branches and to influence
profoundly the religious thought as well as science,
politics and art. But the philosophical approach to
religion was not the only one which played an important role in this development. There was still another
approach to religion, namely the poetical one, which
was perhaps even more important because of its appeal
to the widest circles of population.

Very early, the religious thought developed its own
symbolism, the powerful hold of which upon the mind
of the ancient people can not be overestimated. There
hardly could be, for instance, a symbol more appropriate to convey the identity of the idea of God the
Creator with that of God the Omniscient than the

symbol of an eye which was employed so often in Egypt as well as in Mesopotamia. In poetical imagination, the allegory could encompass an even much larger field. So, for instance, the allegorical story depicting the origin of life as result of matrimonial conjunction between the personified Earth and the spirit of Heaven was not only much older than any attempts of the Greek philosophers to find a primary substance from which all nature had been made, but it also came much nearer to a truth Greek scientists were never able to grasp, namely that of a substantial difference between the realm of physics and the realm of biology. Another instance of such primitive poetical approach to the ultimate truths was the particular cult of Dionysus, in which this god of wine was represented to the Greeks as the deity of all life, of which the sparkling wine is an apt symbol.

The contrast of life and death brought the poets to ponder over the primeval religious tradition concerning the immortality of man. Already the simple and sometimes rude Egyptian stories surrounding the belief in the eternal character of the *ka*, the spiritual component of man's nature, yield occasional glimpses of lyrical beauty. But in one of the Greek myths concerning the life of the dead, the story of Orpheus and Eurydice, we meet with a full appreciation of love as the one thing in the world which is always opposed to death. The most important milestone on the path of the Greek poetical thought was the dramatic representations of the mystic rites of Eleusis in Attica. These ecstatic and mystical ceremonies, which were connected with the cult of Dionysus, aimed—as far as we are informed about them—at a final union with God, obtainable by purifications from guilt and release of the soul from the body by death. Organized by Dionysiac and Orphic confraternities, in whose detachment from political and family bonds we may see a movement similar to the Christian Church, these mysteries were of the greatest importance not only for the origin of the Greek drama, but also for the Greek religious thought. Plato, for instance, could despise them as he did despise poetry in general, but in several of his dialogues—which are all rather poetical in their setting— *Phaedrus*, *Gorgias*, and *Phaedo*, he discussed the immortality of the soul quite along the lines of the Dionysiac and Orphic ideas.

It does not surprise us that the Greek poets liked to express their thoughts within the framework of the myths. Pindar, one of the oldest of them, had a high esteem for every detail of the mythical stories. But Aeschylus used to speak of Zeus as a supreme intelligence and Euripides called him the "Unknown, the base of the world and over the world enthroned, whose nature it is difficult to guess." Plato went even farther and spoke of the Divinity as of a principle with no personal name. What, however, seems a bit illogical when compared with the Greek cult for personality, is the doctrine of the successive incarnations of every human soul, which was rather popular in Greece, especially among the participants of the mysteries. Perhaps it sprang from the conception of purification (*catharsis*) as the only way out of the sufferings of this world.

Suffering itself was a mystery to the Greeks as it had been a mystery to the Semitic tribes of Mesopotamia. Tabi-utul-bel, the sufferer of the Mesopotamian legend, arrives at the only conclusion that he cannot

understand the designs of gods. Has Aeschylus understood them more when he spoke of Zeus who made for
Man the road to Thought and established "Learn by
Suffering" as an abiding law? Most of the Greek
dramas were tragedies; their plots were based on sufferings which could not be reasonably explained. To
learn, to become more perfect, more pure by suffering
or even by contemplating suffering on the stage, such
was the idea which was dear to those initiated in the
mysteries as well as to Aeschylus. The Greek poets did
not shun reality. They realised that suffering as a
basic reality of life must have some meaning. But
they could only express their hope in some future
reconciliation, in which the meaning of suffering
would become manifest.

Among the Jewish literary achievements of the ancient epoch, there are two works of art which are
interested in the same problems: the Psalms and the
Book of Job. They also face the reality of the pains
and griefs of human life. But their poetical power is of
a different character; their vision is a much more
general one, if we compare it with that of the Greek
drama. What they lack in psychological detail, they
can more than compensate in concentration upon the
mysterious relation between man and his Creator.
They clearly discern suffering as a retribution for sin
on one hand and as God's inscrutable device which has
to be accepted with unswerving hope on the other
hand. If, for the Greeks, hope was a dramatical possibility, the author of the Book of Job and the poets of
the Psalms saw in it the most beautiful thing in the
world, a virtue which could be its own reward. Speaking of hope, the Jewish poets spoke of love.

The rational approach to religion started much later than the attempts to express religious ideas by artistic symbolism and poetry. Discussing it, we have, first of all, to say at least a few words about its development in India and in China, because in the sterility of the religious thought of those regions may be seen the most probable reason for their general cultural barrenness. The Hindus, like the Persians, whose seemingly rational but wholly unreasonable dualism of Good and Evil we have already mentioned, regarded suffering as an evil only. In an attempt to renew the older cult of unpersonal spiritual forces in nature, they identified the First Principle of the world, named Brahma or Atman, with the world itself. But soon afterwards, conscious of the constant change and suffering in the world, they declared the limited and multiple existence of the universe a mere appearance and Brahma the only reality. According to their doctrine, however, Brahma does not exist in the way in which evil and suffering nature exists. A wise man, such was the conclusion of the Hindus, can free himself from suffering by destroying his own individuality and uniting himself with the First Principle which is the annihilation of any natural existence. This teaching, perfected in the 6th century before Christ by Gautama, surnamed the Buddha, spread gradually all over the Far East. In China, it met with two slightly different doctrines. One of them, founded by Lao-Tse, who possibly wrote his *Book of the Principle and its Virtue* at about the same time when Buddha flourished in India, speaks of two different aspects of the First Principle, one unmoving and unknowable, the other active and perfecting itself constantly; the final end of every creature is to return to the first one of these aspects. The other doctrine, spread by the pupils of Confucius (Kung-fu-tse), who flourished at the beginning of the 5th century before Christ, does not interest itself in any ultimate philosophical problems; it merely sets down the rules of a certain ethical opportunism, sophisticated and void of love to nearly the same extent as the teaching of Buddha.

The Greeks were as great intellectuals as the Orientals, even more so. The division between traditional religion on one side and philosophy on the other side was greater in Greece than elsewhere. But there was one quality in their thinking which gave the Greek philosophy a firm basis. It was the consciousness of the truth expressed by Anaxagoras: "All things were in chaos until mind arose and made order." The human mind works in conceptions which are expressed in words; and words were one of the chief interests of the Greek philosophers. Not only did they insist on accurate distinguishing of apparent synonyms and on such an employment of expressions which would be in the fullest accordance with reality, but they also studied the structure of the language from the logical as well as from the philological point of view.

Some of the Greek philosophers, it is true, made from such studies an instrument of a rather vain and superficial word-play. But the best of them were striving conscientiously to get behind the words, to the real meaning of things. Even when they could not adequately answer the question, whether the words they were using were necessary or merely arbitrary expressions of the meanings of things, they attained to the essences of things. Plato distinguished the opinions concerning the visible and easily mistaken world from real knowledge which transcends the physical appearances. He subdivided knowledge into *reason*, which is concerned with numbers, and *intellect*, which grasps the meaning of things, the ideas, the only real existences in God's hands. Aristotle, Plato's pupil, was even more rational. He conceived the meanings of things as derived from the world around us by the activity of our own minds. And he demonstrated that they are necessary only as objects of intelligence, as immaterial, but intelligible forms, which give to the things their essence. In his logic, based on the eternal principle of identity or non-contradiction, he formulated the inevitable theoretical foundation of any reasonable knowledge.

Both these great thinkers, Plato and Aristotle, attained a philosophical conception of God. Aristotle conceived him as the final Cause which is the principle of every being and every change. Plato saw him as a Person which is Love and of which he could say: "It is not like any face or hands or bodily things; it is not word nor thought; it is not in something else, neither living thing, nor earth nor heaven; only by itself in its own way in one form it for ever is."

The conclusions of Plato and Aristotle were, however, not acceptable to the great majority of their contemporaries. The time was not yet ripe for them. Other doctrines, not half so profound and consistent, became popular at the close of the ancient epoch in the pagan society. The Stoics preached a certain sort of pantheism and considered the conformity of human will with the so-called soul of the universe a guaranty of happiness. A thinker who was quite popular in the Roman Empire, Plotinus, introduced into the Greek philosophy some of the one-sided oriental idealism when he taught that the spiritual alone had a real existence and that everything material was a mere image of the spiritual and begotten by it. Naturally, such philosophies did not help to break the atmosphere of bitter disillusionment which spread through the ancient world in the last centuries of its life.

There was only one nation whose spiritual civilization stuck relentlessly to the hope that a day would come when the true meaning of human life would become manifest. It was the Jews, the nation whose prophets remained unshaken in their teaching activities even when it was threatened by dissolution and, for a certain time, kept in captivity in Mesopotamia. The Jewish prophets, whose teaching we know from their own writings, Amos, Hosea, Isaias, Jeremias, and, later, also Ezekiel, flourishing from the 8th to the 6th century, were not philosophers. They were theologians, whose doctrine gradually transcended even the profound and pure religious tradition of their tribe. Again and again, in very adverse circumstances, they affirmed their belief in a future epoch, in which God, the Lord of hosts of heaven as well as of earth, would gather the nations of the world and make a new covenant with the faithful. They were uncompromising in their attacks against injustice and oppression of the poor and also in their assertion of individual responsibility and retribution. They also developed the conception of the "holy," stressing the inward life of man and the purification of his mind. "I desire love and not sacrifice, and the knowledge of God more than burnt offerings," said Hosea.

But what was perhaps the most curious thing in the teaching of the Jewish prophets, was their constant interest in an idea which was particularly at home in the Jewish religious tradition: in the future incarnation of God, in the expected coming of the Saviour, who was to open a new chapter in history, a new way towards light. It would have been quite natural if such a prophetical idea was taken as an invitation to dreams of worldly power and glory; and indeed such was its interpretation among many common members of the Jewish nation. But the opinions of the prophets, concerning the coming of the Saviour, were rather unusual. They refused to accept the popular dream about the character of his mission. And Isaias, the most profound thinker among them, presented his picture in a surprising way: "Despised and the most abject of men, a man of sorrows, and acquainted with infirmity . . . Surely he hath borne our infirmities and carried our sorrows; and we have thought him as it were a leper, and as one struck by God and afflicted . . . He was offered because it was his own will, and he opened not his mouth; he shall be led as a sheep to the slaughter . . ."

III

ASPECTS OF
CHRISTIAN CULTURE

The New Testament and the Church

THE CIVILIZATION in which we live and which has developed during the last nineteen hundred years is a Christian civilization. We could perhaps say that it is still a Christian civilization although the spirit in which it was founded does not permeate all its branches to the same extent as it did five or six hundred years ago. Nevertheless, it is a Christian civilization, because it rests preponderantly upon values which originated from the Christian spirit, no matter how distorted they may be. When a Communist agent is exhorted to offer his life for the sake of the Communist idea, he participates in the Christian civilization, because the idea of offering one's life for the sake of an abstract doctrine has been enormously popularized since the pre-Christian era. When a sick person gets gratuitous hospitalization in a state institute where nobody cares about his spiritual welfare, he still benefits physically from an idea which was developed by several Christian saints and by the congregations they founded. When persons or institutes which lend money are restricted in the amount of interest they are allowed to charge, it is because of the remnants of the Christian doctrine on usury and interest. When the United Nations try to establish a code on the rights of man, they are only imitating the fundamental norms of Christian morals. And there are still many millions of Christians living in all parts of the world who are active in every possible field of the cultural developments of today.

That does not mean that the more ancient civilizations have been extinguished without traces. On the contrary, Christians have inherited many of their values, sometimes transforming them, sometimes accepting them as they were. There are even ancient values which have to be defended by Christians against the misconceptions or undervaluations of the present time. The basic principles of logic, for instance, established by the Greeks and included in the works of Aristotle, have been considered as doubtful by many a modern philosopher, but Christian thinkers have never ceased in supporting their validity.

Christian civilization does not consist of a set of entirely new values, but rather in a transformation and perfection of the ancient background by the spiritual stream flowing from the life, death, and teaching of Jesus Christ. The coming of Christ has changed to a great extent the nature of the creative activity of man in all his endeavours. But not in all of them did that mean a complete transformation of the older values. In religion, it meant a revelation of what had been hidden; the ancient guessing had to cede to the glory and power of the Word. In the conception of history, it meant the change of hope into persuasion. In art, it gave to men the possibility of turning their work toward absolute beauty and to solve the problem of the human drama. In political activity, it replaced the sagacious opportunism of the Stoics with the command of love, but it did not touch the things which were Caesar's. In science, it suggested to man how to use his knowledge of things.

If we had to describe in a general way the difference between Christian civilization and its ancient background, we would point out that, whereas the chief moral rule of the ancient man was the proverb "Do nothing too much," Christian culture united knowledge with love almost inseparably. Ancient prudence was superseded by new enthusiasm.

"There is a cry in the waves of the sea as they fall together, and groaning in the deep; a wail comes up from the cavern realms of Death, and the springs of the holy rivers sob with the anguish of pity." Perhaps no other words than these lines from Aeschylus can say more about the spiritual atmosphere of the world in which Jesus was born. The political insecurity of the times, in which the Roman Empire had not yet taken firm root, was one of the lesser evils. The most prominent characteristic of those years was the disintegration of the primeval values, of the family, of belief in a spiritual power, of the traditional moral prescriptions. There was some hope amidst the ocean of disillusion and pessimism, but there was very little of it.

The world has not become more secure since the coming of Christianity. On the contrary, except for the first two centuries, when the Roman Empire was firmly established and its citizens could live in a comparative peace, even more turbulent and insecure times were to come. But the spiritual atmosphere in the Mediterranean area and, later on, in the whole of Europe and its temporary dependencies, was transformed. Was that the result of a new and astonishing philosophical doctrine? Was it the result of the organisation of masses which the Church was able to undertake with such success? It was neither. Both these factors became quite prominent in the cultural shaping of the world in the Middle Ages and in the Modern Times. But even then, they were always only secondary elements in the growth of Christian civilization. It is sufficient to analyse the way in which the whole realm of the Roman Empire and even some countries beyond its frontiers were gained by the Gospel in a space of only two and a half centuries, to discover that it was, first of all, Jesus Christ himself Who became the centre of human hearts and minds.

This is an important thing for anybody who is anxious to understand the very essence of Christian culture and the foundations of the civilization which it has created. Christian culture grew from the blood of the martyrs. But the martyrs did not suffer because of this or that philosophical explanation of a problem. Nor did they suffer because of some hopes in the future of their communities. They accepted tortures and even death because they were persuaded that Jesus Christ was a man and God Who had overcome death and all the evils of this world. He was the anointed of the Lord, Who came upon the earth in the fullness of time.

His life, extending probably from the year 5 before the beginning of our era to the year 29, was as great a failure in the eyes of a distant onlooker as it was a most astonishing thing for those who were near to Him. Some humble Gallilean shepherds and fishermen were the first to witness His youth and to hear of its hidden events which Mary kept and pondered in her heart. A few of them and, later on, whole crowds of their

compatriots accompanied Him for months on His jour-
neys over the Palestinian hills. There was much poetry
and very little haste in His moves from village to village; from the very beginning He knew that the importance of His death would transcend the work of His
active years. As man He was of such a many-sided
character that His biographers were only able to collect
flashes of disparate reminiscences of the three years of
His preaching, discussion, and His dramatic parables.
Such a life, unusual in itself, was crowned by three
events through which the greatest drama in human
history was achieved: the Crucifixion, the Resurrection, and the Ascension.

This drama, as real as it was astonishing, was the
idea, the truth which was professed by the Christians
under any circumstances, because they always saw
and still see in it the central point of all history, without which all human accomplishments, the efforts of
every one among us included, have no sense and no
meaning. The birth, life, death, and resurrection of
Christ, the Incarnation of the Word of God, is the central fact of all the Christian culture. What we do, is
only a participation in Christ's heritage.

There is no doubt that the truth revealed by Christ
to His disciples and transmitted by them orally as well
as by written word to the subsequent generations, is
a preeminently religious truth. Every word in it is
concentrated on the relations between man and God.
It is concerned with the other endeavours of man's
activity to a far lesser degree than the purest of the
ancient religious traditions, the tradition of Israel. In
that respect, the New Testament seems to be more
restricted than the Old Testament.

But when we study the manifestations of Christian

culture in each one of its twenty centuries, we come to the conclusion that such a limitation of Christian truth is a mere appearance. The concentration of revelation gave it such a power that, by its sheer spirit, it has penetrated farther into the different fields of human creative activity than any older religious tradition ever has.

First of all, the facts of Christ's life and His teaching had to be expressed in a doctrine. Such expression, of course, could be only imperfect because of the imperfect nature of human words. All theology is imperfect, because of the incompleteness of its investigations and comparisons. But the truth contained in the doctrine of Christ is perfect, because it has been given to men by God. As such it has to be accepted. Secondly, there is the stream of grace, a sanctifying gift, promised by Christ himself and conveyed, by the Church, through the medium of the sacraments. And thirdly, both the above mentioned elements, the truth and the grace, open the way toward the perfection of all human capabilities, corporeal as well as spiritual, for our body is as capable of satisfaction as our soul.

But this possibility to elevate human nature would not exist, had it not been for the fact that Jesus Christ, God and man, died for us and rose from the dead again and that He founded His church to bear witness to how He had lived and what He taught. Who does not accept this truth without reservation, is not a Christian. Who does not know it, does not know the core of Christian culture. It is true that this culture was always based on a certain abstract doctrine. It is equally true, that its main bearer was always a special organization, the Church. But neither of these two characteristics is the most important in the description of Christianity. The most prominent of its features is the testimony that it bears to the Incarnation of God.

The Church is the central field of Christian culture. It is an exclusive and universal society. Its subsequent generations are bound together by the transmission of the undiminished message revealed by Jesus Christ to mankind. It is true that many a passage of its teaching was and still is repeated by men who are not its members. Many of the principles it has proclaimed have been restricted or distorted by others. Innumerable other ideas, belonging to the spheres of philosophy, history, politics, art, and science, have been conceived and put into practice beyond the sphere of its direct interest. Sometimes its individual members or even representatives of its hierarchy were clearly mistaken in their opinions concerning such ideas and their values. But whenever it came to the ultimate problems of human life, there was no other source from which a really consistent and wholly salutary doctrine could be obtained.

Not only because it accepted from Christ's own hands the mission of distributing grace—the inspiring and strengthening influence which Christ himself promised to men—but also because of its guardianship of Christ's teaching, it is called "holy," sanctified by God. It is firmly believed that its body as a whole and also its visible head, the Vicar of Christ and successor of Peter, the shepherd of the last of Christ's parables, can not depart from the truth of Christ.

But historically, although it is the only society which has existed throughout the duration of this era, the Church is far from immutable. Nor is her teaching defined in such a way that she would not need to make new pronouncements when faced with new developments in the surrounding world. The life of the Church in the world, the human dramas of its leaders, the ever varying destinies of its flock, and above that, its constant exercise of its teaching office even in ages which have estranged themselves from the Christian principles, result in a story which is very similar to that of Christ's own life. Even the Church is being scourged and lots are being cast for its clothing.

The development of the Church's constitution, as well as that of her teaching, is rather similar to the development of an organism which unfolds one of its parts after another when some circumstances require it; these parts are only actualized by the circumstances; they existed before them.

In the very first period of its existence, the Church lived in communities scattered in various towns of the Roman empire and governed by direct successors of Christ's own disciples. The title given usually to these successors of the apostles was that of "presbyteros" or "episcopos." Such was the organization which went through the bloody experience of the first persecutions. At the turn of the first century and in the following period of relative tranquility which ended by the succession of the emperor Commodus, when the Christian communities grew rapidly, the appellation *presbyteros* (priest) began to be employed as designation of the helpers of the *episcopos* (bishop). In the fourth century, when the Church established its communities in all the provinces of the Roman Empire and when the liturgy was celebrated freely in special buildings, the priests were put in charge of smaller communities, which then developed into parishes. The seats of the bishops assumed the role of regional centres; the regions began to be called *dioceses* after the appellation of administrative districts of the Empire. As we know it today, the internal organisation of a diocese with regular registration of births and deaths of its members in every parish, was accomplished only in the 16th century.

Each of the original Christian communities conserved the teaching of the Church. It was the usual criterion of the theologians to look for the general acceptance of any dogmatic assertion, because, as they said, an article of faith common to all the communities must have come from the time when these communities were founded, that is, from the apostles themselves. Whenever an assertion appeared, concerning the revealed truth or any of the moral principles, which was not in accordance with the common tradition, it was the custom to appeal to the authority given by Christ to St. Peter and inherited by the bishops of Rome and his successors. Since the interference of the Roman bishop Clement in the trouble at Corinth, in the year 96, many similar steps testify to this belief in the authority of the see of Rome. From the 7th century onwards, the title *pope* (father) was reserved to designate the bishop of Rome. On the basis of this tradition two distinctive features in the character of the Church were gradually unfolded: its monarchical constitution and its legal order.

Neither the monarchical constitution nor the juridical organisation of the Church was accomplished without considerable difficulties. It was necessary to overcome the opposition against the legal pronouncements of the popes which, together with other ecclesiastical decisions, were assembled, in the course of the 12th and 13th centuries, into the body of ecclesiastical law.

The monarchical constitution, with the pope as the visible head of the Church, went through its critical moments in the 15th century, at the council of Constance, and again in the 19th century, at the council of the Vatican. But if we bear in mind the essential mission of the Church, the transmission of the heritage of Jesus Christ, we can see quite clearly that without such accomplishments this mission would have been long lost and forgotten. Most of the Christian bodies which, in the course of time, have separated themselves from the Church—many of them attempting to return to what in their imagination had been the primitive state of the Church—have sooner or later lost that which had been the essential content of the Gospel, namely the message of the Incarnation and the graces which flow from it.

There is one chapter in the story of the separations from the Church which deserves special mention. It concerns the bodies which are still active in Russia and in the Balkan countries, governed by the archbishops-patriarchs of Moscow and Constantinople respectively and using the Old Slavonic and the Greek as their liturgical languages. The metropolitan see of Constantinople left the communion with the see of Rome for the first time in the 11th century, under the pressure of the East Roman Emperors. And although it attached itself to the centre of unity twice again, in 1274 and in 1439, it was confined, after the occupation of Constantinople by the Turks in 1453, within the boundaries of the Mohammedan Empire, where it grew accustomed to separation. The other body, the original centre of which was Kiev, was founded by missionaries who came from Constantinople. It remained in contact with the see of Constantinople even when Kiev was lost to the Tartars and the metropolitan see was transferred to Vladimir on Klyasma and then to Moscow. Together with the patriarchate of Constantinople it was repeatedly invited to join the Catholic Church again. As late as 1437 the patriarch of Moscow, Isidor, came to the council of Ferrara and Florence to reestablish union with the see of Rome but was abandoned by his own suffragan bishops who ceded to the pressure of their political ruler. As a rather paradoxical effect of their dependence upon the state, these eastern patriarchates—they call themselves Orthodox—have proved sterile in matters of social morals, although they have preserved the Christian tradition almost undiminished. They have been unable to guide their flocks through the violent political and economical disputes of recent times. The patriarchs of Moscow became, moreover, passive tools of the Communist dictatorship.

Developing its internal constitution and organization, the Church at the same time expanded territorially. In the first eight centuries of the Christian era it added Western Europe, including Germany and England, to its Mediterranean field of activity. In the following three centuries, it spread through the Slavonic countries and Scandinavia. After some previous attempts, it began, in the 16th century, its missionary drive into the most distant countries of the world, suffering reverses in some of them but taking firm root in many others.

The world changed as the distances between its various parts became more and more easy to be covered. The Church unfolded its mission at the same pace. We may trace this development also in the public activity

of some of its greatest popes. Gregory I, at the turn of
the 6th and 7th centuries, employed his Roman genius
in safeguarding the remnants of the ancient political
order which was attacked from every side by invading
tribes. Gregory VII, in the 11th century, a man of
common stock and perhaps a bad politician, but a saint
of ascetic piety, had to begin a contest with the worldly
powers over the liberty of the Church and the divine
and natural right. Pius V, in the 16th century, although handicapped by the religious secession of
Northern Europe and by the necessity of carrying out
an internal reform of the Church, led Europe's common defence against the Turks and organized missions
into the recently discovered countries. And finally
two popes of the 19th and 20th centuries, Leo XIII and
Pius XI, were listened to if not obeyed throughout the
world when they pronounced authoritative decisions
concerning moral and social questions of utmost importance.

The relations between the Church and the society
as a whole were always subject to irregular oscilla-
tions. When, in the 5th century, the young Christian
civilization was nearly destroyed by the invasions of
pagan tribes, the man who received Attila, the leader
of the Huns, at the gates of Rome and in presence of
the Roman Senate, was Pope Leo I—although he had
no political function in the Roman Empire and his
legal position in it was rather uncertain. In 1799,
Pius VI, an octogenarian and ruler of the independent
papal state which was founded in the second half of
the 8th century, died as a prisoner of the French dictator Napoleon in Valence. At the middle of the 20th
century, the Pope, owner of several old palaces and

churches, but citizen of no worldly power, is again looked upon as a major factor in the social development of the world.

There are ages in which the life of every Christian is linked closely to the Church not only by daily prayers, fasts, feast days, and weekly and seasonal observances, but also by the glorification of suffering and humble work, by sanctification of marriage and even by principles concerning the human society. But there are also periods in which religious ideas seem to be thrown out of cultural life altogether and only superficial remnants of religious customs remain. Such secularization of the Christian civilization results frequently in an open persecution of the Church. "In the world you shall have distress; but have confidence: I have overcome the world." This prediction of the Saviour has been fulfilled many times in the course of the history of the Church. Almost immediately after it had come into existence the Christian religion clashed with public opinion. At Rome and in other cities of the Roman Empire cruel judicial actions were started against the Christians. Under the Roman Emperors of the 3rd century, Decius, Valerian, and Diocletian, the hatred of Christianity resulted in systematic persecutions based on the assumption that the Christian religion was incompatible with the interests of the state. But the blood of martyrs bore strange fruits; the number of Christians was growing everywhere until, in 313, the emperor Constantine gave them the liberty of worship. From that time onward, if we do not count the numerous martyrdoms suffered by Christians from the hands of nations who had not yet received Christianity, persecutions almost always started at the end of periods in which the moral life of the Christians themselves had disintegrated. The exacting of heavy tributes by the papal curia in the 13th century was the prelude to the imprisonment of the pope in Avignon and to the religious wars in Bohemia. The complacency of the Christians towards the faults of the governments in France and in Mexico led to bloody persecutions of the clergy by French revolutionists in the 18th and by Mexican Socialists in the 20th century. And whenever the hatred against the Church started, it was very hard to pacify.

Nevertheless, the Church always stuck to the ideal of the perfect society in which the Church itself would play the role which the soul plays in the body. The Kingdom of God is not of this world but it is in this world. It has to bear its testimony to it. Such testimony consists in moral influence upon the minds of rulers, legislators, and citizens.

There is, however, always the possibility of a complete divergency between the moral views of the Church and those of a political power. For some time, from the 12th to the 16th century especially, the Church in such a case, having exhausted all the milder means, used to call upon her members to revolt against such a power. In more recent times, this practice was abandoned. In such prominent cases as were the Nazi and the Communist attempts to dominate the world, the Church has condemned the respective ideologies, but left undecided the problem as to what practical steps should be taken against them.

In cases when only some individual members of the Church assume a doctrine contrary to its teaching, the Church reserves the right to punish them. Such has always been the normal procedure in any society. The children of a family are punished by their father, no matter how opposed they may be to the punishment. A citizen of a state is punished if he does not comply with his duties as a citizen, no matter how loudly he may protest that he no longer considers himself a citizen.

In the first centuries of the life of the Church, its moral prescriptions were very strict in spite of its practical powerlessness. Moreover, prominent members of the Church, such as Tertullian, the famous apologist, severed all contacts with it and even, in some cases, founded new communities independent from it, because they were of the opinion that the Church was not strict enough in dealing with sinners and heretics. In the Middle Ages the Church was willing to help the political powers in suppression of any teaching which could be dangerous to the Christian civilization. That, undoubtedly, meant an efficacious protection of the society against doctrines which tried to undermine it. The *cathari* who were against the institution of the family, the *flagellants* who were able to reduce the normal life of whole regions to wreck, the followers of Wiclif and Hus, depriving everybody who was not "in the state of grace" of any authority and even of lawful possession of any property, such were the people with which the courts of the Church and also the so-called tribunals of inquisition used to deal. But among those who were condemned by them was, undoubtedly, a number of innocent people; the process of the physicist and astronomer Gallileo Gallilei is probably the best known of the cases in which the ecclesiastical court committed a judicial blunder.

At the same time, the inquisition became gradually a tool in the hands of the rulers of various countries who used it for political purposes and even for personal vengeance. Joan of Arc was condemned and executed by the English inquisition for political reasons. Juan Mariana, one of the best Jesuit writers of the 16th century, was jailed by the Spanish inquisition for years because he dared to criticize the monetary policy of the king of Spain. With the growing dissension between the State and the Church, especially from the 18th century onward, the Church abstained from punishing the heretics in a judicial way and contented itself with condemnation of their doctrines and, in some cases, with excommunication.

In the same measure in which the Church became more benevolent, however, every one of the political powers tightened its grip on the citizen. At the present time, not only is every state ready to punish severely the heresy of not respecting the laws of the state, but many states are ready to inflict penalty upon any citizen who would dare to have ideas of his own about the education of his children. To distinguish this "liberty" from the liberty of the Church they call it the "democratic" or "people's liberty."

The essence of any conscious deviation from Christian truth is the glorification of the divergent. St. Paul said in one of his epistles: "There must be factions, so that those who are approved may be made manifest among you." (I Cor. 11, 19). Those who are not true metal, are always subjective and one-sided. "I want no Jesus Christ to think that he could ever die for me," says the text of a Russian revolutionary song, sung by people who themselves were ready to die for their comrades. They were themselves ready to die because they had been imbued by the Christian idea of self-sacrifice; but their pride did not allow them even to acknowledge the possibility that somebody could have died for themselves. Such a pride has two inevitable consequences, the multiplication of separations and the loss of faith. In every heresy, the hatred against the Church is stronger than the love for the ideas upon which the heresy is based. As the sects multiply, this hatred remains the only thing they have in common and, actually, the only thing they really profess. Gradually, they lose, one by one, the truths contained in Christ's message. From time to time, a movement springs up among them aiming at a renewal of Christian faith. Such were the endeavours of John and Charles Wesley in the 18th century, the Oxford movement and the attempts of Karl Barth in the 19th and 20th centuries respectively. But none of these movements was able to save much of what had been lost.

We live in a time in which dissensions spread more rapidly than they did in the 4th century, when Arianism prevailed in the Christian communities, or in the 16th century, when Protestantism got the upper hand in many European countries. Materialism and the deification of state are gaining ground everywhere.

Consequently, the question presents itself: is the civilization in which we live going to remain preponderantly Christian or will the non-Christian culture prevail? The thoughts of Aeschylus, Plato, and Aristotle did not prevail in the ancient epoch; on the contrary, they were more or less lost to the ancient world in general. What will happen with the message of Jesus Christ?

No historian can answer such a question. The Christians themselves can answer it through the words of St. Paul: "If Christ is not risen, our preaching is in vain and vain also is our faith." But if he is risen, then he will be with his faithful through the days that are coming, until the consummation of the world.

There is no fatalism in the Christian expectations. Either Christ is risen from the dead, or there is no reasonable explanation of history and the suffering of man is a tragedy which has no sense and no meaning. The remaining chapters of history lie in God's hands.

But the individual progress of anyone among us— the only progress which is reasonably conceivable— depends on his own free will. To be progressive means first of all to know the message of Christ. Any real knowledge of things pushes man toward Christ. To refuse Him is not an act of reason.

To know Christ's message, to divulge it, and to be ready to confess it and even to suffer for it is the historical mission of the Church which is closely connected with its sacramental mission, with the distribution of the grace of God, flowing from Christ the Crucified.

To study and to explain the teaching of Jesus Christ as it is conserved in the gospels and in the tradition of the Church is the task of the theologians. The story of Christian theology is the story of continuous interest in a doctrine which is always actual. Even the objections made to the Christians in various epochs are involved in it, because they usually condition the manifestations of the real compass of Christian doctrine. Among the apostles, John and Paul were able to see the profound internal cohesion of the teaching of their Lord better than others. Their names stand at the beginning of a long series of theologians. Scarcely did John the Apostle die when Ignatius of Rome wrote his theological epistles. A generation later, at the close of the 2nd century, Ireneus, Hippolytus, and Tertullian were engaged in apologetical writings. In the 3rd century, Origen, a most learned man who died under the persecutions of Decius, tried to find his way from the works of the Greek philosophers to the books of the New Testament. In the next century the indefatigable Athanasius and the two learned brothes, Basil the Great and Gregory, bishop of Nyssa, together with their friend Gregory the Nazianzen, developed those parts of the Christian doctrine which were then the most attacked. At the turn of the 4th and 5th centuries, Jerome, the translator of the Bible from Greek and from the Semitic languages into Latin, and Augustin, a master of the Latin style, were the first to encompass all the fields of the sacred science without, however, systematizing it. Then, in the dark ages of the migrations, Maximus of Constantinople, the 7th century theologian of the Incarnation, and John Damascene, the author of the "Fountain of Wisdom," aimed—as was natural—more at collecting what had already been done than at any new development. But they made possible the theological revival of the 12th and 13th centuries, represented by the names of Anselm of Canterbury, Peter Lombard, Thomas Aquinas, and Francis Bonaventura, masters of systematical synthesis. Their endeavours, aiming at an intrinsic unity and based on a careful distinction of concepts, became then a common property, transmitted especially by men of genius like Francisco Suarez in the 16th century and Mathias Scheeben in the 19th century.

Quite an important role in the progressive development of the Christian theology was played also by the general councils, summoned from time to time to clear up theological discussions and to face the moral questions of the time. Prominent among them were the council of Nice in Asia Minor in the 4th century, which defended the divinity of Christ; the fourth Lateran council in the 13th century, which defined the basic Christian doctrine of the Lord's Supper; the council of Trent in Northern Italy in the 16th century, which—besides other definitions—explained justification as an inner transformation, and the council of the Vatican in 1870, which accomplished the juridical organization of the Church and defined the infallibility of its head.

No matter how accomplished theological learning may be, it would never be sufficient to make the Church a decisive factor in the cultural, creative life of the world. The true and most important life of the Church is its life of grace, which rarely manifests itself by any external signs and therefore can not be easily seized by the historian. What is accessible to the historian are the instances in which the inner life of this or that Christian comes into manifest conflict with the surrounding world. The most dramatic of such occasions are, undoubtedly, furnished by the times of persecution. The life of the early Christians in the Roman catacombs, as well as the hidden suffering of the Communist-dominated countries of 20th century Eastern Europe, are rich in heroic deeds, each of which may in a few minutes accomplish more and influence the lives of more people than many solemn professions of faith or a whole life of careful studies.

The Christian name for a hero of faith is "saint." Although a common name, this appellation is given to men and women who differ from each other as human individuals may differ. There is no such thing as a type of sanctity.

Many saints assembled around themselves men and women of similar interests and founded or renovated an order or a congregation which, in some cases, accomplished a revival of religious life in many provinces of the Church. But even the characters of these organizations differ. In the 6th century Benedict of Nursia expressed in his rule a way in which prayer and work could be combined incessantly by communities bound to a fixed place and obeying the paternal authority of their leader. At the close of the 11th century the monasticism of the Benedictines bore a new fruit in the severe observance of the Cistercians, founded by Robert of Molesme and brought to perfection by Bernard of Clairvaux. The need for preachers in the 12th and 13th centuries was met first of all by the Premonstratensians, founded by Norbert of Xanten, and then by the systematical theological training of the Dominicans, whose founder, Dominic de Guzman, accepted also the rule of voluntary poverty, which his contemporary, Francis of Assisi, the great poet of the humble life, imposed upon his friars. The 16th century saw the beginning of such different actions as the foundation of the Jesuit order by Ignatius of Loyola, a man of military discipline and enthusiasm, and the accomplishing of a reform in the contemplative Carmelite order by Teresa of Avila. In the next age, Vincent de Paul began his grandiose work of active charity by founding the Daughters of Charity and the Lazarists, and John Baptist de la Salle started the influential congregation of the teaching brothers. Among the modern groups, that of John Bosco, the

Salesian congregation, devoted to joyful education of youth, is the most prominent.

Although usually detached from the small worries of this world, a saint is never a solitary figure. No matter how anxious he may be to avoid social contacts and to spend his days in quiet work and meditation, he always attracts other people. The communion of saints is usually established in the time of their lives. And it is the firm belief of Christians that this communion surmounts even the frontier between this life and the world of the holy ones who have been granted the eternal companionship of Christ.

All nationalities and all kinds of professions are represented among the saints. Young men and women who did not achieve anything in the world, like Stanislas Kostka, John Berchmans, and Bernadette Soubirous, are among them as well as experienced scholars and politicians like Albert the Great or Thomas More; beggars like Benoit Labre or farmers like Niclas von der Flue as well as kings and women of noble blood like Wenceslas of Bohemia or Bridget of Sweden; humble women who influenced profoundly their surroundings, like Catherine of Siena or Joan of Arc, as well as missionaries who died in foreign countries like Cyril and Methodius or Francis Xavier; soldiers like Theodore or Louis as well as peaceful pastors like Josaphat the Ukrainian or Clement Hofbauer. Most books dealing with the story of mankind usually mention them only if some public events are connected with their names. In a history of Christian civilization it should be otherwise.

The central point of all history is, as we have already pointed out, the Incarnation of the second of the Three Persons of God, the Father, the Son, and the

Spirit, who are the absolute Being, Knowledge, and Love. Through the Incarnation it became manifest that love is the supreme end of every being and every knowledge. Christ's voluntary offer of His body and blood upon the Cross, perpetuated in the central liturgy of the Church, the Mass, is the highest example for any man. And, of course, love can not be other than voluntary; it must spring from a complete freedom to choose between assent and negation, between heaven and hell. In making this choice, man decides about his freedom. If, therefore, any human action has a sense, it is, in the first place among all the others, the action of making this choice. And, consequently, a saint is a more important person in history than an artist, a scholar, a politician or a scientist. He has made his choice a preëminent one. He has known the sense of history.

The Cathedral and the Theatre

THE EMOTIONAL CHARACTER of man is present in all
his creative activity. There is hardly any religious,
political or scientific thought which is not colored by
it. But the various arts are its special field. In music
and dance, in planning buildings, in sculpture and in
painting, in prose and poetry, both lyrical and dramatic, human love for persons and things finds its
most natural expression. Is it not a luxury? The modern man, addicted to the pursuit of his material welfare, has some doubts about it. But even he can not
help looking for the beauty in nature or for the simple
melody of a song.

As all the other branches of cultural activity, and
perhaps to a greater degree than some of them, art is
capable of an ascent towards the greatest values that
we can know. The story of the artistic achievements
of the Christian epoch is the story of such an ascent.
But it is also the story of the ever returning dilemma
of art and amusement.

The Christian doctrine spread through a world in
which two different trends were fighting each other:
the old order of the Roman Empire and the much more
simple order of the tribes which began to cross the

river frontiers of the Rhine and the Danube. As far as
art was concerned, it meant the presence of two cultural levels. There were the complicated and, in many
cases, rather sophisticated achievements of the ancient
Mediterranean civilization which, however, was already stagnant and almost void of any creative force.
And there were the undeveloped capabilities of the
barbarians, whose simple songs, myths and various
types of ornaments could not compete with the Greek
and Roman works of art.

But all that was of secondary importance to the
Christians. They were in possession of the Gospel, the
glad tidings, which were in themselves the most noble
drama ever expressed in human words and which contained parables unsurpassed by any lyrical poet. Even
today, after having heard the words and read the
books of all the prominent poets of the last two thousand years, as well as those of the ancient masters of
word and pen, do we know a book more beautiful than
the New Testament? And reciting slowly the melodious phrases of the Nicene Creed, can we say that there
ever was written anything more majestic and impres-
sive, anything which would sum up in one imposing
sweep of exclamations the beauty of the Creation, the
Redemption and all the hopes of man?

Descending into the subterranean net of corridors
and humble halls, hidden under the suburbs of Rome,
where the Christian cult of the first centuries found its
abode, we come across walls covered with unobtrusive
pictures and symbolical ornaments, all of which are
related to the events of Christ's life and to the main
points of His message. Some of them are rude enough
and certainly none of them can be even compared to
the technical perfection of the wall paintings and

mosaics of the pagan artists of the same or preceding centuries. How are we to judge them? As a manifest decline of style and abilities?

The value of any work of art rests in the fusion of spirit and matter, in the balance between the idea and the artistic form. And it is quite obvious that in this respect Christianity has not made art easy.

The ancient painters and sculptors discovered the beauty of the harmonious features in nature's face. They have also discovered, although to a smaller extent, the realistic beauty of the human countenance. And working hard for many generations, they became accomplished masters in expressing those kinds of beauty in stone and in colors. They achieved a technical mastery which made it, in the end, easy for them to express all they had in their minds. The conceptual and the real form of their most prominent works were in perfect balance. But, at the same time, there were other forces at play in the development of the ancient art beside the genuine astonishment and love for the harmonious forms. A dance, for instance, may express the joy springing from the beauty of movements, but it may also serve as a means of bringing about some sort of nervous excitement. In such a case, the purpose of the art of dancing is very restricted. It does not even encompass the beauty of the movements. It envisages only the pleasure of excitement. And pleasure is definitely not a kind of beauty, because its nature is restrictive. It does not move man to look behind the frontier of his own ego as every true beauty does. A mastery of words, tones, or colors which serves such purposes is therefore not an art but just a technical ability. And in quite a number of minor works of the ancient artists such an ability had obtained the upper hand.

The first step the Christians made in the field of art was in quite a contrary direction. Without being able to use all the technical achievements of the ancient epoch in the arts of sculpture and painting, they immediately set out to express, through works of art, a series of concepts which had never been dreamt of by ancient artists. The love of God, the unequalled sacrifice of Christ, the pure life of Mary, His mother, the mystery of bread changed into Christ's own body and distributed to His faithful, the grace flowing from the sacraments of Baptism, Confession, and Marriage, the bond of fraternity which sanctifies the communal life of Christians—such were the primary objects of their admiration and such were the concepts which the authors of the paintings in the catacombs tried to express.

No wonder that neither the codes of harmonious physical beauty nor the realism of the ancient portraitists proved sufficient for such a task. The realism did not suffice even for simple scenes taken from the narratives of the gospels, because much more than a pictorial view of a scene was usually in the mind of the artist. There was no other solution of the problem than a revival of the symbols. The art of symbolical painting which was developed in the catacombs was not a decay but a transformation of painting. It has lost, perhaps, many of the technical improvements which the ancient epoch had achieved, but, at the same time, it has raised the level of art to a height which had been inconceivable to the ancient world.

Is it possible for an artist to concentrate all his efforts on the expression of concepts which are among the profoundest ever attained by human mind? Have not the Christians, in their attempts to raise the level of art, forgotten that there are, beside the religious ideas and events, numerous other objects which also attract the admiration and love of men?

Such questions have much in common with a conception of Christian art which is as foolish as these questions are misconceived. A Christian painter is not merely one who has spent all his life in painting scenes from the Holy Bible. A Christian composer is not merely a composer who devotes himself exclusively to the composition of masses and hymns. On the contrary, such artists may put very little of Christian character into their works or perhaps they may not be Christians at all. The essence of Christian art is in the presence in the artist's mind of the Maker of all things, material as well as spiritual. The Christian transformation of art does not mean its concentration upon the most profound and eminent concepts. It means the repletion of all artistic activity with a profound reverence for the things and events which we love.

If we make from a thing or a person a mere object or tool of our own passions, it is evident that we do not love it. And feeling no reverence for it we can not increase our reverence for the God who has made it. But if, on the contrary, our art does express a real love, then, by paying a real reverence to the object of our art, no matter how simple or humble it may be, we pay a reverence to its Creator. Thus all good art is an act of worship of God and all good art is a Christian art.

To say, therefore, that the early Christians were not able to grasp the importance of art in the creative life of man—an affirmation which may be found in some books on the history of art—is to miss the very substance of the decisive events at the beginning of our era. The members of the first Christian communities were quite aware of the fact that a work of art can touch truths that go beyond those that are accessible to the impassive reasoning of scientists, politicians or even philosophers. But the conscience of Christ's own message was so overwhelming in their minds that they concentrated all their emotions upon it. The presence in the mind of the spectator of Christ himself was all they tried to produce through the sensible medium of their symbolical paintings. They also knew that ancient art had turned away from a real love and, being anxious to rectify that mistake, they thought it a waste of time for any artist to aim lower than God himself and his Incarnation.

But as early as the third century the Christians were ready to accept the technical achievements of ancient art and to use them in the glorification of God. Not only the adornment of the catacombs, but also the liturgy which was celebrated there and in other places throughout the Roman Empire, gave them sufficient opportunity to do so. The liturgy was concentrated around the sacrifice of the Mass, that is, around the transubstantiation of bread and wine as it had been ordered by Christ himself at the Last Supper. Readings from the Scripture, explications of the Christian doctrine, and prayers were added. Gradually every movement connected with the liturgy was coordinated in a whole, which could well receive the name of a sacred dance. Also the vestments used at such occasions by the bishops and priests were gradually selected and fixed with an unmistakable taste. As to the melodies and rhythms of the prayers, they made a rich tradition out of values which would be otherwise lost to us. They became the basis of all subsequent musical development. The early Christians did not even hesitate to accept liturgical usages from older religious traditions whenever they found their symbolism of value.

The growth of Christian liturgy was based on the worship of God. There never was anything calculated in it. Of its beauty it can be only said that it rose up from the overflowing hearts of the worshipers. Later on, at the beginning of the modern era, generations came whose hearts were rather cold to the beauty of things. They tried to forget liturgy; they ended by forgetting Christ himself.

It has also to be noted, that there was never just one liturgy. The Greeks and the Latins, the Syrians as well as the Abyssinians or the Slavs arranged it according to their own predilections. And although, for some time, there was a tendency in the Church to unify all these different manners of celebrating the Mass and even to abolish all but the Latin language as vehicles of the liturgy, the regional variety in liturgy prevailed. The Slavonic, Armenian, or Maronite liturgy is today as honored in the Church as is the Roman liturgy.

In the 4th century, and in some places even in the third, the Church could at last leave the catacombs and celebrate its liturgy in public. For this it needed certain simple architectural features, such as a distinct place for the table and the lecterns, but its chief need was for a large hall which could accommodate, besides the priest, the greatest number of believers. The ancient temples, consisting of large courts but of only a very small cellule for the statue of the deity, could not be adapted for that purpose. That was the reason why the Church adapted the *basilica*, one of the last achievements of the ancient architecture in the Mediterranean area.

By adapting the basilica as the prototype of its places of worship the Church not only consecrated a prominent work of art but also began a magnificent development. This development continued as long as the Church remained the chief employer and supporter of the architects or, rather, as long as the Christian churches remained the chief buildings of the communities. The Romanesque, Byzantine, Gothic, and Baroque churches became, each in its own epoch, the leading types of architectural achievement, in imitation of which most of the other buildings were constructed. It was in the construction of the churches that each new technical or architectonic element was examined. It was the building of the churches which created the style of each particuar epoch.

Europe and the Near East of the great migrations and of the Carlovingian empire was a crossroads of different aesthetic aptitudes. All of them participated in the formation of the Romanesque architectural expression. Square-ended or semicircular chancels were joined to one of the shorter ends of the basilica and the altar was transferred into them. The circular and polygonal plans, combined with a masterful use of arches and of a central dome, served as basis of an another type of building. The 4th century basilica of St. Paul's outside the walls in Rome was imitated, during the subsequent centuries, in St. Ambrosius in Milan, in St. George in Prague, and in many other churches in Western and Central Europe. The Byzantine wonder of St. Sophia in Constantinople, on the other hand, was followed by the Carlovingian church in Aix-la-Chapelle and by St. Mark in Venice, and even after the 12th century it served as remote prototype of many churches in the Ukraine and in Russia; it also gave rise to the Mohammedan mosques, whose style remained the only non-European architectural achievement of importance beside the pagoda buildings of the Far East and the gradually receding pyramids of the Mexican Indians.

The compact shapes, the round arches, and the small slate windows of the Romanesque buildings were superseded by the steep towers, broken roofs, pointed arches and superabundance of light of a new style which, later on, received the name of the Gothic style. It originated in France and in Sicily in the 12th century and by shifting the weight of the structure from vault and pier by means of outer buttresses it soon achieved structures of admirable lightness. The high windows of stained glass transformed the cathedral of Chartres and even more the Sainte Chapelle in Paris into magic interiors in which it is easy to forget that they were made by human hands. The epoch which invented this style was full of dynamic force. Its architects, for instance, never thought of restoring the older buildings in their original style; what was destroyed they would rebuild in their own way, but always with admirable logic and with a full understanding for the harmony of heterogeneous elements. Also it is to be noted that perhaps no other style has achieved such a perfect interplay of its structural and decorative elements. The sculptures and pictures placed in a Gothic cathedral seem nearly always to be its integral parts.

The regional variety of the Gothic buildings is even

greater than that of the Romanesque architecture. The
13th century French style, as it is displayed in the
cathedrals in Amiens and Reims, found its variants in
Ulm and Vienna, in Milan and Florence, in Canterbury and Lincoln, and it has been transformed to an
even greater degree in the brick churches of Silesia
and Poland and in the late Gothic style of the 15th
century Spain and Bohemia.

Finally, in the course of the 15th century, a third
great architectural style emerged: the Baroque or, as
it is sometimes inaccurately called, the Renaissance
architecture. This style, the reign of which was prolonged until the very end of the 18th century, is a
quite independent creation of the Christian genius.
There is no need whatsoever to speak of it as of a mere
rebirth of the ancient architecture. It is true that its
designers were very much interested in the plans of
the ancient buildings; it is also true that some of the
ornamental elements of the Baroque style, such as the
pilasters or the arch-of-triumph doorways, have been
taken from the remnants of the ancient Greek and
Roman temples. But such details do not make a style.

The Baroque architecture spread not only through
Southern, Western, and Central Europe, but also
through Central and Southern America. In contrast to
the relative anonymity of the architects of the Romanesque and Gothic period, we know the names of the
most prominent representatives of the Baroque archi-
tectonical art. Comparing their achievements we can
notice that the differences between them were much
greater than the differences between the variants of
any previous style. Bramante, Michelangelo, Pal-
ladio, Bernini in Italy, Herrera and Churriguera in
Spain, Mansart in France, Wren in England, Neuman

and Dienzenhofer in Central Europe were much more individualistic in their work than their predecessors. Nevertheless, the structures they built, heavy, as they were, but full of feigned movement and crowned by cupolas soaring to the heavens, belonged to the same noble school of architecture.

Since the end of the 18th century, the art of architecture has been declining. The so called classicism and the various minor styles of the 19th century were no more than imitations—and sometimes very poor imitations—of what had been done already before. The 20th century, of course, has at its disposal a number of new materials which give to the architect a great technical freedom and which may enable him to create a new style. To be able to achieve an architectonic work, however, it is not sufficient to conceive and finish the plans of the building itself. It is equally necessary to situate it in its surrounding. We do not know enough about the ancient and the Romanesque towns or villages to be able to judge their architectonic values. But we know that a Gothic town (whose silhouette was usually perfect), a Gothic castle, or even a medieval farmer's barn were always in harmony with the nature which surrounded them. Similarly, a Baroque town-square or even the setting of a village built in the 17th or 18th century were so arranged that there was no discordance between their component parts or between them and the surrounding country. If we turn, however, to a modern town or village or even to other works of modern architects such as the highways or railway-tracks, we find them very rarely in harmony with their surroundings. Harsh notes of discord accompany them on all sides. Only gradually does the modern architect learn to pay reverence to the works of his colleagues, and to nature, the work of God. He is not as yet, in that respect, a Christian artist in the full sense of the word.

In the history of music, the influence of the Christians is even more evident than in architecture. For nearly twelve centuries the development of music was almost entirely in the hands of the Church, whose plain-song, inherited from older religious traditions, especially from the Jewish one, supplied it with melodies from time immemorial. As far as we know, these melodies were being collected as early as the 4th century. One of such collections was then probably revised and enlarged at the end of the 6th century by order of Pope Gregory I. Because a body of rules concerning the liturgical singing, which still remains valid in the Latin liturgy, is attributed to the same pope, we usually call the plain chant of the Roman liturgy the Gregorian chant. Similar traditions are preserved in the Christian liturgies of the East.

Collecting of melodies required a system of musical signs. At first, the Greek system of notation by letters, then a system of special signs placed over or under the syllables (the neumes), then again the placing of text syllables between lines was tried as a solution to the problem. At the beginning of the 11th century Quido of Arezzo, a Benedictine monk, solved it by placing the neumes on the lines and thus gave rise to our present system of notation. The Church in the West also established a series of fourteen modes, different from the ancient modal system. Beginning with the 12th century, the monks introduced into the notation the signs symbolising the relative length of musical sounds.

With such technical advantages at his disposal the

medieval musician was able to become interested in harmony. Singing of tunes with harmonical accompaniment by other voices developed from the first achievements in contrapuntal art in the age of the *trouvères* in the 13th century to the advanced technical proficiency in contrapuntal compositions of Josquin Desprès and his contemporaries of the early 16th century. Orlando di Lasso and Palestrina, both of them flourishing at the end of the 16th century, could then unfold all the splendors of the vocal polyphony, which often used the treasures of the songs of European nations as thematic bases. Moreover, the instrumental music, which in its ancient and medieval beginnings imitated the melodies of the human voice, succeeded gradually in freeing itself from the influence of vocal music. The Roman organist Frescobaldi was, in the first half of the 17th century, its first great master.

In the meantime, the composers discovered also the musical drama. They found that the purpose of drama —to purify the passions by bringing them into harmony with intelligence—could be eminently heightened by musical expression. In the Middle Ages, singing was employed in the great drama of the passion of Our Lord, as it used to be represented at Easter time before the portals of the churches. Later on, first in the 16th century Roman Oratory of St. Girolamo, under the supervision of St. Philip Neri, and then in many other countries, especially in the Slavonic and German regions of Central Europe, the Christmas and Passion oratorios were turned into a special form of vocal expression and display. Another branch of musical drama, concerned more with worldly subjects, but often full of profound poetry, rose from the 13th century *trouvère* plays and comical scenes to become the 17th century Italian and French schools of opera employing a variety of instruments in their orchestras and displaying arias, duets and choruses: Monteverdi in Italy, Lully and Rameau in France, and Purcell in England brought it to great prominence.

The last two centuries of musical creative activity have each a special character. The 18th century and the first three decades of the 19th century were dominated by five composers, whose genius made it the golden age of music: Bach, Handel, Haydn, Mozart, and Beethoven. The culmination of contrapuntal technique, the development of the symphony orchestra, the unfolding of the theory of piano playing, the establishment of the sonata form and—in Beethoven's work—the fully elaborated art of free thematic composition, all that, and also other ideas foreshadowing the music of subsequent years, may be found in their enormous work. Bach's sublime majesty, Mozart's spontaneity and charm, Beethoven's dramatic emotion gave to the music of those times all the variety of human musical intellect.

The spiritual incertitude of the last hundred and fifty years has left its traces especially in opera, where the composers are nearest to verbal expression and therefore most vulnerable by rational thought. In spite of various technical improvements, the 19th century opera, when compared, for instance, with Mozart's *Don Giovanni*, has preserved its level only in the joyous works of Rossini, Bizet, and Smetana, whereas the decline of its dramatic power, remarkable in the works of Wagner, was not stopped even by the inventive genius of Verdi. The 19th century has witnessed the outstanding imagination of Chopin, the pianist, and also the simple charm of Schubert's art song, but its interest was gradually concentrated on the symphonic poem, represented in the works of composers of almost all the European nationalities, such as Liszt, Franck, Tchaikovski, Saint-Saëns, Dvořák, Debussy, and Sibelius.

The composers of the present age have many ways open. Throughout the Church, a strong movement aiming at the revival of all the treasures of liturgical music has been noticed during the past few decades. There is also a heightened interest in the religious hymns of the Gothic and Baroque epochs. Moreover, various experiments are going on, such as those of Stravinsky in the counterpoint of rhythms, timbres and keys, those of Janáček in the unfolding of the melodical elements of human speech, or those of Respighi in a revived use of the ancient and medieval modes.

When the Church began to build the basilicas, the painters who had adorned the walls of the catacombs found new technical possibilities for their art. As in the ancient epoch, also in the first twelve centuries of the Christian era painting was closely bound to the art of architecture. Wall paintings, accomplished in different techniques, and mosaics were considered more or less a part of the art of building. The vaults of the apses and the walls dividing the nave of the basilicas from the aisles gave the painters magnificent opportunities. In the Gothic architecture, in which the windows replaced the greater parts of the main walls, another branch of painting originated: that of the glass-painting, which made the painter's participation in architecture even greater. As to sculpture,

its works in wood and ivory were relatively independent of the architecture of buildings; its achievements
in stone, on the contrary, became related to the architecture even more closely than they had ever been in
the ancient times. And not only ornamental sculpture,
as had been the use in the preceding ages, but also
figural works were accepted by the architect as an
integral part of his own undertakings. Magnificent
portals assumed the role of ancient friezes and—a
new thing—sculptures as well as pictures painted on
wood were put on the Gothic altars, whose structure
had gradually outgrown the simple tables or tombs of
the Romanesque period. The furniture making found
its own uses for these two arts. An entirely new application for painting was discovered in the illustrating
of manuscripts written on parchment. Such "illuminations" usually adorned the first letters of chapters or
paragraphs. Also the skill of binding manuscripts into
books had its place among the artistic achievements
of the Middle Ages.

Up to the second half of the 13th century, the symbolical tendency remained predominant in the works
of the painters and sculptors. It is true that to some
extent the simple structures of the Romanesque architecture and the strict liturgical ceremonies required
paintings and statues which would be as conformable
as possible to their limitations. But there was also no
other way of expressing the ideas which the artists
were required to express. That is why even today the
symbols are of great value in liturgical art. Their
influence was soon extended also to religious portraits.
Developed especially by the Byzantines, the symbolical portraiture not only enriched the art of the West,
but achieved a great importance in Russia, where the

famous schools of icon painting flourished especially
in the 14th and 15th centuries.

The 6th century mosaics in Ravenna, the 8th century illuminations in the books of the Irish monks,
and the 11th century sculptures in Vézelay in France
and in several places in Central Europe may seem to
us to-day crude and unpolished. It was improbable
that accomplished artists could exist amid the constant
migrations and wars of those times. But what is even
more important to take into account, before we pass a
definite judgment, is the fact that nobody was then
looking for the harmonious beauty of the ancient
times. On the contrary, such beauty was more or less
the thing to be avoided. The ultimate meaning of
things was looked for much more than the ideal
beauty which frequently hides reality.

But gradually more and more things were included
into the horizon of the artist. Glimpses of scenery
emerge in the background of the 14th century pictures
of Italian, Bohemian and Dutch masters. And the
saints portrayed by the sculptors are no more symbolical figures, but real men and women who arrived at
perfection by transforming their passions and vices.
More important than how a scene looked was, of
course, its relation to the idea of the whole picture;
and more important than how a person looked were
his gestures symbolizing his ideas and strivings. Such
was the essence of the medieval art, represented by
Giotto and by the master of Třeboň in Bohemia, as
well as by many anonymous artists.

It proved, however, too high an art for the material-
istic 15th and 16th centuries. Accomplished masters,
such as Leonardo da Vinci or Titian, the painters who
now had the invention of oil painting at their disposal,

or Donatello, the sculptor, were content to grasp the
superficial look of things and even to idealize it. How
vain was their art may be seen when we compare it
to the strivings of their solitary contemporary Michelangelo. The difference between his two pietàs, one in
Rome, the other in Florence, speaks of his anxiety to
find more in the colors and forms than mere material
appearances—even more than he was able to express
in his monumental frescoes and statues.

Since the 16th century both painting and sculpture
regained their dignity again. But the cheap skill of
the preceding epoch left permanent traces in the
works of many of their minor adepts who preferred
amusement and imitation to art.

Prominent portraitists, such as Holbein in the 16th
century, Van Dyck and Velasquez in the 17th,
Reynolds in the 18th, and Renoir and Whistler in the
19th century, found their models in living contemporaries. Not all of them, however, were anxious to discover the very depths of human nature. Others took
more to dramatic scenes than to portraits. Reviewing
their works, we find a much deeper belief in the ultimate sense of things in the canvases of El Greco or
Rembrandt, both of whom flourished in the first half
of the 17th century, than in Goya's pictures, which
are full of despair and frustration, or in the vainglory
depicted by a Delacroix or a Ryepin. But then the 19th
century has seen very little of genuine heroism. As to
the hidden heroisms of our own age, they are probably
still waiting for their artists.

Nearly the same may be said about the sculptors.
Those among them, who worked with the Baroque
architects of the 17th and 18th centuries, like Bernini
or Braun, loved that sort of movement which tells

about the thoughts of the model. Houdon, in the second half of the 18th century, restricted this realism, but did not give it up, whereas the two famous sculptors of the Napoleonic times, Canova and Thorwaldsen, lost it and took to a mere harmony of structure. Only in the relatively recent works of Rodin, Myslbek, Meštrović, and Eric Gill was the balance between form and matter recovered.

A completely new branch of pictorial art emerged in the 17th century in the works of Claude Lorrain and Vermeer van Delft, namely, landscape painting. Foreshadowed already in the previous century by the pictures of Brueghel, it grew rapidly in popularity. And although it suffered a temporary eclipse in the 18th century's sweet imagery, it came out victorious again in the movement of the impressionists who, introduced by Turner in the first half of the 19th century, made their main entré in its later half. Influenced by the old Chinese masters they are represented by Manet, Pissarro, Segantini, Úprka and others. Through their conception of painting as a means to self-release, the impressionists have stressed an old truth, that the inner life of the artist is at least as important as his technical capabilities or his choice of object. But, consequently, the painter may also attack our feeling and our intellect and force upon us his own vision of things. Cézanne or Špála may be cited as representatives of such an expressionist tendency. There is no doubt that many minor artists of poor interior life would jump at such an opportunity and would try to influence the public by making themselves as obscure and mysterious as possible. But in the long run the human intellect will always recognize the art by which it is enriched from an art without content, which is as vain as a speech without ideas.

In choosing the names of the architects, composers, painters, and sculptors whose works have become integral parts of our present civilization we encounter one considerable difficulty: the growing differences between the various national cultures. The works of the Greek authors might not have been known to their contemporaries who were not Greek themselves; but the Greek language was later accepted by the intellectuals of the ancient world as their common language and everybody liked to speak and write in Greek. Throughout the first twelve centuries of the Christian era Latin was the universal language in the West, whereas the Greek and, in a certain epoch, also the Old Slavonic were used as liturgical and intellectual languages in the European East. This bond of common idioms made the flowing of cultural currents from one country into another comparatively easy. But since the end of the Middle Ages, the development of new national languages changed the situation considerably. Especially when art ceased to be anonymous, different artists were remembered by the Portuguese than by the Norwegians. For a general survey we may select representatives of all countries and nations, but we can select only such men of genius whose names are international—and such criterion is not a just one.

This difficulty becomes even more conspicuous when we start to deal with the literary arts, with poetry, prose, and drama. We can not avoid the question whether, in this respect, we still participate in a single civilization. We can answer it in a positive way if we stress the fact that there are, in art, certain currents which the national frontiers are not able to stop. But even when considering these currents the most prominent factors in our civilization we are conscious of the fact that there are many works of art which live untouched by them.

The liturgical poetry with which the Christian literature began went through several phases in which the individual inspiration became more and more remarkable. In the West, the masterpieces of devotional poetry, such as the hymns *Pange lingua* or *Vexilla regis prodeunt*, composed probably in the 8th century by Venantius Fortunatus, had their sequel in early medieval legends of saints, full of realistic frankness as well as of poetical imagination. In the East of Europe the prosaic legends had an even older tradition connected with Greek prose. But in the medieval and modern centuries the lyrical trend of religious poetry prevailed altogether. Pausing at each of the steps of its development—represented in order by Thomas of Celano, Jacopone da Todi, and St. Thomas Aquinas in the 13th century, St. John of the Cross and Bridel in the 16th and 17th centuries, Gerard M. Hopkins, Paul Claudel, and Jan Zahradníček in our own times—we can notice the growing individualism of expression.

Other poets chose a different way. Although living on the verge of religious thought, they were always full of doubt about the real value of Christian revelation and also full of protests against the established institutions. In the Middle Ages, they were faithful friends of musical composers. Most of them, such as Petrarca or Villon, were conscious of the musical qualities of the spoken word. It is true that one of their famous schools, that of the Romantic period at the beginning of the 19th century, represented by Shelley,

Keats, Mácha, and Lermontov, preferred rather a dramatic treatment of emotion. But the modern lyrical poets, such as Verlaine, Machado, Akhmatova, Asnyk, and Yeats, or the members of the youngest generation, write again with more restraint and cherish the beauty of words because they believe more in the musical than in the ideological appeal.

There is no doubt, however, that the centre of poetry, ever since the Gospels made their way through the world, is in the drama. The dramatic works of the Christian epoch are not a direct continuation of the Greek drama; only since the 16th century have the Greeks captured the minds of the Christians again. The late influence of the Greek dramatists was also preceded by that of the mythological traditions of the European nations. In many a dramatic poem which sprang up between the 8th and the 13th century, such as the *Beowulf*, *The Song of Roland*, *The Song of the Niebelungen*, or *The Story of Igor*, the heathen memories made themselves felt quite distinctly. But the true source of the new dramatic accomplishments was the astonishing drama from which Christianity itself arose.

The incomparable story of the Gospels did not need to be reinterpreted. It was read again and again at many occasions in the liturgy. Its chief event, Christ's sacrifice, was and still is continued in every Mass. What could the ancient plays mean to men when confronted with the overwhelming impression created by the "good tidings"? The Christian writers of the first centuries, who were more acquainted with the cheap theatrical amusements of the Roman citizens than with the classical Greek drama, called the ancient theatre sordid. But they knew of another splendid the-

atre, which was not included in the Gospels—that of
the lives of the heroes of faith. Their own world was
one big drama.

It was by the way of this dramatic conception of the
theatrum mundi that the great narrative and dramatic
literature of the last seven centuries came into existence. It entered the world through the portal of the
cathedral. The architects, sculptors, and painters who
built the cathedrals, and the musicians who composed
the liturgical melodies, remained nearly always anonymous. Similar to priests who celebrate liturgy, they
worked as humble servants of God, inspired by the
grace and joy which He gave them. And, as far as
they remained in the cathedral or at least on its door-
steps, the playwrights who created, in Latin or in the
vernacular, the medieval passion and miracle plays,
remained mostly anonymous. Theirs was the drama of
"Everyman" and it was their ambition to include into
it, symbolically at least, all the theatre of the world.

But the task proved to be too complicated. Confronting the drama of Christ's own life with the humble
dramas of Everyman, the medieval playwrights found
that there were too many such dramas: not only those
of the saints, but also those of the weak and evil men
at grips with Grace. Last but not least, there was also
the comical aspect of things, which found its full
meaning in the Christian conception of hope as the
antithesis of irony and despair.

Some of the narrators never lost sight of the cathedral. They knew what Aeschylus would have liked to
know. Dante in his *Divine Comedy* brought all the
world of the 13th century to the portal of the eternal
city of God. Calderón de la Barca and Lope de Vega
in the 17th century used to change the subjects of their

innumerable plays often from a worldly to a religious
one and back again. The incredulous and sceptical
modern times have often forgotten where the cathedral was, but they knew very well of a man who was
constantly admiring it from far away; his name was
Faust and his life was taken up as a dramatic theme
by authors who differed very much from each other,
such as Goethe, Krasinski, and Madách. Dostoievski,
in his turn, descended to the most distant places from
which the cathedral could yet be seen. Among the
dramatists and narrators of our own generation we
may cite Claudel again, because of his plays of immense wisdom and beauty, and also Sigrid Undset,
Bernanos, Mauriac, and Graham Greene.

Others have chosen a place from which the lights of
the cathedral can be seen in the distance, but which is
surrounded by woods of much older myths and traditions. The authors of the medieval epics, the titles of
which we have already mentioned, writers of legends
concerning "King Arthur" and the "Holy Grail,"
anonymous authors of the innumerable folk stories
and fairy tales, and also some poets of a recent past
like the brothers Grimm, Erben, and Andersen have
found their place in this group.

There are, however, many works of narrative and
dramatic art in which the Christian faith appears as
a decoration only or as just one among other human
passions. That does not mean that their authors are
not conscious of the spiritual element in man. On the
contrary, they are very often tortured by such a conscience. Neither does it mean that they have altogether escaped the Christian civilization. Human love,
for instance, which is usually their central object of
interest, is seen by them from a point very different

from that of most of the ancient poets. Their craving for ultimate wisdom tells them that love is much more than one of the blind forces of fate.

The medieval narrators of romantic stories, the *trouvères* and *minnesaengers*, among whose works many are of outstanding freshness, found their undoubted master in Chaucer. But that was still in an age in which the art was concentrated around the seasons of the liturgical year. Only the age of doubt and insecurity, the 16th century, and the subsequent Thirty Years War furnished the proper background for the powerful, ironical stories of Cervantes, Grimmelshausen and Le Sage and for the works of the great dramatists Shakespeare, Racine, and Molière. Thereupon the entrance into the labyrinth was opened. The prudent fables of La Fontaine and Krylov, the lyrical epics of Puškin and Mickiewics, the great novels of the 19th century written by Balzac, Dickens, Turgenev, and Tolstoi, the modern dramas of Ibsen, Synge, Čapek, O'Neill and Pirandello, all try to seize the whole human reality by snatching only one or another of its garments. All this world of genial writers and playwrights moves in the narrow streets of the town under the cathedral, but rarely catches a glimpse of it.

The Idea of the University

❦

FROM ITS VERY BEGINNINGS, Christian culture was set on universal aims. "Going, therefore, teach ye all nations" (Matt. 28, 19), was Christ's last command to the apostles. Christian doctrine was not meant to be a common bond between the citizens of only one state or tribe, but of all mankind. No profession, no class, no nationality, no sex, was excluded from its benefits. Christ's message is the message of God to man. The salvation of man, of every single human individual, is its object. It was given to man to help him to attain the greatest personal freedom. According to the opinion of Aristotle, one of the profoundest thinkers of ancient civilization, the citizen had to be moulded to suit the form of government under which he lived. According to the Christian conception, man had to be educated to be able to unfold his own personality to the greatest possible extent by ascending to God, the source of all being, knowledge, and love. The stress laid on the worth of the individual is the basic feature of what the Christian calls education. All knowledge and all the institutions of society, including the community and the state, are here only to serve this purpose.

That true liberty is impossible without God, is clear to every Christian. God is the Being par excellence, from whom all the other beings came. In the ancient epoch, only the Jews made use of this truth in their schools. In other tribes and nations, the best teachers only tried to temper the elements of human nature in due proportion; but even in such cases, in which they attempted to find the correct proportion by means of logical reasoning or by the Socratic mode of inquiry, they did not have the help of Christ, which a Christian receives in his profession of faith.

Moreover, the spread of the message of Christ also meant the education of man through the justification of all his activities. "I have come a light into the world, that whoever believes in me may not remain in darkness" (John 12, 46). In the opinion of the Christians this promise of Christ is being fulfilled in the individual life of every one of his disciples. There is no obstacle which can stop it. There is no branch of creative activity that can not be sanctified by the grace of God and defended against corruption. The Greeks, for instance, were persuaded that the mechanical abilities of man render his body and intellect unfit for the exercise and practice of virtue. The Christian command *"ora et labora,"* on the other hand, puts even the hardest toil in direct contact with the spiritual growth of man, because any kind of work can be a creative work. And, whereas, in the ancient civilization of the Mediterranean area and also in the oriental civilization, the young generations were taught to observe a certain number of established forms, Christianity encouraged its followers to glorify God, the Creator of all things, by inventing new values, and enlarging the old.

Such are the ideas upon which the Christian conception of attaining knowledge, and transmitting it to others, is based. Its chief consequence is the inseparability of study and education. In any other civilization, studies were pursued in secret societies or closed circles and their results were kept secret. But the Christian ideal is to glorify God by study, and to make the results of the studies as widely known as possible. The art of making knowledge accessible to those to whom it should be transmitted was known by the Founder of Christianity long before modern pedagogues made an elaborate doctrine out of it. His parables were easy to understand, even by the humble fishermen who were His first disciples. Also, the medieval establishment of the university, which was, originally, a "university of students and professors," was an example of the basic unity of studies and education in Christian culture. And as late as the end of the Middle Ages, an observation or a thought put on parchment or paper was considered a common good. Most of the authors were provided for by the Church, but even when they were not, their manuscripts were freely quoted and incorporated into other manuscripts. This custom was not an ideal one, and it had to be abandoned, but it expressed very well the Christian sentiment about intellectual work.

As the natural endowment of man and his interests vary from person to person, schooling always has to be a selective one. Every one, however, is entitled to the basic education which would make him conscious of Christ's message. The family holds the natural obligation and hence also the right to educate its offspring. This right is inviolable and not subject to any power on earth. Only when the parents are found wanting either physically or morally, then society has to protect the rights of the child.

It has to be pointed out that the right to know the message of Christ is the natural right of every child. Therefore, a society would be acting against the natural law if it kept this message away from the children. It has also to be stressed that the Christian definition of basic education is: an education which makes the child conscious of Christian doctrine. This definition can not be superseded by any other definition without wrecking one of the basic principles of Christian civilization. Whenever, in the course of our era, this definition was called doubtful or directly attacked, it always resulted in a movement dangerous to society as a whole. The so called neutrality of the school always turned out to be a trap for people whose conception of human liberty was not clear. Whenever religious knowledge dropped out from the curriculum of schools and "something more useful" was put in its place, it always turned out to be a device of somebody who wished to see himself in Christ's place. The pupils of such schools were taught to believe either in the genius of a military dictator, in the automatic progress of mankind or in the magnanimity of various Bolshevik state bosses. In one word, superstition took the place of religion.

Therefore it has always been the firm opinion of Christians that, not reading, writing, or mathematics, but religion is the most useful thing in all education. Reading, writing, and mathematics are intellectual tools which can be used for any purpose. Religion, on the contrary, is that which gives man the possibility to use his tools in a creative way. Gradually, not only reading, writing, and mathematics, but also history, art, political education, and science were added to basic education. In this task, the Church always led the way—even when some of its representatives were from time to time rather peevish in their anxiety to keep religion in the first place.

The Christian education started with the catechumen groups. These groups were organized in every Christian community. The bishops and the priests were their first teachers and the parish priests remained in this office for many subsequent centuries. In the seats of the bishops the catechumen schools developed into centers of learning, some of which (for instance those in Alexandria, Antioch, Edessa, and Jerusalem) were famous in the whole Christian world of the first centuries. Besides the study of the New Testament and Greek grammar—Greek was the international language of those days—history, philosophy, and logic were taught in these schools. In the subsequent times, when the Roman Empire collapsed under the attacks of the migrating tribes and when there was no secure place in all Europe, the Church made immense efforts to save the intellectual achievements of the ancient times. Scholars like Isidor of Seville in the 7th century and Venerable Bede in the 8th century assembled encyclopedic knowledge to an extent unsurpassed by any individual in modern times, despite the many technical advantages now at the disposal of learned people. Isidor's *Etymologies*, which served as a treasure of learning throughout the whole medieval period, and Bede's *History* were the real transmitters of knowledge of the ancient times.

As soon as political conditions became stable again, the Church reëstablished its organization of schools.

This time besides the cathedral schools, it was also the monasteries which became the most important centers of learning. The monks were free from the fears of the early Christians concerning the loss of time spent in acquiring theoretical knowledge, which was believed to be of little practical use for man. Therefore, in the schools, to the original *trivium*, grammar, historical and philosophical rhetoric, and dialectics, a *quadrivium* was added, consisting of arithmetic, geometry and geography, astronomy, and acoustics or music. These seven disciplines were usually called by one common name: the seven liberal arts. Theology, law, and medicine were treated as major disciplines and studied apart from the others.

It was natural that after such a social catastrophe and many upheavals, of which the age of migrations was witness, not everything could be saved. But certainly more was saved by the Christians from the ancient civilization than has been saved, for instance, by the Greeks from the Aegean civilization when they had captured Crete and the other Aegean islands. The oldest manuscripts of various Latin authors, which we now possess, nearly all date from the 8th or 9th century. It was, however, not until three centuries later that the works of the ancient Greek authors reached the European centers. They had not been known, until then, to the Celtic and Germanic immigrants because of their ignorance of Greek. The Greek manuscripts were preserved by the Christian communities in the East and they were also translated by them into Oriental languages. But the political cleavage between the imperial East and the immigrant West and, later on, also the apostasy of the Christian communities of the East from the Church, stopped their transmittance to the West. Only when the Christian scholars of the West were involved in polemics with the Arabs who occupied Spain and who possessed the works of the Greek authors in Arabic translations, could this gap in the foundations of the Christian civilization be completed.

It was also natural that the diffusion of all this knowledge differed from the channels through which knowledge spreads in our own times. In the ancient epoch and in the medieval centuries only a small number of people could read or write. To copy a book required many months of labor and therefore only great centers of learning could afford to possess books. Nevertheless, these centers had a decisive influence upon contemporary life. From the great theatre of the liturgical year, which is an eminent means of religious and artistic education, to the new methods in agriculture conveyed by the monks to the villagers, all their activity meant a veritable making of Europe.

Out of the most important centers of learning in Paris, Bologna, Oxford, Cambridge, Salamanca, and Prague, to which the students flocked from all Europe, new institutions arose: the universities. Their material existence was based on the so called colleges, residences of students, endowed by pious benefactors and designed to educate the poor. Their system of studies was inherited from the schools of the cathedral cities. It consisted of a course of general studies, called the faculty of Arts or Philosophy, and of the faculties of Theology, Law, and Medicine. The faculties were ruled by elected deans, the whole university by a rector and an academic council. In the course of the 13th and 14th centuries, in their first epoch of prosperity, they acquired not only a firm legal status, but also an authority in nearly every branch of cultural life.

The secret of the success of the universities was in their spiritual unity. The course in arts, divided into two periods marked by the degrees of Bachelor and Master, and taking usually six to seven years, furnished the student with a general formative education in grammar and logic, in history and poetry, in the fundaments of mathematics and science, and, above all, in philosophy. Because of this opportunity to obtain general education in the university, the students usually entered it immediately after leaving the parish school. Many of them were satisfied with one or both the degrees obtainable in the faculty of Arts; others continued their studies for another six years or even a longer period in the other faculties. From among those who had finished the faculty of Arts, teachers were recruited for the parish and town schools. The masters of Arts and the masters and doctors of Theology, Law, and Medicine were entitled, in their turn, to teach the younger generations of students. Thus the unity of the universities was transmitted from generation to generation.

As soon, however, as their spiritual unity was lost in the philosophical controversies of the 14th century, these great schools descended into a state of permanent decay. In the countries which, in the 16th century, left the Church, this decline was prolonged until the late 18th or, in some cases, even the 19th century. In the Catholic countries it was stopped only by the great reform of schools which was accomplished in the period before and after the year 1600.

That reform came after the wave of so called humanism, a rather retrograde movement which considered the ancient civilization the peak of all human achievements and which sought the purpose of education in sheer rhetorical skill. The newly founded Jesuit order could not find a better way to combat this empty trend than by reviving the universities. Following the principles set down in their *Ratio Studiorum*, published in 1599, the Jesuits concentrated their efforts on the six years of lower college, which in their institutions took the place of the faculty of Arts, and also on the first two "philosophical" years of upper college—the rest of the graduate studies being divided into the three usual faculties. They also brought into education quite a number of useful innovations: the illustrative way of teaching foreign languages, which was imitated by Commenius and other Protestant educators, the stressing of education through art and, above all, the indirect influencing of the will through the enlightening and strengthening of reason.

The Jesuit reform was supported by other corporate teaching institutes, which arose in the same or in the following century: the Oratorians, the Piarists, and especially the Brothers of Christian Schools. This last congregation, founded in 1689 by St. John Baptist de La Salle, was interested in basic education and one of the most effective steps it took was the introduction into parish and town grammar schools of the class method of teaching by which several grades of pupils could be instructed simultaneously in a single class.

The 18th century, the age of the so called enlightenment, brought a frontal onslaught on Christian education. At the present time, this attack has not yet spent its force. On the contrary, it may achieve further victories in the near future. It is important for us to know, why it started and what are its tactics.

Christian education is not, as we have already pointed out, an instruction of the citizen. Neither is it a training in a special profession. Both these aims are included among the aims of the Christian schools, but they are only their secondary aims. Their chief and unavoidable purpose is the unfolding of human personality to the greatest liberty which is the knowledge of God.

On the other hand, in the political and social history of modern times, forces have come up which do not wish man to be free at all. It is, in fact, one single force: pride and the will to power which results from pride. In different epochs, this force assumes different faces. The un-Christian absolutism of the 17th and 18th century, the mechanical democracy of the 19th century, and the Nazism, Bolshevism, and other Socialist systems of our own age, have all one and the same purpose: the servile state, in which some people will be omnipotent and all others will be their slaves. On the whole, it is a great reactionary movement which endeavours to bring human society back to the pre-Christian stage of tribal empires. And this movement, naturally, does not like the Christian idea of education.

Its tactics, of course, have changed considerably in the course of the last two centuries. First of all, it tried to use the Christian schools for its own purposes. That was in the 16th and 17th centuries, in the time of the great scholastic reform of the Jesuits and Piarists. We have to remember that in those days, although they achieved very much, the Christian schools were still far from ideal. The idea of the basic education as a natural right of everybody was, of course, accepted throughout the Christian world. That women have the same natural rights as men—an idea strange to the pre-Christian civilization—became also an evident principle; medieval chivalry as well as monastic schools helped to develop it. An ideal curriculum of general studies was set up by the universities. But there were still very few schools and most of the educational burden lay upon the shoulders of the parish priest, whose forces were insufficient. The absolutist rulers of the Catholic states took therefore the easiest course, that of declaring themselves supporters of the Church, in the hope that the Church and its schools would enter their own services. And, what was also true, many Christians did not recognise the ruse.

Such a situation, however, could not last. After a series of conflicts between the Jesuits and the absolutist rulers—starting with Philip III of Spain in the 17th century—all the Jesuit schools were abolished throughout Europe. The first measures against them were taken in Portugal in 1759 and were then followed by similar acts in other countries. At that time, absolutism began to throw away the religious mask and embrace, openly, the so called enlightenment. The ideas, which the founders of this movement had about education, can be best expressed in two quotations, the first from Rousseau's *Emile:* "The poor man has no need of education"; and the second from Voltaire's *Dictionnaire Philosophique:* "It is suitable that some children should learn to read, write, and cipher, but the great mass of them, and above all the children of labourers, should know only how to till the land; we need only one pen to every two or three hundred hands."

The expression "we need" is perhaps the most characteristic of all the epoch which was introduced by
Rousseau and Voltaire. Jesus knew well that such
times would come. "You know that the rulers of the
Gentiles lord it over them, and their great men exercise authority over them," such were his words to his
disciples. "The Son of Man has not come to be served
but to serve, and to give his life as a ransom for many"
(Matt. 20:25-28). But Rousseau and Voltaire said "we
need" and the two words, significantly enough, were
repeated not only by the parliamentary politicians of
the 19th century, but also by Hitler and Stalin in our
own epoch. What the ruling individual or the ruling
group needed was to become law. "Above all, I should
like to harness the Christian Brothers to my ploughs,"
wrote Voltaire in 1763, and in a few years the French
Revolution put his words into practice by abolishing
all the Christian schools, about 22,000 in France alone.

In France, where a large percentage of the population could read and write before the Revolution, only
a few could do it fifty years later, so that the number
of illiterates in France of the postrevolutionary period
equaled that in the Protestant countries like England.
But not everywhere were the tactics of the enemies of
Christian doctrine the same. In Central Europe they
also abolished the Christian schools and made it a
special point in their activities to destroy as great a
number of the monuments of Christian art as possible
so as to get them away from the eyes of the public.
But instead of leaving the farmers and workers without education, according to Voltaire's plans, the Central European enlightened statesmen decided to use
education for their own purposes. Accordingly, they
founded a state system of education and, although

they were not able to take the basic education away from the clergy at once, they brought the higher education, based on the medieval university system, under the strict control of the state. In places where they were also able to lay their hands on primary education, they tried to assimilate it to the system proposed by a Swiss named Pestalozzi, whose chief idea was hatred of Christian schools and whose aims were best expressed by his words: "My system of instruction has the advantage of leaving everyone in the proper sphere and condition in which he was born." The Christian idea of unfolding everyone's liberty and capabilities definitely did not coincide with the aims of the modern wielders of political power.

The present situation in education resulted from the 18th century attack on the Christian schools and can be described as a fight at the crossroads. Throughout the 19th century and up to our own times, the Church has never betrayed its mission and, what is more, a certain residuum of Christian ideas has never left public opinion—not only in Europe but also in other countries to which the civilization had spread from Europe. On the other hand, the nationalist Statism of the last century and the totalitarian Socialism of the present age have not ceased to push society back to that pre-Christian stage where education was the tool of those who were in power.

Up to now, as far as we can judge, the Church has been losing in this fight. There are still Christian schools in many countries and there exists even a small number of Christian universities. But there is not a single country in the world in which Christian education is as predominant as it was in Europe in the

13th century. On the contrary, the Christian schools
are losing ground even in those countries which are
now well aware of the dangers of totalitarianism and
which consequently try to find their own solution to
present difficulties. Even such states can not avoid
being totalitarian in the field of education and although they do not dare to prohibit the existence of
the Christian schools openly, they at least combat
them by forcing their supporters to pay taxes, from
which the anti-Christian, but not the Christian schools,
receive subsidies.

Political power, it is true, has accepted the tenet of
Christian doctrine that to obtain a basic education is
a natural right of everybody. But, at the same time,
the managers of society are very careful to substitute
the word "schooling" for "education" in the definition
of this right. And that, of course, changes the sense of
the definition altogether.

Consequently, the organization of schools which is
now prevalent in the world, has very little affinity
with Christian educational principles. It is divided
into three groups: the grammar and preparatory
schools, the colleges (*lycées*, *gymnasia*), and the universities. The most remarkable fact in this division is,
perhaps, the split in the medieval scheme of the universities. The modern university is no more, to use
Newman's words, a place of teaching universal knowledge. It is, more or less, a collection of highly specialized institutes, which force their students to do original
research work, but succeed, in many cases, only in mul-
tiplying useless information. The educational basis,
which had once been common to both the faculty of
arts and the three special faculties, does not exist any-
more. There is no educational basis common to the

colleges and the universities, because there is no educational basis at all. A special faculty of philosophy has been added to most universities, but it has very little in common with the old faculty of arts; it is a specialized graduate school, and so are also the other faculties established in recent times, such as the faculty of pharmacology, journalism, and others.

The grammar schools, the preparatory schools, and the colleges have a number of subjects obligatory to all their pupils, so that some of the modern teachers may assert that the modern undergraduate schools have taken the place of the old faculties of Liberal Arts. But they have not. They are instructing young people along identical or similar lines, giving them identical or similar amounts of knowledge, but they are not educating them. They do not show them their way to God. On the contrary, many of them show the students the way to racial hatred or to deification of the so called class leaders. And that, of course, is the very opposite of education.

There is, also, one other thing which is characteristic of the modern schools and which is perhaps even more curious than the absence of education. It is the fact that as far as philosophy is concerned the modern teachers, excluding education from their schools, have lost not only all knowledge of Christian philosophy, but also nearly all knowledge of what used to be the top achievements of the ancient, pre-Christian philosophy. This fact deserves special attention.

As we have already pointed out when dealing with the growth of ancient civilization, philosophy was always secondary to religion—somewhat in the way that reasoning is secondary to cognition. There was always a religious tradition. But only gradually had religious tradition become supported, explained, and even criticized by philosophy. We have also pointed out that Greek philosophy ensured its supremacy above all the other philosophical schools of the ancient era—with the possible exception of sparse Jewish philosophical efforts—by its constant interest in logic. The stress laid by the Greek philosophers on the correctness and precision of every expression has saved the ancient philosophy of the Mediterranean area from the stagnancy and decay of the Eastern philosophies and allowed it to change into a living and most important branch of more recent culture.

The doctors of the Church and other Christian teachers, true to the ancient conception of philosophy, which involves the idea of reason as being capable of understanding the meaning of things, continued the work of Socrates, Plato, and Aristotle. There is no doubt that at least some of them were familiar with it from the beginning of their teaching activity. They used the Greek language even when reading the Old Testament (in the so called Septuagint version). When St. Paul wrote his epistles he wrote them in Greek. And St. John did not hesitate to borrow Plato's expressions in order to translate into Greek what he had heard from Christ in Aramaic.

There was some discussion going on, especially in the 4th and 5th century, as to what extent the study of pre-Christian pagan books should be included in the curricula of the Christian schools. Whereas the doctors of the Church who were of Greek nationality (such as St. Basil or St. Gregory of Nazianzus), were friendly to the ancient studies, there was some scepticism about their utility in the West. But the very thinkers who were so conscious of the superiority of Christian doctrine and who, consequently, saw little use in studying the ancient authors in the schools, readily recognized the valuable achievements of the pagan philosophy. St. Jerome, who translated the Bible into Latin (the *Vulgate* is the usual name given to his translation), was imbued with its wisdom. St. Augustine based his philosophy of sin and grace on reasoning which was full of Platonic and also Stoic ideas. And St. Anselm of Canterbury, first of the great medieval philosophers, whose famous dictum "*credo ut intelligam*—I believe that I may understand," expressed the Christian concept of the relation between faith and philosophy in one single phrase, was again building on ancient achievements in logic.

When medieval culture had reestablished its ties with the ancient epoch, severed by the misery of the migrations, the Socratic art of distinguishing between concepts became the cornerstone of the masterful synthesis of St. Thomas Aquinas and St. Francis Bonaventura. And it is still at the base of works on Christian philosophy as disparate in method as *The Grammar of Assent* by John Henry Newman, *Les Degrées du Savoir* by Jacques Maritain, or *Ungewissheit und Wagnis* by Peter Wust, published, all of them, during the last hundred years.

But since the 17th century, not a few influential teachers, living and working in Christian lands, have refused to accept the benefits from the work of the preceding generations. They have refused to accept that which to the Christians seems an inevitable reality, namely that faith always comes before reasoning.

This important split in the Christian culture of the last few centuries is not always fully explained by historians. What happened at the beginning of the modern era was not only that some men of influence refused to believe this or that main tenet of the Christian creed, or that by doing so they gained a certain freedom from the authority of the Church. Such cases had occurred many times before in the history of Christianity. At least four great secessions, dating from various centuries and repeating themselves under different names, can be cited in this connection.

There was the gnostic belief in the duality of all creation, conceiving the world as a battle between the coeternal principles of good and evil; it came up again with the Manicheans, with the Cathari, and with the Puritans of the 3rd, 13th and 17th centuries respectively; it always resulted either in mad asceticism or in moral profligacy. There were the Christological and Trinitarian heresies, originating with the Nestorians and the Monophysites and ending with the Renanists of the 19th century; they missed altogether the basic Christian idea that, when Christ died, it was because God, not merely a man, meant to prove how much he loved us. (Rom. 5, 8.) There was the Donatist doctrine, which re-appeared in the teaching of Wyclif and Huss, asserting that every sinner is excluded from the Church and thus contradicting Christ's symbolical suggestion that whoever is free from sin shall cast the first stone. (John 8:7.) There was Pelagianism, adopted later by the Waldenses and transformed again in several different ways by the Protestants of the 16th century. This doctrine doubted that justification of the faithful is an inner transformation in which the human will and the grace of God cooperate. And there were men and women who could not agree with the Church on many minor points of doctrine.

But the heresy which started with Descartes in the 17th century and which, since then, has been followed by many other modern philosophers, is not merely a theological disagreement. It is much more. It is a disagreement with ancient civilization as well. It is something the entire consequences of which we are probably not as yet capable of evaluating.

For the ancient as well as for the Christian thinker it was an accepted fact that man is endowed with the faculty of conceiving, that is of recognising the meaning of the objects of his cognition. He can express his knowledge by reasoning, that is by unfolding his capability of thinking in words and phrases, and by applying to his thinking the principles of logic. But, first of all, there must be knowledge and there must be some faith in it, some assent to it. This assent can be, and undoubtedly is, heightened by reasoning. But it does not have its root in reasoning, nor does knowledge. Also, the essential meaning of certain objects of our knowledge may be identical. There are, for example, many objects about us which we can call by the common name of "table." Thus the words we use may symbolize universal ideas which are realized in individual objects. And, finally, as everything has a certain meaning, the existence of the Reason which gave the things their meaning is asserted by the very existence of the logical order.

Those modern teachers who follow Descartes in his disagreement with ancient and Christian philosophy, do not accept these basic philosophical principles.

With Descartes, doubt precedes knowledge. Faith and knowledge are for him a result of reasoning. He wishes to have a certitude equal to that given by arithmetical and geometrical demonstrations. He

forgets that there would not be any logical, and consequently any mathematical, order, were it not for our
knowledge of the different meanings of things. For
Spinoza there are no universal notions. An idea is for
him only an expression of the process of eternal movement which never ceases to change. For Hume no
proof of God's existence is possible; but then any proof
of anything would be impossible, if there were not the
universal and supremely rational order of things
which is God's order. According to Kant, we can know
only the appearances of things, although he does not
tell us how he himself knows that the appearances are
different from the things themselves. For Hegel, being
is not being but becoming, so that every idea may be,
at any unexpected moment, identical with any other
idea. Also for Bergson, every meaning changes constantly into another meaning and change is the substance of things. And with Jaspers, the father of existentialism, existence escapes knowledge.

This whole philosophical trend, which reminds one
of the sophistical decay of Greek philosophy, results
in liberation not only from this or that part of the
Christian doctrine, but also from all logic. Its consequence is an incertitude about the existence of things,
because their meaning changes so quickly that we are
not able to know it.

This decadent process has an immense influence
upon the schools of today. Believing, at the beginning,
that all knowledge may be attained by reasoning, and
asserting, after a time, that even Christ's message may
be replaced by so called rational religion, it has ended
by dismissing logic altogether and, consequently, by
giving up all reasoning, with the exception of mathematical calculation which it regards, not as an expres-

sion of truth, but as a mere instrument of observation.

It is true that philology, the science of human language, has made great progress in recent times. It started with the impulse given in 1767 by the Jesuit Coeurdoux to the comparative study of languages. It achieved great precision through the work of Bopp and other 19th century investigators. But to make our verbal expressions an efficient tool, something more is necessary than mere knowledge of the processes, by which languages have grown, or of the laws of phonetics. Who knows how to distinguish, knows also how to teach. The old Socratic maieutic is what we need. And that, of course, supposes a return to the evident truth that our intellect is capable of dealing not only with the vague and ever changing appearances of things or events, but also with their essences.

There is to-day a deep cleavage between the small number of schools which teach the Christian philosophy and the overwhelming number of schools which, if they have any philosophy in their curricula at all, recede every day farther into the dark chasm of existentialism. There is no middle way. It is necessary either to believe in the power—however restricted— of the intellect to know the essences of things or to descend through permanent doubt and liberal indifferentism to philosophical nihilism which is destructive of all education.

If the philosophical unity of the university is reestablished, it will not be difficult to renew also the education through history and art, to overcome the chaos in political doctrines and to give to scientific instruction its proper place.

Whereas in education through art, free reign may

be given to the study of the national monuments of
art in each country (because good art by its nature
transcends the frontiers of its land of origin), the role
of history in education is quite different. Christianity
has created the concept of universal history. It has also
consecrated much of its philosophical efforts to the
formulation of a rational concept of civilization. And
by so doing it has established a standard which may
not be abandoned without serious damage to all cultural efforts.

Eusebius and Sulpicius Severus, the historians of
the 4th century, despite all their shortcomings in critical evaluation of various older testimonies, were the
first students of the past who, in their histories of religious tradition, conceived the story of civilization as a
single stream of events. St. Augustine in his *City of
God* set up the principles according to which all the
individual ideas and events of the human past may be
classified. Both these steps were of immense importance. The local or tribal historical interests of the
ancient era found a common base. Although in the
course of the Middle Ages many chroniclers restricted
their narratives to the story of their own city, region
or nation, they always remained conscious of the fact
that every special history was but a part of the great
story of Christian civilization. And no matter how
poor their narratives might have been, they always
tried to select their facts and to evaluate them according to the standards of their common civilization.

It was only after the historians of the humanist 16th
century had lost the consciousness of a common Christian civilization that historical creative efforts were
splintered into hundreds of narrow, national concepts
soon to become tools in the hands of various political

dictators. The false rationalism of the modern epoch also led many historians to the fallacious belief that instead of selecting and evaluating their objects it was possible for them simply to set forth how things actually happened. But it is very doubtful whether in any particular case any historian is able to determine just how events occurred. With the modern methods he has at his disposal he is probably nearer to this ideal than ever, but with the complicated nature of modern events he is, at the same time, farther from it than ever. The one important thing, however, is that such a task has, in truth, never been his main duty. He has to be the guardian of civilization and the initiator of culture. Only when fulfilling this duty can he truly participate in genuine education.

The Mastering of Matter

IN PROPORTION as education was ousted from the schools a larger amount of instruction took its place. Most of it was instruction in science. Several faculties specializing in various branches of science were added to the faculty of medicine of the medieval universities. Centers of scientific research and instruction were created and placed outside the realm of the universities. And the methods of scientific instruction have developed perhaps to a greater extent than science itself. Knowledge which, in the ancient epoch, was considered accessible only to men of great learning is now freely imparted to young boys and girls. Division of numbers, for instance, which, only four centuries ago, was the subject of special studies, is now included in the curriculum of the grammar schools. Among all the branches of man's creative activity science is now the most popular and the most cherished.

This development went hand in hand with the gradual estrangement of many philosophical ideas of the last four centuries from the Christian conception of the world and of man's life in it. The historian who studies the 17th century origin of the various academies of science and scientific periodicals can't miss their close relation to the popularization of that kind of philosophy the leading principle of which was the catchword of Francis Bacon, an English essayist of the late 16th century, that knowledge means power. It is difficult to say where was the actual origin of this trend of thinking. Has this philosophical concept brought the whole series of scientific discoveries in its wake or have the successes of science made such philosophy possible? In any case, it grew into a rather common persuasion, based on the conception of science as the best means to an extension of the greatness of man and affirming that man might through science become a master of his own fate. The desertion of critical logic, which we discussed earlier, has, of course, in the long run, resulted in a vague existentialism which is unable to affirm anything. Forgetting that we can reason only if we have at our disposal that knowledge of which we are not ourselves the source, the non-Christian philosophers have started with the assumption that all knowledge may be attained by reasoning. In the end, they gave up reasoning altogether. But popular opinion and also the spirit of most modern schools still retain their faith in an omnipotent science.

Moreover, many of the modern thinkers, being aware of the fact that most of the recent scientific discoveries have been made possible by material and moral support given to the scientists by society, started to compare the feebleness of each individual man with the seemingly great power of man collectively. By this path they arrived at the conclusion that the progress of science has changed the whole substance of human society and its civilization. They started to look askance at the other, "non-scientific" branches of culture. Utterances to the effect that the imagination of an Einstein, a Schroedinger, or a Planck may well transcend that of a Shakespeare or a Virgil, may frequently be heard. And not only do they call our civilization a technological civilization, i.e., resting upon science and operating chiefly through machines, but they also lay great stress on its "collective" character.

It is paradoxically amusing to contemplate the recent conflicts between some scientists and some totalitarian regimes in the world. In 1948, for instance, many biologists in various countries found it necessary to protest against an order of the Soviet government which exacted that certain biological theories be held by the teachers of science and propagated by instruction. Why should such situations arise when nobody perhaps has so willingly supported the growth of social totalitarianism than some of the most faithful adepts of science themselves? The subsequent steps by which that has come about are evident enough: first of all the Cartesian mechanical concept of all nature from which the human soul and its realm have been carefully excluded; then the subjection of the spiritual realm to the same mechanical concept by some of the savants of the 18th century; then the new notion of the different levels in which nature is organised as being analogous to the past phases in the history of its development and the resulting theory of evolution; and finally the basic idea of dialectical materialism affirming the unity of all existence which may express itself in qualitatively different forms, but which remains a unity in which neither life—no matter how different it is from inorganic matter—nor personal experience constitute domains apart. If life, spiritual activity, and science itself are only necessary products of the eternal development of nature, then, undoubtedly, the political power which dominates the inhabitants of the world is in possession of truth—which is also a mere product of nature—and the individual scientists who dare to protest against it are comparable to pathological tumours.

Looking back on the development of the philosophy of science in the course of the past few centuries and on the influence it had and still has upon the concept of civilization which prevails in our schools, we can't avoid the general impression that a profound cleavage has split the spirit of Christian culture. Will it really result in the formation of a new, non-Christian civilization? In order to answer this question we must first of all realize the fact that actual scientific knowledge is not identical with the philosophical or quasi-philosophical conclusions based upon some of the scientific discoveries or hypotheses. Such conclusions cannot represent the whole scientific branch of culture. We have to study the story of science itself to be able to evaluate correctly its bearing upon the general civilization of today.

But still another warning is necessary. Historians are always inclined to judge severely those epochs which did not share the predilections of the age in which they themselves live. And nowhere, perhaps, is this truth so manifest as in the way in which the historians of science living in our own day treat the Middle Ages, an epoch which had very little interest in science. As the Middle Ages was a period in which Christian culture comprised many activities, the comparatively minor interest in science manifested in those days is frequently explained as something typical of Christian civilization as a whole. Such a conclusion is then readily accepted by those who look upon the modern development of science as based on an essentially new civilization, different from the Christian and frequently opposed to it.

There is something onesided in such a view of the growth of our civilization. The drama of history, although representing a single stream of events, is essentially not a continuous development. And the history of science is even less continuous than the history of the other branches of man's creative activity. First of all a very long epoch from the beginning of history until the 6th century before Christ was characterized by the preponderance of technology over science. Then, in the period which ended by the formation of the Roman Empire, scientific endeavours were split into the mathematical science, conceived as a pure theory and including also systematical zoology and botany, on one hand, and the despised technology on the other hand. The third period began with the spread of Christianity which coincided with the devastating migrations and with the remaking of Europe in the subsequent ages up to the 14th century inclusive. If we compare this medieval period with the modern one, in which science has achieved its greatest triumphs, we must not forget three most important factors: first, that it cost great efforts on the part of the men living in the dark ages of the migrations to save at least something of ancient civilization; secondly, that it would have been of little advantage to teach Euclid to tribesmen who had not as yet settled down to live in villages and towns, and that therefore it was essential to save Christian doctrine and moral and legal standards first; thirdly, that it was precisely the awe felt by medieval people for ancient civilization which formed the chief obstacle on their way towards independent cultural activity.

Therefore, to be able to judge the medieval world, it is advisable to place oneself, in imagination, in its social surroundings and try to understand it. The life in villages and small towns situated far away from each other had little opportunity and no need for scientific research. On the contrary there still existed many remnants of decayed tribal civilizations, such as the belief in witchcraft and magic, with which the medieval theologians had to fight.

If, however, somebody can not forget that some apologists of the first Christian centuries and even St. Augustine considered as false and ridiculous the doctrine of the spherical shape of earth, let him remember the ridicule and hatred heaped upon Pasteur's germ theory of contagious diseases by professors of the most enlightened 19th century who were themselves outstanding champions of experimental science. No age in human history is free from superstition and narrow-mindedness. Some venerable priests in the 17th century forbade Galileo to teach the new astronomical theory of Copernicus, because they were afraid that it would undermine faith in the Holy Scripture, but they let him go on with his research work. If, in the progressive year 1950, anybody would like to embark upon some research in geography, which is a much more innocent science than physics, he would be able to visit the countries of his own half of the world only with immense difficulty, and he would certainly end in jail, if he dared to enter the other half—simply because a lot of extremely irreligious people are afraid

that he would undermine, not any faith, but their
selfish power.

But perhaps the most foolish thing a historian of
science can do is to base his judgments on a particular
scientific terminology. Terminology is not knowledge
and there is hardly anything of so variable a nature
as the technical expressions used by scientists. Yet how
often have the historians, when speaking of medieval
science, quoted from one of Molière's plays in which
the highly learned Diafoirus explains that opium
makes people sleep because it possesses the "dormitive
virtue." Do they really think that Diafoirus was meant
to represent only medieval scientists? What about the
modern physiologist who, knowing that the osmotic
pressure in a living membrane does not obey the same
laws as the osmotic pressure in an artificial membrane,
speaks of an *epictesis*, a purely experimental notion,
according to his opinion? Or what about the Marxist
biologists who are very sure that the notion of the
"vital force" is a nonsense because, they affirm, it is
quite sufficient to say that the quality of the living
thing, insofar as the living thing is different from
inorganic matter, is just a "new form of movement"?
Is "medieval" science really dead or is modern science
more "medieval" than a progressive historian would
like to believe?

If anyone would like to sum up the history of science
in the course of the medieval centuries, he probably
could not do better than to point out the fact that in
the medieval universities one of the three main faculties was the faculty of medicine. Not a faculty of science, but a faculty of medicine. Much ancient knowledge in the fields of mathematics and astronomy was

included in the liberal arts, but medicine was chosen as the scientific subject worthy of a special faculty. Also we must not forget that only at the time when the universities were founded, one after another, in various European countries, the knowledge of Greek scientific authors spread everywhere. The direct Western tradition had been for a long time ignorant of most of them. From the whole work of Aristotle, for instance, only a few treatises on logic were known in a Latin translation made by Boethius, a Christian philosopher of the early 6th century. But the Christian monks of the 5th and 6th centuries, who lived in Syria, Mesopotamia, and Persia, had translated most of the ancient scientific writers from Greek into the languages of their own countries and it was upon their work that the Mohammedan Arabs founded their own scientific tradition. When this tradition, following the Mohammedan military expeditions, reached the Pyrenean peninsula, it was a matter of time for the scholars of Western Europe to contact them and to get acquainted with the treasures of ancient civilization. Centers of translation into Latin of the mathematical, astronomical, and medical works of the Greeks functioned in the 12th century in Toledo and in Barcelona, and the translators, such as the English monk Adelhard of Bath and Gherard of Cremona, may be considered real builders of medieval science. But of all this knowledge the medieval people cherished the medical experience most of all.

It cannot be said that they made it as important as theology or law. Against Saints Cosmas and Damian, the patron saints of medicine, many names of philosophers and theologians may be quoted, whose faith in immortality was much greater than their interest in the remedies of this world. But there the science of medicine was firmly established as one of the main branches of the university. It was the science which, of all the branches of science, was nearest to the knowledge of man. Because service to one's neighbor, not the attainment of power, was the leading principle of those times, medicine was also more important than any sort of technology.

The practical knowledge of the medieval surgeons was probably greater than can be judged from the books used in the universities. There, the foolish maxim that it is more honorable to err with Galen than to be right with others prevailed even in the 14th century when Mondino de' Luzzi dissected bodies in Bologna and wrote his *Anatomia*, in which he repeated the evident errors of the ancient authors. But anaesthesia had been tried in Salerno and in other Italian towns with some success, and new surgical operations were introduced by Guy de Chauliac, another alumnus of the celebrated medical faculty in Bologna and author of the classical *Chirurgia magna*, written in 1363. Even antiseptical arrangements were recommended by Henri de Mondeville, who taught in the university of Montpellier.

Similar conditions in the study and practice of medicine prevailed until the second half of the 18th century. The two medical authorities of European fame in the 16th century, Vesalius and Paracelsus, one of them interested in anatomy, the other in experimental pharmacology, were more critical of Galen than their predecessors, but the first great medical discovery of the modern epoch was left for their younger English colleague, William Harvey, who in a concise treatise on the movement of the heart, published in 1628,

announced his theory of the circulation of blood.
Otherwise, and notwithstanding the renewed interest
in anatomy, the science of medicine remained in the
shadow of the ancient Galen. As late as the middle of
the 17th century when the Jesuits brought into Europe
the Peruvian remedy for fever, quinine, physicians
refused to use it because it was not mentioned in the
textbooks they had used as students.

One change, however, occurred at the start of
the modern era which has influenced medicine ever
since. It was the general acceptance of the artificial
separation of mind and body. The medieval university, using Aristotle's terminology, conceived the soul
as the form of the whole body. Thus the unity of mind
and matter in man was always held up before the
eyes of the medical student and everybody was well
aware of the fact that in every cure or operation, however restricted, the whole person is necessarily involved. Even the two great psychologists of the 16th
century, Juan Luis Vives and Juan Huarte, both Spaniards and both interested in the scrutiny of mental
manifestations and abilities and in instinctive behaviour, stuck to the realistic conception of the relations
between mind and body. Not so Descartes. In his treatise on the nature of man he separated mind and
matter in such an absolute way that the learned physicians of the 17th century, many of whom were
under the spell of his powerful pen, began to treat
the human body as a sort of mechanical engine. When,
later on, religious thought began to recede from the
schools, this mechanistic concept was transferred also
to the manifestations of the human mind. The celebrated treatise *L'homme machine* by Julien de La
Mettrie was only the beginning of a series of attempts

to explain the whole human personality by mechanistic terminology. Long after such conceptions had been done away with in other branches of science, they still lived in mental medicine and in the studies of the relationship between psychological and physiological phenomena. Even the experiments of the 19th century psychologists like Weber or Wundt and the intelligence testing of Binet were based upon them.

In the meantime, the second half of the 18th and the first half of the 19th century saw a great expansion of various particular branches of medicine, substituting a sound knowledge of the human body and of the functions of its organs for the experimental guessing of the old masters. Albrecht Haller, a great systematizer of medical science, Caspar Wolff, the embryologist, Leopold Auenbrugger, the internist who first used percussion, René Laennec, pathological anatomist and inventor of the stethoscope, and Jan Purkyně, the physiologist, are the best known men of that inquisitive generation. Some of their new ideas already had the support of the remarkable successes of other sciences, made in the same epoch. Such collaboration was to increase even more in the second half of the 19th century. The completely renovated science of biology allowed Rudolf Virchow to apply the cell-doctrine to pathology and Claude Bernard to discover the importance of internal secretion. It has also, in an indirect way, through the study of the phenomena of fermentation, made possible the greatest medical discovery of the new epoch: Louis Pasteur's theory of the bacterial origin of infections. This theory in its turn furnished the basis of the discoveries of the bacilli of tuberculosis and cholera, made by Robert Koch. It also made possible the change of surgery into a "clean and safe art" by Joseph Lister—a task vainly attempted before by Ignaz Semmelweis. Another invention which has completely changed the methods of medical diagnosis was made by a teacher of physics, Wilhelm Roentgen; it is the discovery of x-rays.

Much recent medical research work has been concentrated on preventive medicine and on the various means by which living organisms protect themselves against diseases. Connected with these studies were the investigations of various food factors, essential for the normal growth and sustenance of the human body, which, shortly before the First World War, led Casimir Funk to the discovery of the constitution and function of vitamins.

Although most students of medicine in recent times came from schools in which the Christian concept of man was quite unknown, a firm persuasion is gaining ground among them, resulting from their practical experience, that in every single medical case the personality of the patient is to be considered as a real individuum and not as a mere collection of organs. This is true especially of the new developments in the rather neglected field of psychology and psychopathology. Jean Charcot had to start, in the latter half of the last century, from the fundamental distinction between the psychotic, the epileptic, and the neurotic patient, which had not been known before his times. But in his studies he soon reached the realm of mental phenomena, such as that of hypnotic sleep, which up to his time had only been investigated by men of doubtful intentions like the 18th century hypnotist Mesmer. The difficulty of understanding and explaining these phenomena, which probably cover a much larger field than is usually supposed, is still the most important feature of modern psychology. The conditioned reflexes of the instincts, studied by Ivan Pavlov, the influence of the past experiences of instincts on emotional life, investigated by Sigmund Freud, and other similar researches can cover only a small portion of the mental life of man and, consequently, can be easily overvalued. The real future of medical science lies only in a critical approach to facts, based upon the conception of human personality as an indivisible whole.

Whereas Greek medical knowledge reached Western Europe in the Middle Ages almost unchanged, the case of mathematical knowledge, which arrived in the same way, was different. The Arabs had introduced a new arithmetical notation, much easier to handle, and the Hindus, to whom the mathematical knowledge of the ancient Mediterranean civilization had, in the meantime, also been transmitted, added the concept of zero and, with it, the system of positional numeration. Explained in the books such as the *Liber abaci*, composed at the beginning of the 13th century by Leonardo Pisano, this system became the possession of the medieval universities and, together with the algebraic symbols denoting unknown numerical quantities, which had been also perfected by the Orientals, it gave impetus to new investigations.

The laws of combination for algebraic symbols became the chief interest of the 16th century mathematicians del Ferro, Tartaglia, and Cardano who, besides founding the solution of cubic equations, recognised also the negative roots of equations and the imaginary numbers. The next century changed the methods of numerical calculations considerably through the in-

vention of logarithms by Napier in 1614 and laid the
foundations for the discovery of the differential and
integral calculus, the principles of which were invented almost simultaneously by Newton and Leibniz.
These revolutionary steps, together with the beginnings of the theory of probability, conceived at the
same time by Jacques Bernoulli, brought with them a
considerable broadening of the role of mathematics.
It ceased to be a theory applicable only to astronomical
research and assumed great importance in physics, in
the construction of machines and even in social and
economic statistics.

It is true, of course, that the purely theoretical aspect of mathematics, which had such a great charm
for the ancient Greeks, remained in the foreground.
When Lagrange, the famous mathematician of the
18th century, presented his mathematical theory of
mechanics, it was a pure theory from which practical
cases could be deduced, not an experimental science.
When Gaus and Riemann in the 19th century and also
Lobatchewski and Bolyai put aside Euclid's affirmation that through a point outside a straight line only
one parallel can be drawn, they were also engaged in
pure theory. They began to consider the much less
evident but perfectly logical possibilities of various
other geometrical systems of a purely mathematical
nature in which perhaps an infinity of parallels may
be drawn through a given point or in which the loca-
tion of a particle is determined by many more coordi-
nates than three. But some time was to elapse before
it could be demonstrated that such geometrical systems could be used to describe real phenomena of
physics. They now have their reward and the time has
arrived when the definitions of physics can be mathe-

matical definitions only. Even the development of the function theory, another great mathematical triumph of the last hundred years, which has many important practical consequences and with which the names Cauchy and Poincaré are connected, was based upon the purely rational concept of a limit.

These successes of mathematical reasoning have undoubtedly furnished a good argument for those historians who see the foundations of a new civilization in the full development of logical reasoning. It is also true that the growth of mathematics is still in a full swing. By logical conclusions a whole theory of numbers, comprising the whole as well as the negative, the rational, the real, and the complex numbers, was constructed by Cantor shortly before the First World War. In quite recent years, Russell and Whitehead have developed in their *Principia mathematica* a complete grammar of mathematical analysis. Further developments along the same line are not impossible.

But the question, which is more fundamental than all this, is to what extent mathematics really is the only language of science. It will remain, with all probability, the exclusive language of physics and of the sciences closely connected with physics. But as we have seen already when discussing the development of medicine, physical notions are not paramount in science. There is also the realm of life which is of much greater importance to mankind than the realm of inorganic matter.

Many special sciences which have helped man to master nature are based on mathematics. Geography, for instance, owes to it all its cartographical and geo-

detical accomplishments from the maps made by
Mercator in the 16th century up to the modern atlases.
Also astronomy has, since the Middle Ages, renewed
its ancient contacts with mathematical investigation.

Astronomy, it is true, had at its disposal the telescope, which had already been invented in the 13th
century, perhaps by the Franciscan monk Roger
Bacon, or maybe even before. This instrument was
then perfected by a whole series of astronomers and
opticians. In recent times, the use of telescopes of great
focal length has been combined with photography, so
that the accuracy of astronomical observations has
been very much increased. Direct observation was
greatly improved in its methods by the two famous
astronomers of the turbulent period before the Thirty
Years War, Tycho Brahe and Johann Kepler. Tycho
Brahe was able to publish the first modern catalogue
of stars. Kepler studied and defined the movements of
the planets. Also by direct observation, William
Herschel, the 18th century amateur astronomer, discovered Uranus and studied the movement of the sun
through the universe. To-day the scientists working
in the great observatories are able to investigate the
spectra of the stellar rays, from which not only the
distances of the stars but also the elements from which
the stars are composed can be inferred. And only
direct observation can lead to the solution of problems included in such strange phenomena as the sun-
spots, with their magnetic properties, or the spiral
nebulae.

But on the other hand, the theory of the axial rotation of the earth and its orbital rotation around the sun,
published in 1543 by the mathematician Copernicus,
Newton's theory of the law of gravitation pervading

the whole universe, published in 1687 in his *Principia mathematica*, and Albert Einstein's general theory of relativity, published in 1915 and offering an explanation for gravitation which, since then, has been supported by many practical experiences—all these discoveries were in the first place mathematical discoveries.

Behind this development of astronomy are hidden the major discoveries in the field of physics and chemistry, concerned with all the properties of nature which can be expressed in numbers. The medieval people did not care much for them; they accepted, for instance, the anonymous discovery of the properties of magnetized iron as a great wonder, too great to be analyzed. The modern age took another extremist view: it made physics and chemistry much more comprehensive than they really are. When, in the 17th century, Galileo formulated some of the laws of motion, his contemporaries, like Descartes and Hobbes, full of confidence in human reasoning, came quickly to the conclusion that all nature is merely space and motion, which can be expressed in equations and which, as Hobbes, at least, put it, comprise even living bodies and our own mental life. After three centuries have elapsed, the physicists and chemists can not define space, nor matter, nor motion any more than they were ever able to do. But they have achieved a great deal in grasping those occurrences in nature which are regular and therefore mathematically ascertainable.

The man who first embarked upon this great scientific adventure was Isaac Newton, whose *Principia* we have just mentioned. By introducing into physics the idea of force he made it clear that even when we leave out the phenomenon of life it is not sufficient to deal with bodies at rest or in motion, but that we have to be interested also in the agencies which make a mass of matter depart from rest or from uniform motion. The universal law of gravitation, which he conceived, is the mathematical expression of the regular ways of one of such agencies. Light, which he also tried to investigate, is another such factor. Magnetic force is a third. To these were soon added the phenomena of electricity, already observed in much older times, but investigated thoroughly in the 18th century and again, in the first half of the 19th century, by Michael Faraday, whose great imaginative power led him to the discovery of the induction of electric currents, and by the mathematician Gaus, whose attempts to express numerically the positions and motions of imponderable electrified particles opened the gate to fields hitherto undreamt of.

In the meantime Robert Boyle, whose *Sceptical Chemist* appeared in 1661, started another investigation: that which is concerned with the structure of matter. His definition of the chemical element as a perfectly unmingled body which is not made of any other bodies, did not prove, in the course of the time, a sufficient definition, but it has proved a very useful hypothesis. Through the 18th century experiments of Lavoisier, conducted on a quantitative basis and accompanied by the introduction of a modern nomenclature, and through the 19th century interest in the atomic theory proposed by Dalton, a basis was furnished, which enabled the physicists to use the results of chemical investigations with much profit. Especially was this so when the atomic weights of different elements had been thoroughly studied and used, in

1865, by Dimitri Mendeleeff for the arrangement of a periodic table of elements; for then a new interpretation of the structure of matter was made possible.

Studying the phenomenon of heat the physicists of the 19th century abandoned the older idea that heat was a material substance and began to see in it the effect of the force of atoms which had been set in motion by friction. They also established ways of measuring the different kinds of forces, or energies, as they used to say. And finally they came to the conclusion that energy is neither created nor destroyed in any physical transformation—a conclusion similar to that of the chemists, who believe that there is neither creation nor destruction of matter in chemical changes. But they also had to conclude that a certain amount of the energy which had been changed into heat was no longer available for any other purpose. Thus the ideas came into existence which led first of all to the postulate that energy is something as material as matter and, later on, to the conception of energy and matter as just two names of one field of events expressible by numbers.

But still another chapter of physical discoveries was to pass. In his treatise on the *Dynamic Theory of the Electromagnetic Field*, written in 1864, Maxwell conceived light as an electromagnetic vibration, thus bringing light and the electromagnetic force into one concept. When Roentgen, in 1895, studying the phenomena connected with the passage of electricity through rarefield gases, made his discovery of the x-ray, and when Becquerel, in the same year, discovered the radiation of uranium, and when, later on, the Curies succeeded in separating the even more active radium, attention was concentrated on the particles which form such emanating rays. It was soon proved, chiefly through the experiments of Thomson and Rutherford, that every atom contains such electrified particles of different sorts, the behaviour of which can be in certain cases influenced but neither defined nor expressed by any laws. As the behaviour of these particles can change the character of the atoms, the elements of Boyle became a mere theoretical postulate and, curiously enough, the dreams of some medieval philosophers about the transmutation of one metal into another have been at least partially realized.

Moreover, the subsequent investigations of the microcosmic interior of the atoms, beside putting aside the concept of their mass and describing the changes in them only by mathematical terms similar to those by which the changes of energy are described, led to other conclusions which mean a deep cleavage between the old physics and the new. The old way of "explaining" things in terms of the material cause and the effect—which was not quite logical in itself as the material cause is no real cause—had to be abandoned in favor of mere mathematical descriptions of situations. Even the equality of action and reaction, a basic postulate of Newtonian mechanics, became a principle the validity of which cannot always be proved. And the principle of indeterminacy, proclaimed in recent years by Heisenberg, shows that a simultaneous ascertaining of both the position and the motion of an electron—the name given to one sort of the electrified particles in the atom—is impossible, so that we cannot even specify precisely the state of anything at any particular moment.

For many years the physicists have hoped that they would be able to find the so-called key to the universe,

that is, an all-embracing theory which would unify
the laws obeyed by all the energies. A step toward this
goal was undoubtedly made by Albert Einstein.
Founding his investigations upon the observation that
the velocity of light is independent of its direction and
using the four-dimensional geometry, developed by
the mathematician Riemann, in which the geometrical invariant is conceived as a distance function in
which time also enters, Einstein has shown that all
measurements are relative to a certain frame of reference. Thereupon he built a more general doctrine,
bringing the concepts of space, time, matter, and gravitational energy—by which even light is affected—
into a single mathematical "field" theory. The electromagnetic force is, however, still outside this unified
theory. Recent studies, connected with the names of
Planck, de Broglie, and Schroedinger, have found that
this force can only enter or leave atoms in certain
finite amounts, the so called "quanta"—a behaviour
which has not yet been observed in gravitation. It has
also been discovered that the electrons can be with
much advantage conceived as the maximum points of
something existing everywhere and behaving in a
wave-like manner.

It is possible that the cleavage between the electromagnetic realm on one hand and the gravitational
realm on the other will be found, in the course of future investigations, deeper and deeper. It is also possible that the two fields will be united by some clever
mathematical symbolism. But even in this latter case
it will not be a key to the universe. The whole science
of physics is still and will probably always be founded
on the pure mathematical theory of the ancient
Greeks. This theory is derived from the much superior

logical order and expresses only a portion of it. It is useful only as far as the observed facts can be accommodated within its boundaries.

The overwhelming number of natural events may be measured and also classified to a certain extent, but it will never be fully expressed by numbers only. That was well known by the ancient scientists and also by the medieval scholars. It is rather easy to reproach them for their lack of interest in measuring. They were not numerous and they could not afford to specialize. Nevertheless, St. Albert the Great, in the 13th century, was a good botanist and his contemporary, Roger Bacon, was already envisaging the construction of a miscroscope. The botanists and zoologists of the 16th century, such as Mattioli or Gesner, were direct heirs of the medieval scholars whose chief aim had been to name and to classify. Later on, when the schools were more numerous and also when the modern development of mathematics was already in full swing, the classification of scientific objects became even easier. But it remained evident that there are more things to be observed than could be measured.

Among the first the basic discipline of geography was systematized in a new way by Bernard Varenius in his *Geographia Generalis*, one of the most interesting works of the 17th century. Geography's main special branch, physical geography, found its chief initiator at the beginning of the 19th century in Alexander Humboldt. Also, the interest in sedimentary rocks and in volcanic activities crystallized gradually into the sciences of geology and paleontology, both of which testify that the earth has a story behind it which was evidently all but a regular process. A number of learned men like Hutton in the 18th century, Barrande in the last, and Termier in our own times, have expounded these two disciplines.

But the discipline which in the course of time proved to be the basic science of all this realm of knowledge is biology. Its ascendancy dates from the 17th century, the age of the perfection of the microscope by the brothers Jansens, the age in which Redi, by protecting decaying meat from contamination by flies, demonstrated that all life has its origin in pre-existing life, the age of Malpighi, the first modern student of morphology and physiology, and the age of Hooke's *Micrographia*, the book which for the first time mentioned the cells of organic structures.

The preponderancy of mathematical reasoning in those times was, of course, great. Few people were interested in the life of organisms. Most friends of science preferred to study only such interrelations in nature which could be characterized by measurable distribution of matter in space. But gradually the number of biologists increased. In the 18th century Leeuwenhoek discovered bacteria, protozoa, and spermatozoa; Wolff showed the falsity of the hitherto prevailing conception of the germs as organisms in miniature; and Linné invented his ingenious classification of plants and animals with the help of a nomenclature which expresses the morphologic connections between different species. With the beginning of the last century, when the term "biology" was also used for the first time, the age of temptations for the new science arrived. First of all Cuvier, in his anatomical studies, pushed to the foreground the functional unity of organisms, a subject also approached by comparative embryology, founded at the same time by von Baer.

Then came the cellular theory of Schwann and Purkyně, affirming that all living things originate and grow in very small structures, called cells, which are all filled with the same essential material, called protoplasm. But simultaneously another theory, a much more general one, but closely related to biology, began to gain ground: the theory of evolution.

The geologists were probably the first to become conscious of the fact that nature had a past which was different from its present. The very term "natural history" testifies to the presence of such ideas. The botanists and the zoologists knew that the species could be arranged in a "natural scale," but even Linné did not see any genetic connection between them. But then some of the geologists conceived the idea that by studying present geological agencies they would be able also to guess the past of nature, and Lamarck, a contemporary of Cuvier, was the first to announce the theory that past changes in nature have gradually produced all the forms of natural existence, from the simplest to the most complex. This hypothesis was later completed by the idea of Charles Darwin about the survival of the fittest and became one of the most popular doctrines of modern times. Even to-day many scientists still believe that inorganic molecules produced living cells—the origin of which evidently depended upon environmental conditions—that such cells produced metazoan organisms, and that primitive organisms produced the higher ones.

Although this theory had hardly any real significance for science, it included at least two problems which attracted the attention of the biologists of the latter half of the 19th century and of our own times: the origin of life and the ways of heredity.

The first problem is the more general one. To search for the origin of life means to search for the frontier between the living and the non-living. But to draw such a precise line is almost impossible. There are living bodies which consist only of a single protein molecule. There are non-living molecules which are almost equal to the cellular units of the living. What is the property by which a body of infinitesimal magnitude becomes an organism? It is certainly not its chemical composition, because the organic compounds were already prepared artificially more than a hundred years ago, in 1824, but nobody has as yet been able to create a living being. There are many single properties of living beings which are also single properties of non-living beings and vice versa. The biologists of today have at their disposal many new instruments, such as the ultramicroscope, the electron miscroscope, and the ultracentrifuge, for isolation of minute particles; yet it may be doubted whether further fragmentation will bring us any nearer to the essence of life. But if, as the so-called *holists* say, life is an expression of functional unity, is not every electron a functional unity? Then, of course, would all "dead matter" mean conglomerations of living beings which are governed by a certain number of statistical laws.

The problem of heredity is not so far-reaching. The first scientist to tackle it seriously was the abbot Gregor Mendel who, in the latter half of the last century, by the cross-breeding of peas in the garden of his Augustinian monastery in Brno, proved that the transmission of characteristic properties proceeds along definite lines and not by chance variation and that, consequently, such properties may be treated as indivisible and unalterable units. His younger contemporary Weismann, whose treatise on the *Germ Plasm* was published in 1892, de Vries, and Morgan, the most systematic of all the investigators of heredity, have not only confirmed Mendel's results, but also substantially enlarged our knowledge of the ways in which every characteristic passes from one organic individual to another. Thanks to their endeavours we now know that the tissue of each cell-nucleus consists of a number of thread-like bodies, the chromosomes, the material of which is the bearer of hereditary characteristics. We know also that there is no sufficient proof that acquired properties are inherited. But there are certain discontinuous variations of the bearers of the hereditary characteristics which we call mutations, a phenomenon which would hardly account for an evolution of one species from another.

At the end of the last century, it was also shown by Driesch that in many eggs interferences could be made without affecting the embryo which is to be born from the egg and that, consequently, there is something which pushes the nascent organism to complete its own unity. It does not matter whether we call this something *entelechy* as Driesch himself did or *determination* as some of the materialist philosophers insist on calling it. Nor does it matter whether this something is within the embryo or outside it, in its environment. The only thing which matters is the existence of this something because it means the existence of a positive finality of living beings.

Whoever wants to know the source of the idea that our present civilization is a scientific civilization—an idea which is still propagated in many schools—has to read Francis Bacon and Descartes. And he has also to read the scientists who invented the theory of evolution. The principles of the first two named, especially the idea of induction of everything else from that which is evident, have been popular for a long time. They are no more. As T. H. Huxley, who was not much of a Christian, put it in his *Progress of Science:* "It is a favorite popular delusion that the scientific enquirer is under a sort of moral obligation to abstain from going beyond that generalization of observed facts which is absurdly called Baconian induction." Bertrand Russell, another of the modern pagans, went even farther by saying: "All science rests upon induction, and induction rests upon what Santayana calls animal faith." Going beyond induction and having an animal faith was the favourite sport of Laplace, one of the first apostles of the theory of evolution. In his *Essai philosophique sur les probabilités*, published in 1814, he dreams of a human intelligence which will be capable enough to know all the forces which animate nature and all the situations of all beings in time and space; such a person would be able to embrace in one single formula all motions beginning with those of the largest bodies of the universe and ending with those of the meanest atom; and by doing that he would know everything: past, present, and future. No wonder that spending his days in such titanic dreams Laplace conceived a very unreal theory.

But even going beyond induction and having an animal faith does not give us much power. What we know, even if we take all the branches of science into consideration, always stops before the individuality. The highest entity of medicine is the human person. Physics and its satellite sciences stop before the individual behavior of the electron, biology stops before the functional unity of the living individuum. Mathematics does not know anything about the individuum; therefore mathematics cannot be the final language of science. Having no power over the individuality, which is the only source of culture, science cannot create a civilization. Science needs a civilization. It needs faith to be able to explain. It needs philosophy and especially logic to be able to express itself. It needs history to remember its own successes and mistakes. It also needs society within which to work.

The Law and the Nations

~~≈~~

THE POLITICAL STRUCTURE of the civilization in which
we live is built on three different levels: the family,
the autonomous community or region, and the state.
Each of these three different institutions has had a
different history, nor have their mutual relationships
been always the same. The family, a primeval institution, has been considered by Christians a necessary
basis of every society; but, at the same time, Christian
moralists and sociologists have been conscious of the
fact that the family is an imperfect society, since it
has not in itself all the means for its own complete
development. The state, on the other hand, defined as
a political unity governed by the same laws, is, in
spite of all its variability, considered a perfect society,
having in itself all the means for its end. The end of
every civil society is, according to Christian teaching,
the temporal well-being of its members. As the family
is much nearer to its individual members than the
state to its citizens, it is usually considered by Christian sociologists as the prototype of all civil societies.
Even the state is more or less regarded as an extension
of the "patria potestas"—"the paternal power." The
father exists for the well-being of his children; the

state exists for the well-being of its citizens—not the other way around.

As for the autonomous community or region, its importance varies with the extension of the state. It helps to defend the family and the freedom of the individual against the state. It ceases to exist in a small state. It comes again into existence whenever the state exceeds by its territorial growth the natural process of unification of customs and tendencies of its various provinces.

Generally speaking, two things may be considered as the main characteristics of the Christian conception of civil society: the subordination of every civil society to the well-being of man as an individual person and, secondly, the firm belief that whosoever holds the right to govern holds it from one sole and single source, namely God. These two tenets of Christian social doctrine are closely related to each other. The two biblical texts: "Render unto Caesar the things that are Caesar's, and to God the things that are God's" and "We ought to obey God rather than men," remind every Christian that it is common sense for an individual to live in civil society not only because otherwise he would not be able to provide himself with the necessary requirements of life, but also because only as a member of society can he procure for himself the means of developing his mental and moral faculties. Therefore, a member of a civil society can not place his whole personality in unrestricted service to that society even if it would mean for him complete material security. He can fully develop his faculties only if he transcends all the interests and aims of civil society. On the other hand every civil society—and also every social authority—has its source in nature and has, consequently, God for its author. That is what the Christian means by affirming that all public authority proceeds from God; by affirming it he reminds the civil authorities that they are here only to serve God and not to glorify themselves.

The Church as the guardian of Christian moral doctrine watches constantly the developments of civil organisations. It is not interested authoritatively in its technicalities, although St. Thomas Aquinas, for instance, did not hesitate, in his commentary on the *Politics* of Aristotle, to name the republic and the mixed forms of aristocracy as the best political systems which are in fact attainable in average cases. Its secular experience makes the Church a little sceptical about the belief that this or that new system of government may create better government leaders than did the older systems. But, to quote Pius XI's encyclical letter *Ubi Arcano Dei:* "If the Church considers it improper to meddle without reason with the government of wordly affairs and purely political matters, she is within her rights in seeking to prevent civil power from making that an excuse to oppose in any way whatsoever the superior interests which involve man's salvation, to endanger or injure those interests by unjust laws or commands, to attack the divine constitution of the Church, or tread underfoot the sacred rights of God in the civil society of men."

The political history of the Christian era presents us, however, with a picture which is far from monotonous, for almost every one of the Christian countries went through different political developments. It is only by selecting some of the particular characteristics of the various regional or national histories, that we can arrive at a general classification. For that purpose, the whole development of political life since the beginning of the present era may be divided into five epochs terminated by the years 395, 800, 1453, 1789 and by our own times respectively.

The first of these epochs belongs more to the ancient than to the Christian civilization. The Roman Empire was still in existence and its geographical extent only slightly decreased in the second half of this period. The administrative and military institutions were remodeled several times, but they were still essentially ancient institutions. The laws were only to a certain extent influenced by the moral principles of the Church. It was an age when the Christians found it necessary to accept and learn many things which were later useful to their own cause: many of the basic concepts of the Roman law, the discipline of the Roman army, the rules of an orderly administration, the value of towns as centres of cultural life.

The real history of Christian political culture begins with the second epoch which, as an epoch of migrations and turbulent changes, is rightly called the Dark Age of Europe's past. If we have chosen as the date of its beginning the year 395, it was not only because, at the end of the 4th century, the Roman Empire was split into two independent units, but, in the first place, because, at about the same time, Roman administration and the military defense of the Empire gave way to the assault of the immigrating tribes. Seen from the purely political point of view, this date is perhaps a more important milestone of history than is the beginning of the Christian era. Whereas the political development of the ancient era and of the first three or four centuries of the Christian era can be summed up as the development of the Mediterranean area or of the Roman Empire, the period from 395 to 1453 may be characterized as the age of the making of Europe and the centuries after this as the age of the making of the modern world.

But for several hundred years to come, the idea of the Roman Empire was still to be considered the best expression of the political unity of Europe. Men like St. Jerome, wholly addicted to theology and other abstract studies, admired the virtue, the military and administrative capabilities of the ancient Romans, and their political history; they considered the Empire an institution of permanent value. Even the Celts and the Germans, although they entered the territory of the Empire in isolated groups of tribes and although they destroyed much more than they preserved, had a common respect for the ancient traditions of the empire. They were not able, of course, to understand them fully, but the image of the emperor which they often used on their own coins was a sufficient testimony of the spell cast by the ancient political order on the newcomers.

The bishops, the priests, and the monks of the Church also did their best to preserve the idea of the political unity of the Christendom. When, at the beginning of the 7th century, the Arab tribes, stirred up by the visionary commands of Mohammed-ben-Abdallah, brought under their subjection the territories of Mesopotamia, Egypt, and Iran and began their drive westward, occupying gradually the whole coast of North Africa, Sicily, Sardinia, and the Pyrenean Peninsula and overflowing beyond the Pyrenees, it could almost have been expected that the Church would be obliged once more to live underground and that the influence of its moral doctrine upon the principles of politics would be destroyed. But the idea of the unity of Christendom had become strong and, out of the defense of Europe against this new invasion, the Carolingian Empire emerged not as a survival, but as an answer to a living need.

Moreover, it can not be forgotten that in the meantime, in Constantinople, the series of the eastern Roman Emperors went on unbroken. The famous Justinian, by whose orders the Roman law was codified in the 6th century, was among them. Although a country rather stagnant in its culture and not connected with the trend of events in the West, the Eastern Empire never ceased to be considered a substantial part of Christendom and it was to exert a great influence upon the Slavs who were slowly moving westward and southward following the steps of their Celtic and Germanic predecessors.

The era between the years 800 and 1453 may be characterized, in so far as its political culture is concerned, by its happy compromise between the customary institutions of the new tribes and the Christian conception of the social order. Its basic political unit was the monarchy. Derived from the function of the tribal chieftains, the office of the regional monarch was first of all adorned by the title of "duke"—originally a military rank—which was quite compatible with the supreme authority of the emperor. Later on, when the Western Empire became more an ideal than a reality, many of the dukes assumed the title of "king." But before this last development had been accomplished, the inthronization of a new monarch began to be accompanied by a religious ceremony, which developed into the coronation of the king by a bishop. This ceremony meant more than a mere benediction; although it was never considered a sacrament, it signified a consecration which, once granted, could never be nullified. Thus the principle of authority and discipline was maintained in a world in which political rivalries were perhaps even more frequent and more unscrupulous than in our own time.

At the same time, however, it was generally expected that the dukes and kings would settle their affairs in consultation with, and by the judgment of their subjects. It is not easy for the historian to find the true source of this salutary custom. In all probability it was a legacy of the former patriarchal civilization of the tribes, a legacy unspoiled as yet by long ages of division of work, in which the business of government was frequently changed into the autocracy of one man.

The development of the representative system could not, of course, avoid the consequences of the division of work inside every tribe. The function of the warrior and defender was divided from that of the farmer. Later on, it was ennobled and, in a certain sense, consecrated in the institution of knighthood. Not all the knights came up to the standards of their class. But generally their standards were much higher than those of the public officials of the ancient city-states and empires and perhaps also higher than those of the public servants of the modern epoch. It was these knights and the dignitaries of the Church and, later on, also the representatives of the cities, who were summoned by the medieval dukes and kings to decide with them the more important affairs of the state. The collection of taxes, which in those times was regarded

as voluntary aid given to the head of the state when
he was under some special strain, was especially considered their business. The ordinary expenses of administration were paid by the head of the state out of
the income from his private possessions.

It has to be pointed out that modern historians are
frequently inclined to deal with these things from the
aspect of popular persuasion—which probably originated with the poets and novelists of the Romantic
school at the beginning of the last century. They believe that modern democracy is a renovation of primitive society which the feudal system of the Middle
Ages abolished. The truth is that such a primeval
democracy never existed. The feudal system, in which
the duke or king acted with the approval of the nobles,
was in fact a developed patriarchal system. Only the
patriarchs were able to dispose of the possessions of the
tribes. Similarly, all the land in a medieval country
was considered to be the nominal property of the duke
or king who gave it to the heads of the foremost families as his liegemen. They in their turn ceded, again
nominally, the largest part of it to their villagers.
And, as the patriarch used to summon the experienced
men of the tribe to his council, so the medieval duke
or king summoned the heads of noble families to the
assembly, upon which also his own recognition as
duke or king was dependent when he ascended the
throne. It is truer, therefore, to speak of modern democracy as an aristocracy for all than to regard it as a
reestablishment of an order which has existed only in
the imagination of some poetical minds.

So great was the respect for autonomous administration and the consent of the citizens in medieval times
that the feudal, agricultural society was usually free

from the encroachements from the part of the central authority. Also the cities which either survived from ancient times or were newly founded by kings, dukes, nobles, and Church dignitaries and which made their living from industry and commerce and were therefore strange to the agricultural society, were from the very beginning given an extensive autonomy. Inside their walls again a substantial autonomy was enjoyed by the different branches of industry in the professional corporations or guilds which protected the interests of their members but which also controlled the production and took care of the quality and the prices of the products.

It is evident, of course, that such a development of tribal social customs was possible only under the powerful influence of Christian doctrine and the Church as its bearer. This influence was perhaps more effective in proportion to the demands of the Christian moralists. Some of the Christian thinkers considered the state a sort of "magnum latrocinium"—a "great roguery." And the ideals put forward in many books on politics, from St. Augustine's treatise on the *City of God* to Dante's *On the Monarchy* were undoubtedly more fitted for utopia than for human reality. Nevertheless, it was probably this intransigence of the theorists which achieved the most. It was not an easy task to persuade the new members of Christendom to accept the principles of the indissolubility of the family, the equal right of women and men to inherit, or the unlawfulness of usury—which, by the way, the medieval moralists were slow to distinguish from the legal interest on long-rate loans. But gradually all these difficulties were surmounted and a legal order emerged from the combination of Christian moral principles with the tribal customs.

Such a creative process naturally had its dangers, the most remarkable among them being the power conceded to the political authorities in the enforcing of the new principles. So, for instance, the procedure known in western Europe as the Inquisition, by which the judicial powers could summon a person and compel him upon oath to reveal what crimes had been committed, was an instrument open to misuse. Similarly the enforcing of this or that moral principle gave the dukes and the kings the opportunity of taking the more important cases from the regional courts of the nobles to their own courts, a procedure which could be used in the interest of selfish political motives. No wonder the nobles themselves, even when they had already accommodated their customary laws to Christian moral principles, did not like any legal innovations, especially the procedural principles of Roman law which presupposed the supreme and very broad authority of the head of state.

Thus a situation gradually developed in which the Church had to remind its faithful again and again that God is the only source of authority and that even the dukes and kings, and, of course, also the emperors, are bound by the law of God and by the natural law manifested in the logical conclusions of the human mind. Many examples of such conflicts between political leaders and Christian theory may be cited from medieval history; St. Adalbert of Bohemia, St. Thomas of Canterbury, Robert Grosseteste, bishop of Lincoln, and John of Jenštýn, archbishop of Prague, illustrate this struggle between the natural and the positive law.

Being common to all Christendom, this development was bound to influence the political history of the Christian world as a whole. The fact that everybody was conscious of being not only the subject of his duke or king but also the citizen of Christendom was an international factor of importance. In the field of international politics, the Middle Ages were miles ahead of the absolutist epoch to come with its mechanical conception of the balance of power. To the medieval man the idea of peace was based on the conception of moral duty and not upon that of diplomatic skill and military power. International privileges protecting by a special peace the various places of worship, the fairs, the feast days, or even—as was the case of the 10th century "treuga Dei—the peace of God"— some days in the week, were generally observed. And even such international clashes, which resulted from the ambition of the rulers, were frequently represented as conflicts of legal claims.

The idea of the Roman Empire as a definite political order comprising all the Christian countries was never abandoned in the course of medieval history. Many theologians, politicians, and poets considered the realization of a Christian Roman Empire a moral obligation. They were fond of remarking with Dante that, in the past, the Empire arose from the fountain of ancient piety and that, therefore, Christians would have to reestablish it. At the same time they considered it an essential part of the civilization they had inherited; they liked to receive the titles of the ancient statesmen and they hardly ever admitted that the ancient Empire had ever been destroyed.

There existed, however, two Roman Empires

throughout the years between 800 and 1453. The eastern, with its central seat in Constantinople, was perhaps the more real and consolidated, although its extent was restricted to Southern Balkans and—for some time at least—to Asia Minor. When the Turks took over Mohammedan expansion from the Arabs, the emperors of Constantinople had to evacuate Asia Minor—although they could return there, but only temporarily, in the 12th century, the epoch of the Crusaders. In the Balkans they had difficulties without end with the Slavonic Bulgarians and Serbs, whose rulers were always ready to assume the title of Roman Emperor themselves—as Simeon of Bulgaria and Dušan of Serbia actually did in the 10th and the 14th centuries respectively, testifying thus to the international significance of the title. After the fall of Constantinople in 1453 into the hands of the Turks, all the territory of the Eastern Empire came under the domination of the Mohammedans.

The Western Roman Empire, as it was reestablished by Charlemagne in 800, comprised the territories of France, Italy, Switzerland, the Netherlands, Germany, and Austria of today, but it only survived half a century in that geographical extent. From 843 onwards, until the middle of the 15th century, it was restricted, more or less, to the territory of Germany and Austria of today, as France had fallen off altogether and the imperial power in Italy, Switzerland, the Netherlands and the newly added kingdom of Bohemia was very weak. Some of the emperors of those times, such as Otto III in the 10th century or Charles IV in the 14th century, were statesmen of high ideals; many others, however, were not up to their task. The most fatal development in the history of the medieval Western Roman Empire was the conflict between some of the emperors and the popes, concerning the extent of their authority. The core of this conflict was the contest between the Church as the guardian of moral principles and the Empire as the protagonist of the positive laws issued by the civil authority. But much in it was determined by the personal policies of the various emperors and popes. As the popes, in the course of time, became political heads of a quite large territory in Italy, their spiritual role in those developments was not always allowed to come clearly to the foreground. In such a way the prestige of the Western Empire was gradually declining and when, in 1452, the city of Rome saw for the last time the coronation of an emperor, Frederick III, a member of the Habsburg family, everybody knew, that his real authority was problematic even in his native duchy of Austria.

Nevertheless, Christendom was still a kind of political unity. And Christian Europe of the Middle Ages existed in a world which was far from quiet and pacific. Already before the year 800 it had to endure the lightning-like invasion of the Mongolic Huns and to stop the onslaught of the Arabs in the Pyrenees. In the 10th century, the attack of another Mongolic tribe, the Magyars, had to be stopped by the Central European Slavs and Germans; the Magyars then settled down in the Danube valley and became Christians. But still another and perhaps the greatest danger was in store. When the Arabs, at the beginning of the 8th century, took possession of the region of Samarcand, in Central Asia, they included into the Mohammedan sphere the tribe of the semi-Mongolian Turks. The Turks, imbued with the imperialist spirit of Islam, adopted soon afterwards imperialist policy. They invaded India and, in the 11th century, Persia and Mesopotamia, occupying even Baghdad, the political center of the Arabs, and then Palestine and Jerusalem. The Holy Places of the Christians, made accessible in the meantime to the pilgrims from the Christian countries—with certain interruptions—by the more or less tolerant Arab rulers, were desecrated and access to them forbidden. And the Turks proceeded farther westwards, into Asia Minor. Europe, threatened in its very existence, tried to defend itself by counterattacks, organising, from the end of the 11th to the second half of the 13th century, the Crusades. After some initial successes, this military move could only postpone the main Turkish attack. By the end of the 13th century the last stronghold of the Christians in Palestine fell again into Turkish hands and the Turks were free to advance against Europe.

In the same 13th century the Mongolian tribes which still lived in Central Asia were assembled by Temoudgin, who assumed the title of Genghis-Khan. He launched an attack, first of all, against China and then against Europe, pushing as far as the Dnieper and annihilating the recently erected Slavonic duchy of Kiev. The sons of Genghis-Khan not only extended their attacks to southern Asia and the Far East where China especially was to bear long the traces of their brutalizing occupation, but also proceeded from the Kiev region against the Slavonic kingdoms of Poland and Bohemia and were only repulsed after bloody battles at Lehnice and Olomouc. Afterwards, when their immense empire broke down completely, some of their units, the Tatars, as the Slavs called them, still remained in the Kiev region.

The feudal period of the Middle Ages was followed by three centuries of moral and political decay, known as the age of absolutism. There are very few political values whose origin could be traced to the years between 1453 and 1789. Nevertheless even that age is part of the political story of Christendom.

The initial desertion from moral duties, called the "renaissance," which destroyed the feudal social order, was soon followed by the desertion from the Church of various reformers, each of whom in his turn condemned the others and was ready, in the words of Martin Luther, to "stab, slay, and strangle" their "thieving and murderous bands." The spirit of the barbarous tribes had revived. Mere commonplaces without logical connection, the so-called humanist truths were kept by those who turned their backs on the moral doctrine of the Church. The door of the future stood open for the most immoral developments in politics.

The Eastern Roman Empire was no more. The Western Roman Empire remained, nominally at least, until 1806, in the hands of the Habsburgs who then exchanged their title for that of the Emperors of Austria. They were able, it is true, to defend their territories against two major onslaughts of the Turks and they even freed the kingdom of Hungary from their domination. But they lost all authority in Germany and at last only the duchy of Austria and the kingdoms of Bohemia and Hungary remained in their hands and were governed by them in the same autocratic, absolutist fashion as were the other European states by their own rulers.

The new Europe consisted now of a constellation of states which were ready to form alliances against each other, being jealous of each other's power, but which cared no more for any sort of political unity; the so-called European leagues of George of Podiebrad or Leibniz were considered mere utopias. Great Britain with occupied Ireland, France, Spain, and Portugal— the last two freed from the Arabs—in the west, the Scandinavian kingdoms in the north, the Netherlands, the various German and Italian states and cities, and the Habsburg monarchy in the centre, and Poland with Russia in the east, such was the political map of divided Europe. Internally, these states were administered in a highly centralized manner. The nobles were deprived of their public duties but they preserved their privileges. Regular taxes were introduced and almost all their burden laid on the shoulders of the peasants. Most of the state revenues went into the building and maintaining of large professional armies. War was a more normal state than the period of peace. The medieval doctrine of God as the only source of authority was falsified into a semi-deification of "Kings by Divine Grace" whose main right was their moral irresponsibility.

Outward competition between the various rulers— called, euphemistically enough, the upkeeping of the balance of power—went so far that the kingdom of Poland was completely destroyed and divided by an alliance of its neighbours. The same spirit of unscrupulous competition was introduced into the sphere of economics. The peasants who had ceased to be nominal holders of land either became free owners, among whom the greed for soil soon brought the distribution of property out of any proportion, or they were enslaved by the privileged nobles. In the towns the disci-

pline of the guilds passed away and the owners of
factories and commercial enterprises discovered the
misery, as well as the advantages, of an unbridled
competition. Commercial patriotism, called "mercantilism" and aiming, in each country, at the annihilation of all foreign production and the security of home
production, was accepted as a fashion of the time
everywhere.

But Europe was also slowly changing into the
World. The naval explorations of the Portuguese, and
then also of the Italians, the Spaniards, the English,
the French, and the Dutch, resulted in a series of great
geographical discoveries. Knowing very little or nothing about the 10th century voyages of the Norsemen
across the Atlantic Ocean and about the later contacts
of the Venetian merchants with the Far East, the
European explorers of the 15th century reached India
by the way of the Cape of Good Hope and the West
Indies by a direct westward route. In the course of the
16th century they discovered most of the American
continent and circumnavigated the world. In the 17th
and 18th centuries they extended their discoveries to
New Zealand, Australia, and the islands of the Pacific.

The discovered territories were promptly appropri-
ated by the European states as their "colonies," that is,
as possessions completely dependent on the centralized
administration of the mother-countries. The noble
doctrine of international law, elaborated by Francisco
de Vitoria on the basis of the Christian conception of
the natural law, was repudiated by his Spanish countrymen—in spite of their repeated professions of faith-
fulness to the Catholic doctrine. The less logical
doctrine of Hugo Grotius, when applied to practical

politics, resulted in a system of treaties, the validity of which was completely dependent on the good will of its sponsors. Consequently, the fate of the native inhabitants of the colonies was a sad one. Even the "Reductions," founded by the Jesuit fathers in Paraguay in the 17th and 18th centuries and consisting of communal land under common management and of allotments held by the Indian families, were finally destroyed by the Spanish civil administrators in 1767. In the same time, the colonies were at stake in every major war between the European absolutist rulers and they were exchanged by peace treaties as if they were pieces of private property.

The last epoch of political history, initiated by the "enlightened" trends in the political thought of the 18th century and started by the French Revolution of 1789, is not easy to characterise. Living in the very centre of its stream, we do not perhaps evaluate correctly the significance of its various features. And we are hardly able to distinguish which of its various characteristics is the leading one. Is it really the age of democracy in which we live? Or is nationalism its most significant trend? Shall we perhaps speak of it as the epoch of total wars? And what about the industrial revolution and the social problems connected with it? All of these points of interest are represented, in this or that way, in the events of our own days. We cannot close our eyes to any one among them.

If we examine the Declaration of the Rights of Man, the major ideological document of the French Revolution, and the Declaration of Independence by which, thirteen years earlier, several British colonies in North America separated themselves from their mother-country, we may find in them, undoubtedly, ideas which were much closer to the Christian conception of society than most of the political theories of the preceding absolutist era. That there are "certain inalienable rights of man," that "the aim of every political association is the preservation of the natural and imprescriptible rights of men," such ideas are in perfect accord with the Christian teaching that man, as rational creature, can participate through his reason in the knowledge of the eternal law of God and that, consequently, he can know what he ought to do in relation to his fellow men. The Christian sociologists, presuming these principles, came to the conclusion that every human law should be derived from such natural knowledge of right—or law of nature—and that no human law could be valid if it contradicts the law of nature. This conclusion was always looked upon as one of the cornerstones of Christian society.

Thus the Declaration of the Rights of Man seemed the best way to a new realization of the old Christian principles. It also accepted the principle that "social distinctions can only be founded on common utility" —an idea which had been one of the leading principles of medieval society. Thus far the new turn of events could be looked upon with great expectation. But there were also other ideas, of quite different character and consequences. Whereas the American Declaration of Independence stated cautiously that "governments are instituted among men deriving their just powers from the consent of the governed," the French Declaration of the Rights of Man affirmed in its 6th article that "law is the expression of the general will." There is a great difference between just powers—one has to stress the word "just"—to the exercise of which a consent is given and an expression of the general will. What is a general will?

The chief apostle of this unhappy idea was an "enlightened" philosopher, Jean Jacques Rousseau. He himself was never clear about this idea in his writings. But it took root. And what the modern epoch has made out of Rousseau's theory can be best illustrated by a quotation from a famous modern lawyer, Hartley Shawcross, attorney general of the Socialist government which came into power in Great Britain in 1945. He said: "Parliament is sovereign. It can make any laws. It could ordain that all blue-eyed babies shall be destroyed at birth. But it has been recognized that it is no good passing laws unless you can be reasonably sure that, in the eventualities which they contemplate, these laws will be supported and can be enforced. Parliamentary jurisprudence, you may observe, is a nice calculation of force." In other words, the belief in the general will—no matter whether expressed by a dictator or by a parliamentary majority—has clashed with the doctrine of inalienable rights.

There was a perfectly natural and good tendency in modern democracy to reestablish the ancient consent of the governed. But perhaps the theoreticians flourishing at the close of the 18th century were naive enough to think that the governed could never turn against their own liberties? If they had been told that the German people would, in free elections, give Hitler 107 seats in the Reichstag, they would probably not believe it. They confused the consent of the governed, if not with the mystical "general will," then at least with the absolute will of the multitude, expressed by mechanical voting.

In the course of time, the idea of the general will

has, of course, found various and rather differing elucidators. Some of them, the "liberals," affirmed that every man is a law to himself and that the general will results from the occasional agreement of the majority of such absolutely free personal wills, which are all equal, however different might be the reasoning abilities of the minds which they express. They never took care to explain why a citizen should obey—without any reservation—the majority of his neighbours.

Others chose a different way. They accepted the idea of the general will in its mystical, romantic aspect. They identified it with the State and transferred upon the State its infinite wisdom and absolute power. They did not forget to remind everybody that the general will, or the will of the State, is or should be the will of the people or the class. But—and in that such statesmen differed from the liberals—an individual member of the people or the class was not allowed to say anything about it. There were the press, the radio, posters, propaganda leaflets, and also the secret police ready to teach what was the will of the people or the class. Socialists of all kinds, theoreticians as well as practicians, Proudhon and Marx in the 19th century, Mussolini, Hitler, and Stalin, all affirmed that the general will of the people was manifested by their activities.

What is a rather interesting, although a secondary aspect of this development, is the opinions of the jurisprudents. Most of them are not favorable to the Christian conception of the superiority of natural rights—derived in their turn from the Christian conception of man—above the positive laws of the State. But, among themselves, they are divided into two big groups. One, the so-called normative school, derives all laws by a "concretization" from an initial legal hypothesis of the constitution. Thus the sign of equality is put between the State and the Law and there remains no criterion according to which the steps taken by the State could be judged. The other, the sociological school, goes even farther from the conception of natural right and would like even a district magistrate to judge whether the laws really express the general will of the people or the class. No wonder that in some states of the 20th century proscription, forced labor and concentration camps, tortures and fear of sudden death, and other terrors became common, which even the Absolutist Age, so fond of burning witches at the stake, did not know.

National feeling grew, in the course of the last hundred and fifty years, into another mythical religion, as popular and as unreasonable as the religion of the general will of the people. There had always been some tribal or regional patriotism in medieval Europe. Later the "reformers" and the absolutist rulers frequently profited from it in their selfish endeavours. But in the 19th century this patriotism grew into a veritable frenzy which, for instance, would not allow two peoples speaking the same language to live in two separate states nor two peoples speaking two different languages to live in the same state.

The striving for the political independence of the nations living in the Habsburg monarchy on the upper Danube and in the Turkish empire in the Balkans did not stop when complete autonomy had been achieved; it went on, concentrated on the petty problems of national boundaries, until every political collaboration between them was made nearly impossible. The feuds inherited from the absolutist rulers, like those between France and Prussia and between Prussia and her other neighbors, took on a nationalist character and continued in undiminished force. The building of big national states to replace smaller political units was considered almost a moral duty in the 19th century. As a tool in the hands of those who preached the divinization of the State, nationalism was directed against any regional autonomy which did not coincide with the boundaries of languages. Under the leadership of Prussia—the medieval duchy of Brandenburg—and with the help of British statesmen, a colossal German state was erected. With similar help of the French politicians, a united Italy was constructed upon the soil of old kingdoms, duchies and free cities.

Gradually, modern nationalism spread overseas. Following the 18th century example of the North Americans, the racially mixed inhabitants of Central and South America succeeded in establishing their own independence in the first half of the last century. Soon the tendency began to be imitated by members of other races. Japan was the first among the native states of Asia to accommodate itself not only to European nationalism but also to modern progress in the fields of science and industry—without, however, accepting the religious and moral foundations of the Christian civilization. After 1918, a number of independent native states like Iran, Persia, Irak, and Transjordania, emerged in the Near East and nationalist revivals in Turkey, Egypt, and Abyssinia completed the reorganization of that region.

The main triumphs of nationalism were, however,

to come after 1933, when a pseudoscientifical theory, formulated for the first time by anti-Christian Frenchmen and Englishmen of the 19th century and concerning the superiority of the "Nordic race," took root among the Germans and when, subsequently, the Communists began to use nationalism in propagating their social theories among the Slavonic nations of Europe and among the nations of Eastern and Southern Asia. The result was a sharp cleavage between the Slavonic countries on one hand and the countries of Western Europe and the Americas on the other hand and also a complete change in the political organisation of Asia, where independent states of Indonesia, Burma, India, Pakistan, and others took the place of former colonies.

Under such circumstances, the idea of an international legal order suffered a further retrogression. It is very interesting to note that this was connected with the development of military science which even the highly moral Middle Ages could not curb. From the Lateran Council in 1139, which tried in vain to forbid the use of crossbow and arch as "deadly and odious to God," to the attempts of the United Nations in the years 1945 to 1950 to make the production of atomic weapons illegal, a long time has passed but nothing has restricted the progress of that deadly science. Moreover, many a modern state, no longer recognizing the religious sanctity of an obligation, had ceased even to look for legal pretexts for a declaration of war and was ready to attack its neighbors whenever it pleased the "will of the people."

Hope and Despair in Modern Society

❦

Discussing the progress made during the last few centuries in the mastering of matter we have mentioned the frequent assertion that the civilization in which we live is based upon science and machines. Analysing this belief we find that it is due to a certain anxiety which to-day pervades almost all the countries of the world. Many people around us live in material insecurity which was unknown in the past ages. Until the beginning of the last century, even if a man had lost all his property, it was nearly always possible for him to find work and, what was equally important, to find it without having to leave his family. Such security exists no more. As it is evident that without being able to work and earn his living no one can develop his abilities, everybody looks for a solution of the economic and social problems and for a weapon against economic insecurity. And many people find such a solution and such a weapon, or at least a hope for them, in science and in technology. Or, as others put it, in the social utilization of science and technology, in the social rule of these two branches of culture, that is, in technocracy.

There is no doubt that the complex of social and

economic problems is one of the prominent aspects of the present state of our civilization. It can not be its only and exclusive aspect. A unilateral civilization would not be a civilization at all. Even a complete technocracy would not be able to satisfy man if it did not help him to find his way to God, to create works of art, and to contemplate the drama of the human past. But perhaps the economic and social difficulties of our own times are a prelude to a major reorganization of our society. They may be, of course, a prelude to an age of total destruction as well.

Everywhere around us we see society divided into two classes: the owners or managers of productive property, and those who work for them. Almost everything seems to be permitted in the mutual struggle of these two groups, especially in the totalitarian societies, where all the old ideas of legality have been forgotten. Moreover, Europe, the cradle of the Christian civilization, which for ages has radiated cultural initiative, seems to be in the greatest social and economic difficulties of all the parts of the world. Will the struggle between the classes annihilate Europe? Will it disintegrate society? The words of the encyclical letter issued by Pope Benedict XV at the outbreak of the First World War may be quoted in this connection even today: "Such has been the change in the ideas and morals of men that unless God comes soon to our help, the end of civilization would seem to be at hand. Thus we see from the relations of men the absence of mutual love; the authority of rulers is held in contempt; injustice reigns in relations between the classes of society; the striving for transient and perishable things is so keen that men have lost sight of the other and more worthy goods they have to obtain."

The modern epoch of political history, dating from the end of the 18th century, has several characteristics of its own, the study of which is indispensable for a clear understanding of the contemporary economic and social problems.

The first of its features is the retrogression of agriculture as the main occupation of men. In the preceding epochs of history agriculture was man's chief economic activity. The commercial cities of the ancient epoch, the re-established cities of the Middle Ages, or even the state-supported industries of the absolutist period did not affect its position of importance. Besides, up to the end of the 18th century, the technical aspects of agriculture, with its natural fertilizers, fallow fields, and simple breeding of animals, were also almost unchanged. The 19th century achieved a real revolution in this respect. The rapid development of industry, and the accompanying development of commerce and transportation, pushed agriculture aside and in many countries those who are engaged in it are now in minority. Many other countries already show indications of approaching the same condition.

Several factors accompanied the industrial revolution. The main two among them were the growth of capitalism and the help of science in the production of goods.

Although the word "capitalism" has nowadays many different meanings—the most popular among them being perhaps that which indicates the economic systems prevalent in the countries which have not accepted the Marxist economy—its original and also most logical sense denotes an economy (production and consumption of goods) in which any kind of money plays a preponderant and indispensable role.

The origin of money is connected with the division of professions in the tribes which had settled down to live in villages and towns. As their members were not always able to use direct barter, they turned to a medium of exchange which was given and received by measure or by weight. They preferred, and still prefer to use as such a medium, a material which could be also used for other purposes: hard metals, for instance. Only much later, when they had confidence in the system, did they use symbolical money (letters of credit, printed money, cheques). The heads of states or other wealthy people frequently coined money, supporting thus the exchange of goods.

But as far as exchange of goods was concerned, the invention of money could not change the economic aspect of the world. Throughout the ancient epoch and the Middle Ages even the proprietors of the workshops had but little use for it. The quantity of money—mostly coined from silver—which circulated in more or less restricted areas, did not concern the great majority of the population. Most of the exchange of goods was still a simple barter. Also it was very easy to estimate the cost of producing goods, because usually only one craftsman manufactured a complete article. The societies, which were formed when the Roman Empire was at its height and which used money to finance their enterprises in mining and in agriculture, were very rare and soon crumbled with the Empire in which they lived. The financial usances of the ancient merchants, renewed by the Italian, Flemish, and Hanseatic merchants of the Middle Ages, with their international gold currency and bills of exchange, were restricted to commerce and with the exception of the production of textiles had no influence upon production in general.

In such circumstances it was only natural that the Christian moralists considering money as a good among other goods or as a simple medium of exchange going quickly from one hand into another, classified all interest on money loans as usury which was a thing not permitted to any Christian.

Circumstances changed, however, with the decay of feudal society at the end of the Middle Ages and at the beginning of the absolutist epoch. Feudal society was a social order in which the composing parts directly exchanged their services. The villagers produced the food and the clothes and the lord defended them and acted as their judge; the duke or king ruled, living on his own estates; whenever the rulers had to exact the help of their subjects, it was given to them either in direct service or as a part of their goods—among which also the precious metals were counted. When this order began collapsing, money rents were substituted for direct services. The farmers changed from nominal tenants into holders of their land and, what was even more important, their lands could be charged with fixed annual payments, which, in their turn, developed into a complete mortgage system. The lords and the burghers began to place their money into breweries, textile manufactures, and overseas commercial expeditions which were bringing precious goods from the newly discovered countries. And what can be considered a final development in this process, the absolutist rulers, who were not able to support their bureaucratic and centralized administrations and their standing armies from their own personal revenues, had to introduce regular tax collections and also to borrow money from the wealthy merchants.

Thus a new economic system was introduced into the Christian countries and into their overseas colonies and, consequently, also into the other countries with which the European merchants were in commercial contact. In this new system money assumed an indispensable role in the production and consumption of goods and also in the administration of political units. Hence the appellation "capitalist."

It is perhaps better to point out at once that all the economic systems of the modern epoch are capitalistic. Soviet Russia, as well as the United States, has an economy, in which money is no longer a simple medium of exchange but an institution indispensable to the production and consumption of goods and in which all the economic processes are based on financial calculations. The difference between the two systems is only in the degree in which the enterprises are owned by private individuals or by the state. To use the word "capitalistic" to describe the non-Marxist economies only, is faulty and misleading.

The Christian sociologists observed this development with much apprehension. They never ceased to stress the primary importance of peace and justice in the community, to which every economic enterprise is only secondary. Most of them would have also preferred to consider money in the old way as a medium of exchange which, as they used to say, could not beget other money. They were quite aware of the dangers inherent in the new economy. But their influence was not large and effective enough to stop the process. At last, after many deliberations, especially at the General Council in Trent at the middle of the 16th century, the theory of the escaping gain, the *lucrum cessans*, was accepted as the basis of a legal interest in a money loan. According to that theory, at the beginning, the owner of the money was permitted to take interest, provided only that a short period of gratuitous lending was allowed to lapse. Later on, the taking of interest was permitted for the whole period of the lending, but even then care was taken that the amount of the interest was not exorbitant.

Another temporary advantage of the medieval feudal order was that the economic capability of each person was so much more evident than it is today. Not a few injuries, undoubtedly, were inflicted and there were unjust and selfish people in the Middle Ages as in any other period. But as the mutual services were direct and personal and, consequently, it was clear to everybody what could and what could not be done, it was not so easy to be unjust or even cruel in social and economic relations. The introduction of money, however, has changed nearly all the mutual relations into indirect services, where the economic partners are only rarely known to each other. Thus, the evaluation of the cost of the production of an article became a complicated task, involving many factors.

That all these dangers were real enough, became evident in the course of the absolutist age, between the years 1453 and 1789. The financing of the centralized systems of political administration and of the great standing armies put a hitherto unknown and often unjust burden on the average citizen. The social relations between the employers and the employees be-

came strained. In the Protestant countries, especially
in those of the Calvinist denomination, it became almost a tenet of faith that economic prosperity in this
world is a sign of predestination to eternal salvation,
whereas the poor were considered as those who somehow had not pleased their Saviour. In the Catholic
countries things were only slightly better. Many people began to believe that the Church had no business
to meddle in social relations.

Nevertheless, up to the end of the 18th century, the
economic structure of the world, although already permeated by the capitalist usances, was still predomi-
nantly agricultural. The great change was achieved
only by the industrial revolution of the subsequent
decades. The industrial revolution means the substitution of machines for work done by hands. Machines
can liberate energy at a much slower and also a much
faster pace than man himself. It means also the substitution of industry for agriculture as the principal
occupation of many countries. The industrial revolution is, as we have already pointed out, a combined
result of the fusion of capitalist economy with the
developments and inventive activity of science.

When we read in the works of the 13th century
Franciscan monk, Roger Bacon, about the machines
which would relieve man from his toil and about the
rays which would pass through every substance, we
almost shudder before his powerful, prophetical vision. And yet the Middle Ages had no more use for
scientific inventions than the ancient epoch did. The
compass needle, which appeared in Europe during the
12th century and which had been probably known before in the Far East, and the primitive telescope, the
windmills and the improved ploughs were the only in-

struments of any importance introduced by medieval man in the service of mankind. What Roger Bacon saw in his dreams began to be prepared only by the heightened interest of the absolutist age in physical mechanics. Various simple instruments were invented by the 16th century miners. And it was also in the mines that the first steam engine of Thomas Newcomen was used at the beginning of the 18th century. The same century saw the invention of textile machines, such as the flying shuttle, spinning jenny, spinning frame, and power-loom, replacing the ages-old hand-spinning and hand-weaving, and the introduction of coal as the chief fuel and of iron as building material for the new machines. At the end of the 18th century the long looked-for process of manufacturing an iron alloy that would be lighter and more resistant than natural iron was discovered and led to the production of steel. That in its turn enabled the revolutionary improvement of the steam-engine by James Watt.

Thus the stage was set for that big 19th century development in the use of natural energy for the production and transportation of goods. Throughout the previous ages the energy available to man for that purpose came either from his own body or from that of the animals and was only to a slight degree supplemented by the force of falling water and of wind and by the heat of burning wood. All such use of natural energy could be easily mastered by one man or by a family and there was no need of assembling a greater number of people to one place for productive purposes and to submit them to the direction of one or very few proprietors or managers of an enterprise.

Out of the combination of coal and steel production

with the investments of accumulated money the new industry arose and with it—following the construction of the locomotive by Stephenson and of the steamship by Fulton—the new, immense net of transportation facilities. In a few decades, the steam-engine was driving steel machines producing many kinds of comestibles, clothing materials, furniture, and other commodities in great factories. But as the organic material of dead plants and animals embedded in sedimentary rocks yielded not only coal but also petroleum and natural gas, the opportunity was created for the construction of the internal combustion engine by Otto, Daimler, and Diesel, which was then employed not only in industry but also and especially in transportation, making possible the invention of the automobile by Diesel and the airplane by the brothers Wright.

A third source of energy was added by Faraday's discovery of the induction of electric currents. Machines generating powerful electric currents by mechanical power and electric motors were then constructed by the efforts of Faraday himself and also by those of the brothers Siemens. This development led to the invention of the incandescent filament lamps by Edison and of the transmission of symbols and of sound by electricity, connected with the names of Morse and Bell.

The 20th century, besides having perfected all the inventions of the preceding age, profitted, with much success, from some of its physical theories. Maxwell's hypothesis that electromagnetic radiation with waves much longer than those which create light could be achieved by purely electrical methods, was used by Hertz and Marconi and led gradually to the invention of wireless telegraphy, broadcasting, and television.

The theory of radiation, supported by the theory of relativity—affirming that matter can be converted into radiant energy—resulted in the construction of devices, by which atomic energy can be freed—possibly the greatest industrial achievement of the modern epoch.

Another branch of industrial production was founded on the progress of chemistry. The artificial fertilizers, propagated by Liebig in the first half of the last century, the silver compounds used in the photographic process of Daguerre, the extensive use of cellulose in producing paper and various artificial materials, the use of chemicals in refrigeration and in the preservation of comestibles, the use of cement in concrete construction, the production of artificial rubber, of nylon and other similar materials, may be quoted among the most important achievements in that field.

Numerous historical books mention these facts with natural satisfaction, stressing their significance as manifestations of human ingenuity. Such a one-sided evaluation can, of course, be acceptable only to historians who are not concerned with the dramatic aspect of the story of mankind and who consider history a sort of abstract, theoretical science. A full picture of the modern epoch, based not only on enumeration of individual historical facts but also on the consciousness of the dramatic element in history, has to stress in an equal way the profound changes in the social life which are closely connected with the development of production. The collaboration of capitalist economy with science has proved to be a social factor of the greatest importance. A great number of positive achievements can be put to its account. But the social problems which have resulted from these achievements are equally important. And especially for our cultural aims they are of vital interest.

Let us first consider the situation in agriculture. The chemical fertilizers and the agricultural machines have heightened the crops in such a remarkable way that an incomparable lesser number of men is needed on the fields which produce several times the quantity of wheat and other products they used to produce a hundred years ago. The breeding of animals, put on a scientific basis, has been improved to a similar extent. Moreover, the transportation facilities have made it possible to supply almost all the countries of the world with the agricultural products of those regions in which they can be produced in the easiest and cheapest way. The chemists, it is true, in spite of long research work, are not yet able to imitate in their laboratories the process of photosynthesis—in which the chlorophyll of living plants employs the energy of light in breaking the molecules of carbon dioxide and water and uniting them into glucose, the simplest of sugars. Nevertheless, it is quite possible, that this task will be accomplished in due time. What that would mean for agriculture, may be easily imagined. But even as it is now, agriculture is no more the primary and most usual profession of mankind. Hundreds of thousands of people who had previously worked on farms have already migrated to the towns. Other hundreds of thousands will follow.

Moreover the mechanization of agriculture has included the farmers among the immense number of the purchasers of energy. It is estimated that the expenditure of energy in the world is now about fifteen times

as large as it was in 1800. The production and use
of petroleum alone has increased approximately
twenty-five times in the last fifty years. The resources
of such energy as petroleum are naturally limited.
Their exhaustion would mean a social catastrophe.
But even if we suppose that a sufficient number of new
sources of electricity will be built and that atomic
energy will be made available for industrial use, other
problems will surge up. And they are of the kind
which concern not only farmers but people of all
professions and ways of living as well.

Trying to discuss these problems we have to bear
in mind still another phenomenon of modern political
history: the enormous growth of population. We call
it enormous because, in spite of scarcity of documents
it can be estimated, for instance, that the population
of Europe has changed from about 100 millions at
the end of the Middle Ages to 140 millions in 1800;
in 1900, however, it was 400 millions and in 1930
506 millions. Most abnormal of all was the growth of
the big cities, while the population of some agricultural regions has even declined. The factors which
contributed to this development can hardly be discussed in this brief survey.

It is not necessary to share in the pessimistic calculations according to which the number of births should
be limited because of the danger that in the near future
there will not be food enough on the earth for such a
great number of people. The statistics show that even
a greater number than dwell on the earth today
would be able to live if the food which is available
were distributed among them. But the essential question is whether our present society is morally strong
enough to cope with such a task. This problem now

stands out in clear perspective. A quarter of a century ago the pseudo-philosophers who restricted the meaning of civilization to the meaning of scientific and industrial progress could perhaps find a hearing among undiscerning people. But the main experience of our generation is that even a military dictatorship may use science or industry as instruments of power and that irresponsible individuals may use it for the increase of their personal comfort only. We also know that science and industry may become the humble servants of anybody powerful and wealthy enough. Science—and also industry which is only applied science—is only a branch of the cultural activity of man and, consequently, a branch of civilization. But when it is deprived of contact with the other branches of culture and especially with religious culture, which is the main progress of man, it may lead mankind into a bottomless abyss.

With all the sources of energy open or at least under scientific observation, with all the regions of the earth known to the geographers—Central Africa, Tibet, and the Arctic and Antarctic regions were among the last to be investigated in the 19th century—and with a regular production of food which, theoretically, would be sufficient for all the inhabitants of the earth, where are we now socially and economically? In a period of profound and turbulent discontent.

All the preceding historical periods knew social clashes, but in none of them did the social difficulties have such a menacing aspect for society as a whole. The first wave came and went in the first half of the 19th century when the factory workers in various industrial regions, dissatisfied with their meager

wages, excessive working hours, and periodic unem-
ployment, began to organise their professional groups.
The 1840s were especially a time in which the situation of the workers had given rise to much theoretical
discussion. Sušil, Ketteler, and Ozanam were the first
Christian sociologists who stressed the importance of
the social problems of the workers and pointed to their
solution according to Christian moral teaching.
Against them were not only the adherents of irresponsible individualism in economic relations, but also
those who proclaimed the necessity of a future society
in which there would be no private property and, consequently, according to their hopes, no social injustice;
the latter were, however, divided into two groups: the
Anarchists of Bakunin, who wished to abolish all property as well as all political authority at once, and the
totalitarian Socialists of Marx, who were persuaded
that the social reforms which they were envisaging
could be realized only through a dictatorship.

A betterment of the social situation seemed to appear in the second half of the century, when the general increase of wages and shorter working hours
appeased to a certain extent the discontent of the
factory workers. The First International, founded by
Marx himself, broke into pieces. The workers' parties
in Germany and elsewhere seemed more inclined to
peaceful propaganda of their ideas than to civil warfare. But to careful students of the situation darker
things already loomed on the horizon. Pope Leo XIII
chose the year 1891 to proclaim the principles of a
social reform according to Christian moral doctrine;
his proclamation, prepared by many careful preparatory studies by individual Christian sociologists, appeared in the form of an encyclical letter, *Rerum*

Novarum. His warning, however, could not stop the general trend of events. One bloody war, started in 1914 by Germany's fanatical nationalism, was sufficient to let the totalitarian hatred loose. Three dictatorships started almost at the same time. In Russia Lenin refashioned the original doctrine of Marx in his own way, in Italy Mussolini, former editor of a Marxist paper, marched with his followers into Rome and became head of the state, and in Germany Hitler founded his National Socialist Party which, a decade later, secured a dominating position in the state. Two of these movements combined nationalism with Marxist tenets from the very beginning; the third seemed for a time to prefer internationalism, but then accepted national imperialism of the worst sort. The leaders of all three were real masters of the "general will" doctrine of Rousseau; their highly efficient police, concentration camps, and chambers of torture existed only to do the "will of the people."

Hitler started another cruel war annihilating his neighbors one after another and was soon joined by Mussolini. Stalin, the successor of Lenin, wanted to keep apart for the moment, but did not escape Hitler's jealousy and had to participate in the war against him. After the end of Hitler and Mussolini, however, he began immediately to prepare a world revolution by force, compelling all the Slavonic nations and also the Chinese to join him in preparations for another gigantic war.

The lack of logic, a symptomatic characteristic of our era, is illustrated by the extent to which public opinion has been confused by the personal rivalry of the totalitarian leaders into believing that there are essential differences between nazism, fascism, and communism. In reality, all these systems profess the so-called will of the people without ever asking—after they have been installed—any individual citizen to express his will; all three have perhaps not nationalized property; but they have done something much worse: they have given the state the power to choose the professions of its citizens; and what was most important, because it is the very essence of totalitarianism, all three recognised the prerogative of the state to decide what should be thought and done in religion, art, history, philosophy, politics, and science; in short, all three have denied the human personality.

Therefore, in studying the present social and economic situation, we do not have to bother with the various branches of totalitarianism and with the secondary and passing differences between them. There is only one totalitarian doctrine as there is but one Christian doctrine. The first denies the human personality, the other upholds it. The civilization in which we live sprang up from the free creative activity of the human personality. Consequently, the fate of our civilization depends on the outcome of the ideological struggle between Christianity and totalitarianism.

But is there not a third partner in this contest? Does one not frequently mention also a doctrine called individualism?

Individualism is a philosophical doctrine opposed to the Christian conception of man, because it teaches that man is his own measure and thus, paradoxically enough, deprives man of the possibility to develop fully his personality. Man can develop his capabilities only to the extent to which he is able to come near to the full Being, Knowledge, and Love which is God. If he does not accept God and the immense wisdom of his revelation and if he declares himself the measure of all things, he does it, undoubtedly, of his own free decision, but by doing it he restricts his own development. Therefore philosophical individualism is opposed not only to Christian doctrine but also to the full liberty of man.

There have been attempts in the past to apply the philosophical doctrine of individualism to human economy. The ancient epoch knew such attempts. The rising capitalism at the end of the Middle Ages and at the beginning of the Absolutist Era knew them also. The capitalist merchants of those days did not bother about the moral aspect of their dealings nor about the well-being of the communities in which they lived. They accepted their own prosperity as the final measure of all their actions. But whereas full liberty comprises everything, restricted individualism is always opposed by another restricted individualism. Therefore the economic individualism of the merchants in the 16th century soon found itself opposed by the individualism of the absolutist kings, who equally declared their own power to be the only measure of all things. This power of theirs in the field of economy was obtained by securing the influx of bullion into their countries and by economic "mercantilism," which we have already described.

The natural opposition to this individualism of the kings swung the balance again in favor of the individualism of the merchants. In 1776, Adam Smith published his *Wealth of Nations* which is still its most famous theoretical exposition. But practically this renaissance of the individualism of the merchants had very little influence on economic development. In the latter half of the 19th century it was greatly favoured in Great Britain, but, as the British legislation soon restricted free trading with human labor—by enacting the "factory acts," regulating the conditions of individual employment—even in that country renowned by Smith's classic conception of the individualism of the merchants its ideals never became a full reality. In other countries, economic nationalism and the idea of economic autarchy—which is another sort of individualism, this time the individualism of the nations and of their leaders—was much stronger. The overseas colonies themselves, which had been considered merely as the suppliers of raw materials for the mother-countries and which were preëminently suited for agriculture, deliberately established new and autonomous industries. Finally, during the period before the first World War, even Great Britain accepted the individualism of the nations and relinquished the individualism of merchants and enterprisers.

It is evident, therefore, that there is no such thing as a general economic doctrine of individualism. There are only different kinds of individualism, such as the individualism of the merchants and enterprisers, the individualism of the absolutist rulers and builders of standing armies, and the individualism of the managers of nations and classes. This last sort of individualism almost coincides with totalitarianism. None of these petty individualisms constitutes a doctrine applicable to humanity as a whole. As to the original, philosophical doctrine of individualism, based on the tenet that man is his own measure, it would result, when applied to the economic field, in a war of all against all.

It was only in their poetical proclamations that the adherents of totalitarianism revolted against the individualism of the 19th century merchants. Their visions of a future stateless and classless society in which there would be no private property and no authority have never been fulfilled anywhere. Even if they could be realized, they would result again in the philosophical individualism, that is, in warfare between individuals; to outlaw property does not mean, as yet, to bring order into production and the use of goods. But most of the totalitarian theoreticians have postponed the realization of such visions into an indefinite future. They prefer the individualism of the managers or leaders of classes and nations to any other sort of economy. That is why they have accepted so readily the theory of the general will of the people, which gave them the power to realize the ideals of the managerial individualism. In some countries, such as Nazi Germany, Fascist Italy, and Soviet Russia, they have succeeded in establishing their individualism quite firmly: their personal comfort and ambitions were enthroned as the measure of everything else. In other countries they must still fight with the individualism of the enterprising owners. In such countries, they say, the "will of the people" has not yet been manifested clearly enough.

We may therefore return to our assertion that the future of our civilization depends on the result of the struggle between the two conceptions of man and human society—the Christian and the totalitarian. The conflict between these two ideologies may be defined as a conflict between a conception of society which, accepting God as measure, puts the natural rights of the human personality above all organisation and its opposite which sums up its aims in a mystical, and dangerously undefinable, general will. According to one, human society exists to aid the full development of every one of its members. According to the other, it exists to serve the managers of the state.

The totalitarians are sometimes willing to concede to their citizens as many political rights as possible, but they grant political rights only. The Christians believe that political rights without economic rights have no meaning. What are economic rights? Certainly not the so-called economic equality which in the totalitarian language merely signifies that the entire population of the state is employee of the managers. Real economic equality can be attained only on the basis of an unnatural operation which would put all diligent people on the level of the laziest. A natural conception of human society can not accept such a mutilation of nature. The true foundation of the natural economic rights is the right of every individual to obtain by work such property—or means freely convertible into property—that would enable him and his family to live and develop.

In a sense quite contrary to the practice of the totalitarians, who put all property into the hands of the managers, the Christian sociologists have always considered private property an inevitable institution of this world and have carefully distinguished the natural right to it from the evil greed for gain. The encyclical letter *Rerum Novarum* says: "The main tenet of socialism, community of goods, must be utterly rejected, since it only injures those it would seem meant to benefit, is directly contrary to the natural rights of mankind, and would introduce confusion and disorder into the Commonwealth." But the Christian sociology is also conscious of the fact, that there is a twofold aspect of ownership: individual and social. Everyone owns his property for his own good, but also for the common good of mankind. That is why any property except the basic one, necessary for the bare life of the owner and his family, can be lawfully seized or distrained by the society if it is necessary to appease another citizen's hunger. But even in that case the right endures for the owner to possess, as soon as possible, not only the property necessary to live but also the property necessary to develop.

The totalitarians, refusing to accept the natural right of the individual to earn property, affirm usually that private property in a totalitarian state is not necessary, because, in such a state, everyone is supported according to his needs. In practice, of course, this principle is always immediately changed into another maxim, namely that everybody is supported according to his usefulness to the managers, which means that he has the right to die in a forced-labor camp. But even if we accept the totalitarian theory we see at once its fatal point: the needs of every individual are not evaluated by himself, but by the managers of the state. And that, of course, is equal to the direct enslavement of the human person. No one but the man in question can evaluate his own needs and fix the ways of his development. The correct principle therefore is: to everyone according to his abilities and to no one below his necessity; such a principle can only be fulfilled by the institution of private property.

The economic life, however, does not entirely consist in owning and living. It also consists in producing.

Very few things are given to man in our age gratui-
tously. We have stated already that even the right to
property is, exactly speaking, the right to earn property by work.

The practical organization of production is the crucial economic problem of our era. And here again a
profound difference divides the two main points of
view: the totalitarian and the Christian. Totalitarianism is equivalent to economic dictatorship, in which the
sources of energy are at the disposal of the state managers and all the branches of production are directed
by them; there is no private initiative in trade. On the
internal market the prosperity of the managers is
paramount. As such, totalitarianism is a veritable com-
pletion of individualism. Economic individualism is
the direct opposite of free competition, because it means
that everyone is free to destroy the other competitors
instead of competing with them. In a similar way,
every totalitarian manager takes good care to destroy
all the colleagues who could be dangerous to his personal power.

The Christian sociology is against individualism
and, consequently, also against totalitarianism, because it considers free competition an essential condition of healthy economy. It affirms that the sources
of energy must be at the disposal of every producer.
Producers are themselves the directors of their efforts
and they are entitled to associate themselves in buying
and selling or in financial cooperatives, in guilds or
trusts, even on the international level, as far as such
forms of business organization are open to every new
competitor under equal conditions and do not deprive
anybody of raw materials necessary for production.
Nationalization can be permitted only in the case of

enterprises producing some sort of energy or basic material necessary for other branches of production; if such an enterprise puts obstacles of any sort into the way of free competition, the public authority is entitled to put it—in the cheapest way possible—under its control. To nationalize any other enterprise is entirely useless, because the public authority always can start a production of its own, if it can be done cheaper than by the private producer.

As for the indirect ownership of enterprises and their financing, again the totalitarian principle, according to which only the state managers are permitted to finance production and to profit from the invested capital, is not acceptable to the moral teaching of the Christians. Everybody has the right, and even the moral duty, to participate in the creation of economic values by his capital. The employees also are entitled to ask, if they deem it advantageous for them, that the sum of their wages be considered as capital investment in the enterprise. In fact, it is advisable for the proprietors and share-holders to have the employees interested in such a way in the prosperity of the enterprise.

Both wages and the profit from the invested capital depend upon the prices of the products. And here again the basic opinions differ. Totalitarianism, true to the selfishness of individualistic principles, allows prices to be fixed by the state managers who, of course, are interested exclusively in their own advantage. Natural rights demand, on the contrary, that the price of every product be fixed by the demand. An authoritative stabilization is permissible only in cases of emergency and should not be extended over a long period. The same thing is true of the money as medium of exchange and investment; not a government dictate but an open market and constant convertibility of paper money can provide a good control of credit in the national as well as in the international field.

The immense growth of population, the congestion of the workers in the cities, and other conditions, the relative importance of which is not easy to estimate, have caused the industrial fluctuations which result in social insecurity. Such periods as that of 1929-1934 recur, in a lesser or greater degree, again and again. Products do not sell, people are unable to find employment, and although the supply of food products is undiminished, there is hunger in the world. It is quite possible that it will take some time before we are able to investigate these phenomena properly and to make the flow of economic life more regular. But before we are able to do so, we shall be always confronted with social insecurity. What remedies can we apply against it?

The individualistic remedies are simple. In fact, they are restricted to one single gesture: to get rid of the unemployed and hungry. A society of economic individualists throws the unfortunate unemployed away and lets him die in the street. A society of national or managerial individualists, the totalitarian state, is even more selfish; it does not like the sight of corpses in the streets; therefore it charges the unemployed with sabotage, conspiracy or no matter what else and transfers him into a concentration-camp where it can, in addition, profit from his slave toil.

No such thing is allowed to a Christian. Every one of our neighbors has the natural right to earn by his work the basic property which is necessary for him and for his family, even if that means the restriction of our own economic possibilities. Society is responsible that this right does not remain on paper only.

It is possible, of course, to point to the voluntary or perhaps even obligatory insurance as the most obvious way to security. But that is a rather expensive way. It may be necessary for the economic security of the ill and disabled; but it takes too much money away from the hands of the citizen, with which he would otherwise be able to buy private property—the best way to social security. If, therefore, the Christian conception of society stresses in many other fields the independence of the citizen and also the independence of the working groups, which may defend their interests even by strikes—a right forbidden by the totalitarian managers—it stresses equally the collective responsibility of society to give the opportunity of work to everyone in times of economic crises.

To a critical student of these problems many of them may seem difficult to solve. He tackles first one of them, then another—obstacles appear everywhere. No wonder he acquires a distrust of all general instructions. And he does not have much confidence in the lessons of history either. Observing how quickly the circumstances change, he doubts the applicability of old precepts to new predicaments.

He should remind himself, however, that if there is no regularity in history, there certainly is a meaning of history and, consequently, a reason for everything which history has created or will create: the freedom of man which enables him not only to deny, but also to love. Consequently, no real solution of any problem in history can be directed against the freedom of man. To know that and to be able to envisage the current tasks in the light of such a principle is of priceless value.

Of course, to be conscious of the necessity of personal freedom has perhaps never been the main difficulty. Even in the mature years of the Absolutist Age there were men and institutions, such as the *parlements* in France in Mazarin's days, whose firm persuasion it was that the Law is above the State. And in our own days, when totalitarian tyrannies seem to rule the world annihilating private initiative inside each one of their spheres and building iron curtains as well as tariff walls on their frontiers, the citizens of the United States have shown how the problems of creative collaboration between the management and the employees can be solved by negotiation and adjudication; they even have had the courage to come forward, in 1946, with the "Proposals for Consideration by an International Conference on Trade and Employment," the realization of which would be the best weapon against economic nationalism. Thus the appreciation of freedom still lingers in this world.

But as to the source of freedom, there has not been even that much interest. Even those who should be interested find themselves frequently in the place of Edmund Burke who, criticizing the French Declaration of the Rights of Man, asserted that the rights which he enjoyed were an "entailed inheritance" rather than the result of a concept of man and of the world. An inheritance, however, which is not constantly related to the basic concepts of philosophy, may be lost at any moment. The citizens of Russia before 1917 or those of Germany before 1933 had not a few positive rights; they lost them all, nevertheless, in a few days.

77051

DATE DUE
